COMMENTARY ON
ROMANS

COMMENTARY ON
ROMANS

MARTIN LUTHER

Translated by
J. Theodore Mueller

kregel
PUBLICATIONS

Grand Rapids, MI 49501

Commentary on Romans by Martin Luther.

© Copyright 1954 by Zondervan Publishing House.

Reprinted in 1976 by Kregel Publications, a division of Kregel, Inc., P. O. Box 2607, Grand Rapids, MI 49501, under special arrangement with Zondervan Publishing House. All rights reserved.

Cover Design: Don Ellens

Library of Congress Catalog Number 76-12077

ISBN 0-8254-3119-0

19 20 21 22 Printing/Year 99 98

Printed in the United States of America

Contents

Foreword

In the fall of 1515, Dr. Martin Luther, professor of Sacred Theology at the University of Wittenberg, Saxony, began to expound to his students the Epistle of St. Paul to the Romans.

This was three years after he had joined the Wittenberg faculty and two years before he posted his famous ninety-five theses. The lectures were begun on November 3, 1515, and continued till September 7, 1516. Luther did not follow the modern semester divisions, but lectured on each book of the Bible until he had completed it. There were no summer vacations for professors at that time, but only brief interruptions of their work when they were called away on official business.

As Luther slowly and painstakingly prepared his lectures, he gradually came to a clear knowledge of the central teaching of Scripture, the doctrine of justification by grace through faith in Christ without works. Unfortunately, Luther never repeated his lectures on Romans. Had he done so, he no doubt would have revised much that he had written at so early a time in his teaching career. Later Melanchthon took over Romans, and from his lectures came the first Lutheran manual of Christian doctrine called *Loci Communes,* the "Common Topics," of the Christian faith.

The manuscript of Luther's commentary on Romans was lost for a long time. It was only in recent times that a good copy of it was discovered in the Vatican Library at Rome. This copy, it is thought, had belonged to the library of the University of Heidelberg, which Emperor Maximilian I had given to Pope Gregory XV. Later, the original was found in the Prussian State Library at Berlin. It was published in September 1908 under the able editorship of Professor Johannes Ficker. Thus it was given anew to the world about four hundred years after Luther had prepared it for his lectures at Wittenberg.

Luther's method of Scripture interpretation is original. It represents a radical departure from that of the medieval teachers and constitutes the beginning of modern exegesis, which is both textual and historical. For his students Luther published a special text of the books of the Bible on which he lectured. In these special editions there was ample space for notes both between the lines and on the wide margins. Between the lines Luther recorded his "glosses," or notes on words and expressions. On the margins he wrote his "scholia," or comments on the theological content or doctrine of the text. These at times became quite lengthy. Both the glosses and the scholia were primarily designed for Luther's own guidance. As the notes taken by the students show, he often departed from his written commentary, adding, modifying and eliminating as the impulse of the lecture mood moved him. He was an inspiring teacher, gifted with quick and deep insights and ready, persuasive speech. There is no doubt that he had much to say also on those verses on which he wrote no comment. In the center of his teaching was Christ, crucified and risen for our sins, as his whole teaching, according to his own statement, was the "theology of the Cross."

Luther's Romans, as here presented, is a digest rather than a complete, scholarly edition. Its purpose is to present to the reader the most important thoughts of the great Reformer. It is to be a companion volume to the abridged edition of Luther's Galatians edited by Theodore Graebner and published by the Zondervan Publishing House some years ago. This first work found many friends both within and outside Lutheran areas. In preparing this edition I followed Luther's commentary on Romans in the famous Weimar edition of Luther's works, Volume 56. For guidance I also used the fourth edition of Dr. Eduard Ellwein's German translation (Muenchen, Germany: Christian Kaiser Verlag, 1937). To all who have helped to make these two scholarly editions a success I express my cordial thanks.

Since Luther's comments are often terse and disconnected, explanatory words are inserted in parenthesis in italic type. While these at times may be somewhat disturbing, they nevertheless help in bringing out Luther's meaning more clearly. I divided the chapters into paragraphs with special headings to give the reader a general overview of what the great reformer's notes treat. I did not endeavor to produce a literal translation. My object was rather to reproduce the sense of Luther's notes in clear and concise language. At times Luther's notes lack clarity, but the fundamentals of his message of sin and grace are always precise and perspicuous.

There soon may appear a scholarly edition of Luther's Romans. Such an edition will be warmly welcomed by all who are interested in the great evangelical works which the Reformation has brought forth. But a scholarly edition will not render superfluous this shorter practical and devotional edition of Luther's commentary. For one thing, a scholarly edition must be complete, and that means much repetition, for frequently the glosses and scholia cover the same material. Again, it must offer much that is unclear and so it requires careful explanatory notes. Then, too, a scholarly edition must be concerned in detail with Luther's medieval background and must clarify such agreements with and departures from it as are found in his commentary on Romans. There is, needed moreover, a good deal of textual criticism, which a scholarly edition dare not ignore. Lastly, a scholarly edition will have to offer much material that is not essential to Luther's central teaching, and which, since it was written specifically for the reformers own time, no longer interests the modern evangelical reader.

In short, a scholarly edition of Luther's Romans must satisfy all scholarly demands, while this popular and abridged edition seeks only to acquaint the average Christian reader with the fundamentals of Luther's evangelical teachings. We might add that Luther's commentary on Romans contains some thoughts which later he modified or discarded altogether. In order to avoid confusion, such portions are largely omitted in this practical edition.

I am greatly indebted to the splendid work by such able scholars as Professor Johannes Ficker, Licentiate Eduard Ellwein, and their fellow workers, whose valuable research studies I gratefully used; to the Zondervan Publishing House for undertaking the publication of Luther's Romans; to my student helpers, Messrs. Martin Frederking, Edward Rauff and John Lemkul for their help in preparing the manuscript; to many pastors for their encouraging assistance. May God's blessing rest upon Luther's commentary on Romans as it goes forth to witness to many the truth of Christ's precious Gospel.

J. THEODORE MUELLER

Concordia Seminary
St. Louis Missouri

Publishers' Note:

In the interest of clarity the following policy has been adopted on parenthetical expressions within this book. Those expressions which appeared in the original work by Luther are enclosed within parenthesis, in regular body type. Those expressions which have been added by the translator, Dr. J. Theodore Mueller, are enclosed in parenthesis in italic type.

Luther's Preface

Preface

by Martin Luther (1552)*

This Epistle is really the chief part of the New Testament and the very purest Gospel, and is worthy not only that every Christian should know it word for word, by heart, but occupy himself with it every day, as the daily bread of the soul. It can never be read or pondered too much, and the more it is dealt with the more precious it becomes, and the better it tastes.

Therefore, I, too, will do my best, so far as God has given me power, to open the way into it through this preface, so that it may be better understood by everyone. For heretofore it has been evilly darkened with commentaries and all kinds of idle talk, though it is, in itself, a bright light, almost enough to illumine all the Scripture.

To begin with we must have knowledge of its language and know what St. Paul means by the words, law, sin, grace, faith, righteousness, flesh, spirit, etc., otherwise no reading of it has any value.

The little word, "law," you must not take here in human fashion, as a teaching about what works are to be done or not done. That is the way it is with human laws—the law is fulfilled by works, even though there is no heart in them.

But God judges according to what is at the bottom of the heart, and for this reason, His law makes its demands on the inmost heart and cannot be satisfied with works, but rather punishes works that are done otherwise than from the bottom of the heart, as hypocrisy and lies. Hence all men are called liars, in Psalm 116, for the reason that no one keeps or can keep God's law from the bottom of the heart, for everyone finds in himself displeasure in what is good and pleasure in what is bad. If, then, there is no willing pleasure in the good, then the inmost heart is not set on the law of God, then

*From *The Works of Martin Luther*, Volume vi (pp. 447-462) used by permission of Muhlenberg, Press, Philadelphia. This material has been known throughout the years as Luther's famous *Preface to Romans*. Although it is really an introduction to his commentary we have retained this title.

there is surely sin, and God's wrath is deserved, even though outwardly there seem to be many good works and an honorable life.

Hence St. Paul concludes, in chapter 2, that the Jews are all sinners, and says that only the doers of the law are righteous before God. He means by this that no one is, in his works, a doer of the law; on the contrary, he speaks to them thus, "Thou teachest not to commit adultery, but thou committest adultery," and "Wherein thou judgest another, thou condemnest thyself, because thou doest the same thing that thou judgest"; as if to say, "You live a fine outward life in the works of the law, and judge those who do not so live, and know how to teach everyone; you see the splinter in the other's eye, but of the beam in your own eye you are not aware."

For even though you keep the law outwardly, with works, from fear of punishment or love of reward, nevertheless, you do all this without willingness and pleasure, and without love for the law, but rather with unwillingness, under compulsion; and you would rather do otherwise, if the law were not there. The conclusion is that at the bottom of your heart you hate the law. What matter, then, that you teach others not to steal, if you are a thief at heart, and would gladly be one outwardly, if you dared? Though, to be sure, the outward work is not far behind such hypocrites! Thus you teach others, but not yourself; and you yourself know not what you teach, and have never yet rightly understood the law. Nay, the law increases sin, as he says in chapter 5, for the reason that the more the law demands what men cannot do, the more they hate the law.

For this reason he says, in chapter 7, "The law is spiritual." What is that? If the law were for the body, it could be satisfied with works; but since it is spiritual, no one can satisfy it, unless all that you do is done from the bottom of the heart. But such a heart is given only by God's Spirit, who makes a man equal to the law, so that he acquires a desire for the law in his heart, and henceforth does nothing out of fear and compulsion, but everything out of a willing heart. That law, then, is spiritual which will be loved and fulfilled with such a spiritual heart, and requires such a spirit. Where that spirit is not in the heart, there sin remains, and displeasure with the law, and emnity toward it; though the law is good and just and holy.

Accustom yourself, then, to this language, and you will find that doing the works of the law and fulfilling the law are two very different things. The work of the law is everything that one does, or can do toward keeping the law of his own free will or by his own powers. But since under all these works and along with them there remains in the heart dislike for the law and the compulsion to keep it, these works are all wasted and have no value. That is what St. Paul means in chapter 3, when he says, "By the works of the law no man becomes righteous before God." Hence you see that the wranglers and sophists are deceivers, when they teach men to prepare themselves for grace by means of works. How can a man prepare himself for good by means of works, if he does no good works without displeasure and unwillingness of heart? How shall a work please God, if it proceeds from a reluctant and resisting heart?

To fulfil the law, however, is to do its works with pleasure and love, and to live a godly and good life of one's own accord, without the compulsion of the law. This pleasure and love for the law is put into the heart by the Holy Ghost, as he says in chapter 5. But the Holy Ghost is not given except in, with, and by faith in Jesus Christ, as he says in the introduction; and faith does not come, save only through God's Word or Gospel, which preaches Christ, that He is God's Son and a man, has died and risen again for our sakes, as he says in chapters 3, 4, and 10.

Hence it comes that faith alone makes righteous and fulfils the law; for out of Christ's merit, it brings the Spirit, and the Spirit makes the heart glad and free, as the law requires that it shall be. Thus good works come out of faith. That is what he means in chapter 3, after he has rejected the works of the law, so that it sounds as though he would abolish the law by faith; "Nay," he says, "we establish the law by faith," that is we fulfil it by faith.

Sin, in the Scripture, means not only the outward works of the body, but all the activities that move men to the outward works, namely, the inmost heart, with all its powers. Thus the little word "do" ought to mean that a man falls all the way into sin and walks in sin. This is done by no outward work of sin, unless a man goes into sin altogether, body and soul. And the Scriptures look especially into the heart and have regard to the root and source of all sin, which is unbelief in the inmost heart. As, therefore, faith alone makes righteous, and brings the Spirit, and produces pleasure in good, eternal works, so unbelief alone commits sin, and brings up the flesh, and produces pleasure in bad external works, as happened to Adam and Eve in Paradise.

Hence Christ calls unbelief the only sin, when He says, in John 16, "The Spirit will rebuke the world for sin, because they believe not on me." For this reason, too, before good or bad works are done, which are the fruits, there must first be in the heart faith or unbelief, which is the root, the sap, the chief power of all sin. And this is called in the Scriptures, the head of the Serpent and of the old dragon, which the seed of the woman, Christ, must tread under foot, as was promised to Adam, in Genesis 3.

Between grace and gift there is this difference. Grace means properly God's favor, or the good-will God bears us, by which He is disposed to give us Christ and to pour into us the Holy Ghost, with His gifts. This is clear from chapter 5, where He speaks of "the grace and gift in Christ." The gifts and the Spirit increase in us every day, though they are not yet perfect, and there remain in us the evil lust and sin that war against the Spirit, as Paul says in Romans 7 and Galatians 5, and the quarrel between the seed of the woman and the seed of the serpent is foretold in Genesis 3. Nevertheless, grace does so much that we are accounted wholly righteous before God. For His grace is not divided or broken up, as are the gifts, but it takes us entirely into favor, for the sake of Christ our Intercessor and Mediator, and because of that the gifts are begun in us.

In this sense, then, you understand chapter 7, in which St. Paul still calls himself a sinner, and yet says, in chapter 8, that there is nothing condemnable in those who are in Christ on account of the incompleteness of the gifts and of the Spirit. Because the flesh is not yet slain, we still are sinners; but because we believe and have a beginning of the Spirit, God is so favorable and gracious to us that He will not count the sin against us or judge us for it, but will deal with us according to our faith in Christ, until sin is slain.

Faith is not that human notion and dream that some hold for faith. Because they see that no betterment of life and no good works follow it, and yet they can hear and say much about faith, they fall into error, and say, "Faith is not enough; one must do works in order to be righteous and be saved." This is the reason that, when they hear the Gospel, they fall-to and make for themselves, by their own powers, an idea in their hearts, which says, "I believe." This they hold for true faith. But it is a human imagination and idea that never reaches the depths of the heart, and so nothing comes of it and no betterment follows it.

Faith, however, is a divine work in us. It changes us and makes us to be born anew of God (John 1); it kills the old Adam and makes altogether different men, in heart and spirit and mind and powers, and it brings with it the Holy Ghost. Oh, it is a living, busy, active, mighty thing, this faith; and so it is impossible for it not to do good works incessantly. It does not ask whether there are good works to do, but before the question rises; it has already done them, and is always at the doing of them. He who does not these works is a faithless man. He gropes and looks about after faith and good works, and knows neither what faith is nor what good works are, though he talks and talks, with many words, about faith and good works.

Faith is a living, daring confidence in God's grace, so sure and certain that a man would stake his life on it a thousand times. This confidence in God's grace and knowledge of it makes men glad and bold and happy in dealing with God and all His creatures; and this is the work of the Holy Ghost in faith. Hence a man is ready and glad, without compulsion, to do good to everyone, to serve everyone, to suffer everything, in love and praise to God, who has shown him this grace; and thus it is impossible to separate works from faith, quite as impossible as to separate heat and light fires. Beware, therefore, of your own false notions and of the idle talkers, who would be wise enough to make decisions about faith and good works, and yet are the greatest fools. Pray God to work faith in you; else you will remain forever without faith, whatever you think or do.

Righteousness, then, is such a faith and is called "God's righteousness," or "the righteousness that avails before God," because God gives it and counts it as righteousness for the sake of Christ, our Mediator, and makes a man give to every man what he owes him. For through faith a man becomes sinless and comes to take pleasure in God's commandments; thus he gives to God the honor that is His and pays Him what he owes Him; but he also serves man willingly, by whatever means he can, and thus pays his debt to everyone. Such righteousness, nature and free will and all our powers cannot bring into existence. No one can give himself faith, and no more can he take away his own unbelief; how, then, will he take away a single sin, even the very smallest? Therefore, all that is done apart from faith or in unbelief, is false; it is hypocrisy and sin, no matter how good a show it makes (Romans 14).

You must not so understand flesh and spirit as to think that flesh has to do only with unchastity and spirit only with what is inward, in the heart; but Paul, like Christ in John 3, calls "flesh" everything that is born of the flesh; viz., the whole man, with body and soul, mind and senses, because everything about him longs for the flesh. Thus you should learn to call him "fleshly" who thinks, teaches, and talks a great deal about high spiritual matters, but without grace. From the "works of the flesh" in Galatians 5, you can learn that Paul calls heresy and hatred "works of the flesh," and in Romans 8 he says that "the law was weak through the flesh," and this does not refer to unchastity, but to all sins, above all to unbelief, which is the most spiritual of all vices. On the other hand, he calls him a spiritual man who is occupied with the most external kind of works, ás Christ, when He washed the disciples' feet, and Peter, when he steered his boat, and fished. Thus "the flesh" is a man who lives and works, inwardly and outwardly, in the service of the flesh's profit and of this temporal life; "the spirit" is the man who lives and works, inwardly and outwardly, in the service of the Spirit and the future life.

Without such an understanding of these words, you will never understand this letter of St. Paul, or any other book of Holy Scripture. Therefore, beware of all teachers who use these words in a different sense, no matter who they are, even Jerome, Augustine, Ambrose, Origen, and men like them, or above them. Now we will take up the Epistle.

It is right for a preacher of the Gospel first, by a revelation of the law and of sin, to rebuke everything and make sin of everything that is not the living fruit of the Spirit and of faith in Christ, so that men may be led to know themselves and their own wretchedness, and become humble and ask for help. That is what St. Paul does. He begins in Chapter 1 and rebukes the gross sin and unbelief that are plainly evident, as the sins of the heathen, who live without God's grace, were and still are. He says: The wrath of God is revealed from heaven through the Gospel, upon all men because of their godless lives and their unrighteousness. For even though they know and daily recognize that there is a God, nevertheless, nature itself, without grace, is so bad that it neither thanks nor honors Him, but blinds itself, and goes continually from bad to worse, until at last, after idolatry, it commits the most shameful sins, with all the vices, and is not ashamed, and allows others to do these things unrebuked.

In chapter 2, he stretches this rebuke still farther and extends it to those who seem outwardly to be righteous, but commit sin in secret. Such were the Jews and such are all the hypocrites, who, without desire or love for the law of God, lead good lives, but hate God's law in their hearts, and yet are prone to judge other people. It is the nature of all the hypocrites to think themselves pure, and yet be full of covetousness, hatred, pride, and all uncleanness (Matthew 23). These are they who despise God's goodness and in their hardness heap wrath upon themselves. Thus St. Paul, as a true interpreter of the law, leaves no one without sin, but proclaims the wrath of God upon all who live good lives from nature or free will, and makes them appear no better than open sinners; indeed he says that they are hardened and unrepentant.

In chapter 3, he puts them all together in a heap and says that one is like the other; they are all sinners before God, except that the Jews have had God's Word. Not many have believed on it, to be sure, but that does not mean that the faith and truth of God are exhausted; and he quotes a saying from Psalm 51, that God remains righteous in His words. Afterwards he comes back to this again and proves by Scripture that they are all sinners and that by the works of the law no man is justified, but that the law was given only that sin might be known.

Then he begins to teach the right way by which men must be justified and saved, and says they are all sinners and without praise from God, but they must be justified, without merit, through faith in Christ, who has earned this for us by His blood, and has been made for us a mercyseat by God, Who forgives us all former sins, proving thereby that we were aided only by His righteousness, which He gives in faith, which is revealed in this time through the Gospel and "testified before by the law and the prophets." Thus the law is set up by faith, though the works of the law are put down by it, together with the reputation that they give.

After the first three chapters, in which sin is revealed and faith's way to righteousness is taught, he begins, in chapter 4, to meet certain objections. And first he takes up the one that all men commonly make when they hear of faith, that it justifies, without works. They say, "Are men, then, to do no good works?" Therefore he himself takes up the case of Abraham, and asks, "What did Abraham accomplish, then, with his good works? Were they all in vain? Were his works of no use?" He concludes that Abraham was justified by faith alone, without any works; nay, the Scriptures, in Genesis 15, declare that he was justified by faith alone, even before the work of circumcision. But if the work of circumcision contributed nothing to his righteousness, though God commanded it and it was a good work of obedience; then, surely, no other good work will contribute anything to righteousness. On the other hand, if Abraham's circumcision was an external sign by which he showed the righteousness that was already his in faith, then all good works are only external signs which follow out of faith, and show, like good fruit, that man is already inwardly righteous before God.

With this powerful illustration, out of the Scriptures, St. Paul establishes the doctrine of faith which he had taught before in chapter 3. He also brings forward another witness, viz., David, in Psalm 32, who says that a man is justified without works, although he does not remain without works when he has been justified. Then he gives the illustration a broader application, and concludes that the Jews cannot be Abraham's heirs merely because of their blood, still less because of the works of the law, but must be heirs of Abraham's faith, if they would be true heirs. For before the law—either the law of Moses or the law of circumcision—Abraham was justified by faith and called the father of believers; moreover, the law works wrath rather than grace, because no one keeps it out of love for it and pleasure in it, so that what comes by the works of the law is disgrace rather than grace. Therefore, faith alone must obtain the grace promised to Abraham, for these examples were written for our sakes, that we, too, should believe.

In chapter 5, he comes to the fruits and works of faith, such as peace, joy, love to God and to every man, and confidence, boldness, joy, courage, and hope in tribulation and suffering. For all this follows, if faith be true, because of the over-abundant goodness that God shows us in Christ, so that He caused Him to die for us before we could ask it, nay, while we were still His enemies. Thus we have it that faith justifies without any works; and yet it does not follow that men are, therefore, to do no good works, but rather that the true works will not be absent. Of these the work-righteous saints know nothing, but feign works of their own in which there is no peace, joy, confidence, love, hope, boldness, nor any of the qualities of true Christian works and faith.

After this, he breaks out, and makes a pleasant excursion, and tells whence come both sin and righteousness, death and life, and compares Adam and Christ. He says that Christ had to come, a second Adam, to bequeath His righteousness to us through a new spiritual birth in faith, as the first Adam bequeathed sin to us, through the old, fleshly birth. Thus he declares, and confirms it, that no one, by his own works, can help himself out of sin into righteousness, any more than he can prevent the birth of his own body. This is proved by the fact that the divine law—which ought to help to righteousness, if anything can—has not only helped, but has even increased sin; for the reason that the more the law forbids, the more our evil nature hates it, and the more it wants to give rein to its own lust. Thus the law makes Christ all the more necessary, and more grace is needed to help our nature.

In chapter 6, he takes up the special work of faith, the conflict of the spirit with the flesh, for the complete slaying of the sin and lust that remains after we are justified. He teaches us that by faith we are not so freed from sin that we can be idle, slack, and careless, as though there were no longer any sin in us. There is sin; but it is no longer counted for condemnation, because of the faith that strives against it. Therefore we have enough to do all our life long in taming the body, slaying its lusts, and compelling its members to obey the spirit and not the lusts, thus making our lives like the death and resurrection of Christ and completing our baptism—which signifies the death of sin and the new life of grace—until we are entirely pure of sins, and even our bodies rise again with Christ and live forever.

And that we can do, he says, because we are in grace and not in the law. He himself explains that to mean that to be without the law is not the same thing as to have no laws and be able to do what one pleases; but we are under the law when, without grace, we occupy ourselves in the work of the law. Then sin assuredly rules by the law, for no one loves the law by nature; and that is great sin. Grace, however, makes the law dear to us, and then sin is no more there, and the law is no longer against us, but with us.

This is the true freedom from sin and the law, of which he writes, down to the end of this chapter, saying that it is liberty only to do good with pleasure and live a good life without the compulsion of the law. Therefore this liberty is a spiritual liberty, which does not abolish the law, but presents what the law demands; namely, pleasure and love. Thus the law is quieted and no longer drives men or makes demands of them. It is just as if you owed a debt to your overlord and could not pay it. There are two ways in which you could rid yourself of the debt—either he would take nothing from you and would tear up the account; or some good man would pay it for you, and give you the means to satisfy the account. It is this latter way that Christ has made us free from the law. Our liberty is, therefore, no fleshly liberty, which is not obligated to do anything, but a liberty that does many works of all kinds, and thus is free from the demands and the debts of the law.

In chapter 7, he supports this with a parable of the married life. When a man dies, his wife is single, and thus the one is released from the other; not that the wife cannot or ought not to take another husband, but rather that she is now really free to take another, which she could not do before she was free from her husband. So our conscience is bound to the law, under the old man; when he is slain by the Spirit, then the conscience is free; the one is released from the other; not that the conscience is to do nothing, but rather that it is now really free to cleave to Christ, the second husband, and bring forth the fruit of life.

Then he sketches out more broadly the nature of sin and the law, showing how, by means of the law sin now moves and is mighty. The old man hates the law the more because he cannot pay what the law demands, for sin is his nature and by himself he can do nothing but sin; therefore the law is death to him, and torment. Not that the law is bad, but his evil nature cannot endure the good, and the law demands good of him. So a sick man cannot endure it when he is required to run and jump and do the works of a well man.

Therefore St. Paul here concludes that the law, rightly understood and thoroughly comprehended, does nothing more than remind us of our sin and slay us by it, and make us liable to eternal wrath; and all this is taught and experienced by our conscience, when it is really smitten by the law. Therefore a man must have something else than the law, and more than the law, to make him righteous and save him. But they who do not rightly understand the law are blind; they go ahead, in their presumption, and think to satisfy the law with their works, not knowing what the law demands, viz., a willing and happy heart. Therefore they do not see Moses clearly, the veil is put between them and him, and covers him.

Then he shows how spirit and flesh strive with one another in a man. He uses himself as an example, in order that we may learn rightly to understand the work of slaying sin within us. He calls both spirit and flesh "laws," for just as it is the nature of the divine law to drive men and make demands of them, so the flesh drives man and makes demands and rages against the spirit, and will have its own way. The spirit, too, drives men and makes demands contrary to the flesh, and will have its own way. This contention within us lasts as long as we live, though in one man it is greater, in another less, according as spirit or flesh is stronger. Nevertheless, the whole man is both spirit and flesh and he fights with himself until he becomes wholly spiritual.

In chapter 8, he encourages these fighters, telling them not to condemn the flesh; and he shows further what the nature of flesh and spirit is, and how the spirit comes from Christ, who has given us His Holy Spirit to make us spiritual and subdue the flesh. He assures us that we are still God's children, however hard sin may rage within us, so long as we follow the Spirit and resist sin, to slay it. Since, however, nothing else is so good for the mortifying of the flesh as the cross and suffering, he comforts us in suffering with the support of the Spirit of love, and of the whole creation. For the Spirit sighs within us and the creation longs with us that we may be rid of the flesh and of sin. So we see that these three chapters (6-8) deal with the one work of faith, which is to slay the old Adam and subdue the flesh.

In chapters 9, 10, and 11, he teaches concerning God's eternal predestination, from which it originally comes that one believes or

not, is rid of sin or not rid of it. Thus our becoming righteous is
taken entirely out of our hands and put in the hand of God. And
that is most highly necessary. We are so weak and uncertain that,
if it were in our power, surely not one man would be saved, the
devil would surely overpower us all; but since God is certain, and
His predestination cannot fail, and no one can withstand Him, we
still have hope against sin.

And here we must set a boundary for those audacious and
high-climbing spirits, who first bring their own thinking to this
matter and begin at the top to search the abyss of divine
predestination, and worry in vain about whether they are
predestinate. They must have a fall; either they will despair, or else
they will take long risks.

But do you follow the order of this Epistle? Worry first about
Christ and the Gospel, that you may recognize your sin and His
grace; then fight your sin, as the first eight chapters here have
taught; then, when you have reached the eighth chapter, and are
under the cross and suffering, that will teach you the right
doctrine of predestination, in the ninth, tenth, and eleventh
chapters, and how comforting it is. For the absence of suffering
and the cross and the danger of death, one cannot deal with
predestination without harm and without secret wrath against
God. The old Adam must die before he can endure this subject
and drink the strong wine of it. Therefore beware not to drink
wine while you are still a suckling. There is a limit, a time, an age
for every doctrine.

In chapter 12, he teaches what true worship is; and he makes all
Christians priests, who are to offer not money and cattle, as under
the law, but their own bodies, with a slaying of the lusts. Then he
describes the outward conduct of Christians, under spiritual
government, telling how they are to teach, preach, rule, serve, give,
suffer, love, live, and act toward friend, foe and all men. These are
the works that a Christian does; for, as has been said, faith takes
no holidays.

In chapter 13, he teaches honor and obedience to worldly
government, which accomplishes much, although it does not make
its people righteous before God. It is instituted in order that the
good may have outward peace and protection, and that the
wicked may not be free to do evil, without fear, in peace and

quietness. Therefore the righteous are to honor it, though they do not need it. In the end he comprises it all in love, and includes it in the example of Christ, who has done for us what we are also to do, following in His footsteps.

In chapter 14, he teaches that weak consciences are to be led gently in faith and to be spared, so that Christians are not to use their liberty for doing harm, but for the furtherance of the weak. If that is not done, then discord follows and contempt for the Gospel; and the Gospel is the all-important thing. Thus it is better to yield a little to the weak in faith, until they grow stronger, than to have the doctrine of the Gospel come to nought. This is a peculiar work of love, for which there is great need even now, when with meat-eating and other liberties, men are rudely and roughly shaking weak consciences, before they know the truth. In chapter 15, he sets up the example of Christ, to show that we are to suffer those who are weak in other ways—those whose weakness lies in open sins or in unpleasing habits. These men are not to be cast off, but borne with till they grow better. For so Christ has done to us, and still does every day; He bears with our many faults and bad habits, and with all our imperfections, and helps us constantly.

Then, at the end, he prays for them, praises them and commends them to God; he speaks of his office and his preaching, and asks them gently for a contribution to the poor at Jerusalem; all that he speaks of or deals with is pure love.

The last chapter is a chapter of greetings, but he mingles with them a noble warning against doctrines of men, which are put in along side the doctrine of the Gospel and cause offense. It is as though he had foreseen that out of Rome and through the Romans would come the seductive and offensive canons and decretals and the whole squirming mass of human laws and commandments which have now drowned the whole world and wiped out this Epistle and all the Holy Scriptures, along with the Spirit and with faith, so that nothing has remained there except the idol, Belly, whose servants St. Paul here rebukes. God release us from them. Amen.

Thus in this Epistle we find most richly the things that a Christian ought to know; namely, what is law, Gospel, sin, punishment, grace, faith, righteousness, Christ, God, good works, love, hope, the cross, and also how we are to conduct ourselves toward everyone, whether righteous or sinner, strong or weak, friend or foe. All this is ably founded on Scripture and proved by his own example and that of the prophets. Therefore it appears that St. Paul wanted to comprise briefly in this one Epistle the whole Christian and evangelical doctrine and to prepare an introduction to the entire Old Testament; for, without doubt, he who has this Epistle well in his heart, has the light and power of the Old Testament with him. Therefore let every Christian exercise himself in it habitually and continually. To this may God give His grace. Amen.

MARTIN LUTHER

Romans One

Content of the first chapter: The Apostle expresses his love to the Christians at Rome and rebukes the vices of those who follow their lusts.

St. Paul a Messenger of the Gospel of Jesus Christ

Paul, a servant of Jesus Christ, called to be an apostle, separated unto the gospel of God, (which he had promised afore by his prophets in the holy scriptures,) concerning his Son Jesus Christ our Lord, which was made of the seed of David according to the flesh; and declared to be the Son of God with power, according to the spirit of holiness by the resurrection from the dead: by whom we have received grace and apostleship, for obedience to the faith among all nations for his name: among whom are ye also the called of Jesus Christ: to all that be in Rome, beloved of God, called to be saints: Grace to you and peace from God our Father, and the Lord Jesus Christ. First, I thank my God through Jesus Christ for you all, that your faith is spoken of throughout the whole world. For God is my witness, whom I serve with my spirit in the gospel of his Son, that without ceasing I make mention of you always in my prayers; making request, if by any means now at length I might have a prosperous journey by the will of God to come unto you. For I long to see you, that I may impart unto you some spiritual gift, to the end ye may be established: that is, that I may be comforted together with you by the mutual faith both of you and me. Now I would not have you ignorant, brethren, that oftentimes I purposed to come unto you, (but was let hitherto,) that I might have some fruit among you also, even as among other Gentiles. I am debtor both to the Greeks, and to the Barbarians; both to the wise, and to the unwise. So, as much as in me is, I am ready to preach the gospel to you that are at Rome also. For I am not ashamed of the gospel of Christ: for it is the power of God unto salvation to every one that believeth; to the Jew first, and also to the Greek. For therein is the righteousness of God revealed from faith to faith: as it is written, The just shall live by faith (1:1-17).

GENERAL COMMENTARY
Man's Own Wisdom and Works Do Not Save

The object of this Epistle is to destroy all wisdom and works of the flesh no matter how important these may appear in our eyes or those of others, and no matter how sincere and earnest we might be in their use. In its place it implants, deepens and magnifies (*the sense of*) sin, no matter how little of it (*in our opinion*) there may exist, or how much of it may be there.

For this reason St. Augustine says in his book *Concerning the Spirit and the Letter* that the Apostle "vehemently inveighs against the proud, arrogant persons who glory in their works." Among Jews and Gentiles there were many who believed that virtue and wisdom suffice (*for salvation*) provided they are exercised not for show or for pleasing men, but with truest singleness of heart as was the case with some philosophers. However, even though these did not assert their righteousness before men or boast of it, but followed it with genuine love for virtue and wisdom (and to these belonged the best and sincerest, though with the exception of Socrates we know only few of such), yet in the inmost recesses of their hearts they could not refrain from self-complacency and boasting, at least not in their thoughts, of being wise, just and good. The Apostle says of them, "Professing themselves to be wise, they became fools" (Rom. 1:22).

But here we learn that the very opposite is the case, and in the Church we declare that our righteousness and wisdom are in vain, so that we must neither praise nor extol them by false pretense. Everything turns about the point that our righteousness and wisdom must be destroyed and rooted out of our hearts and our self-complacent minds. God thus speaks through Jeremiah (Jer. 1:10): "I have this day set thee over the nations and over the kingdoms, to root out, and to pull down, and to destroy, and to throw down," namely everything — (*all righteousness*) — that is our own and in which we glory; and "to build, and to plant," namely everything — (*all righteousness*) — that is outside us and from Christ.

We are Saved by Christ's Righteousness

God certainly desires to save us not through our own righteousness, but through the righteousness and wisdom of someone else or by means of a righteousness which does not originate on earth, but comes down from heaven. So, then, we must teach a righteousness which in every way comes from without and is entirely foreign to us. Christ desires to have our hearts so free and divested (*of our own righteousness and wisdom*) that for our sins we fear no denial of grace and for our virtues we seek no glory and vain satisfaction. We even should not boast before men of the righteousness which is ours from Christ; nor should we allow ourselves to be cast down by the sufferings and afflictions which are sent to us by Him. A true Christian should so renounce all things — (*all righteousness and wisdom*) — that in honor and dishonor he always remains the same, assured that whatever honor comes to him belongs to Christ, whose righteousness and gifts of grace shine forth from Him, and that whatever reproach he endures is inflicted on Christ, (*who is in him*).

To reach such perfection, we require not only much spiritual grace, but also much experience. Because of our natural and spiritual gifts, men may regard us as wise, righteous and good. But God does not regard us as such, especially not if we so esteem ourselves. We therefore must remain so humble, as if we as yet had nothing, (*neither righteousness nor wisdom in Christ*), but were still waiting for the tender mercies of God, who for Christ's sake regards us as wise and righteous. There are many who indeed for God's sake, regard temporal blessings as nothing and gladly renounce them, as, for example, Jews and heretics. But there are very few who regard also their spiritual gifts and good works as nothing, seeking to obtain only the righteousness of Christ. Of this Jews and heretics are incapable, though without this no one can be saved. They invariably desire and hope that their own (*righteousness*) will be esteemed and rewarded by God. But His verdict forever stands: "So then it is not of him that willeth, nor of him that runneth, but of God that sheweth mercy" (Rom. 9:16).

Why the Apostle Wrote the Epistle

Regarding the Epistle, I do not believe that its recipients, who are addressed as "beloved of God" and "called saints," were in such a situation that the Apostle found it necessary to intervene because of existing dissensions and to regard them all as (*gross*) sinners. If really they were Christians, they knew this, (*the need of peace*

and concord), as believers. I rather think that he used the opportunity of writing to them because they were Christian believers.
They were to have a testimony of their faith and doctrine from
the pen of the great Apostle for their controversies with Jews and
Gentiles. These continued in unbelief and glorified in their flesh
over against the despised wisdom of the believers, who had to live
among them and listen to their opposing views. The Apostle thus
writes to the Corinthians: "For we commend not ourselves again
unto you, but give you occasion to glory on our behalf, that ye
may have somewhat to answer them which glory in appearance,
and not in heart" (II Cor. 5:12).

The True Christian Minister

As we study the text, from verses 1-17, we see that it contains
not so much academic instruction as rather teaching by example;
for, here in the beginning, the Apostle teaches by his own example
how a minister should conduct himself over against his parishioners.
It behooves a wise minister of God to hold his office in honor
and to have his hearers show it proper respect. As a believing
servant of God, he must not transgress the bounds of his ministry
nor abuse it by pride, but must administer it to the welfare and
benefit of his parishioners.

The servant of Christ, then, must be both wise and believing.
If he fails in wisdom, he will prove himself a sluggard, who is
self-indulgent and so unworthy of his high office. Such a person
will permit the divine office, entrusted to him by God, to be treated
with contempt, though he should exalt it. If he fails in faith, he
will prove himself a tyrant who terrifies the people by his
authority and takes delight in being a bully. Calling these two
vices by name we might describe them as frivolity and severity.
Of the first Zechariah says (Zech. 11:17): "Woe to the idle
shepherd that leaveth the flock!" Of the second Ezekiel writes
(Ezek. 34:4): "With force and with cruelty have ye ruled them."
These are the two chief sins from which all other pastoral offenses
flow. They are the roots of all evil. It is therefore very dangerous
for anyone to receive the office, before these two monsters have
been slain. The more power they exercise, the greater is the
harm they do.

Why Paul Exalts His Ministry

Against these two monsters, the Apostle, in this entire prologue, or introductory part of his letter, pictures his ministry as a pleasing pattern. In order that he might not be despised by his hearers as faint-hearted or frivolous, he depicts his apostolic office in all its greatness and glory. Again, in order that he might not appear to them as a despot or tyrant, he wins their hearts by charming friendliness, and all this to make them amenable to the Gospel both by dignity and love. After the pattern of the Apostle every minister in the Church should clearly distinguish between his person and his office, between the "form of a servant" and the "form of God" and always regard himself as the least of all, in order that he with dignity and love might administer his office with the sole object in mind to promote the welfare and salvation of his parishioners. Indeed, knowing that his office has been entrusted to him solely for the benefit of his people, he should be willing to give up his ministry if it is no longer profitable, rather than become a hindrance to it. It certainly is a great offense on the part of the minister if by one of these vices, or also by both, he renders his office unfruitful. The final account which he must give of his stewardship shall in that case be very grievous.

VERSE COMMENTARY

Paul a servant of Jesus Christ (1:1). This phrase expresses both modesty and majesty. It expresses modesty (*humility*) because the Apostle does not regard himself as a lord or master as do the arrogant tyrants. It expresses majesty because he glories in his being a servant of the Lord. Now, if it is already disastrous to deny to the servants of an emperor honor and respect, what will happen to those who do not receive with due honor the servants of God! The expression "a servant of Jesus Christ" is indeed overwhelmingly terrifying. Here it does not so much describe Paul's personal reverent submission to God, as rather the exalted dignity of his office. Paul calls himself a "servant" to confess that he has received the apostolic office from God above others. What he means to say is perhaps this: I preach the Gospel, teach the Church, baptize, and do other pastoral works, which truly are God's. But I do them not as a Lord to rule over you, but as a servant to whom the ministry means nothing else than that which Christ desires me to do among you. This cannot be said of that other ministry with regard to which all believers are in equal measure called servants of God. The one is a special ministry of some; the other is a general ministry, which applies to all believers.

Called to be an Apostle (1:1). These words describe his ministry more fully; for there are indeed may servants or ministers of Jesus Christ, but not all are apostles. All apostles, however, are also servants or ministers who are to do the work of the Lord among others in Christ's stead as His stewards.

He directs these words against three classes of men. The first consists of false prophets who at that time were to be found by the thousands, for the Devil sowed them as "tares among the wheat" (Matt. 13:25). The second class consists of such as invade the parishes, prompted by selfish ulterior motives. They might not be lying apostles, for they might teach what is true and proper and rightly direct the people. Still, the words, "called to be an apostle" condemn them; for even though they might not be "thieves and robbers" (John 10:1) as the first, they are hirelings who seek their own advantage and do not promote the cause of Christ. The third class consists of such as enter the congregations by force or are forced upon them against the will of the people. They are worse than those of the second class, but not as bad as those of the first.

Since, then, the holy office is so highly exalted, we must guard against this danger as greater than all other perils in this world and that to come, indeed as the very greatest there is, namely to enter the ministry without a divine call. If even those are not safe in it whom God has called, as Judas (Luke 22:3), Saul (I Sam. 15:3) and David (II Sam. 11:2f.) — and at that the two last were called by a special call — woe to those pitiable persons (*who take upon themselves the pastoral office without a divine call*)!

By the word "apostle" Paul magnifies the dignity of his ministry and impresses upon his parishioners and hearers reverence for his office. We should indeed receive every servant of God with respect as one who does the work of the Lord among us, but much more so an apostle! He is the highest ambassador of the

Lord and the greatest angel of the Lord of Hosts, Jesus Christ. Besides the other blessings of God that come to us in so abundant a measure, we must recognize, with due praise and deep gratitude, the blessing that in His boundless mercy God has given to men the exalted prerogative (*of being His ministers*). For our salvation and the Lord's work might be hindered by our excessive fear, if He Himself either in His own person or through His angels would do His work among us. But now, as a faithful physician considering our weakness, He has chosen men of our own flesh and blood, creatures whom we need not fear at all, in order that (*in this way*) His work might be most richly blessed and prove itself most successful.

In ancient times the prophets felt the greatest fear when they received a message from God or an angel. Even Moses could hardly endure this great terror. Since the Word had not yet become flesh, they could not understand it because of its abounding glory and their own great weakness. But now, after the Word has been made flesh, it has become very captivating and is imparted to us through men of our own flesh and blood. That, however, does not mean that we should love it less and treat it with less reverence. It is the same Word as before, even though it does not come to us with terror, but with winning love. Those who do not want to love and honor it now, must at last endure all the more anguish.

Separated unto the gospel of God (1:1). These words may be understood in two ways. In the first place, in the sense of Acts 13:2: "The Holy Ghost said, Separate me Barnabas and Saul for the work whereunto I have called them." In that sense the words mean: Paul alone was separated as an apostle of the Gentiles, as were Peter and the other apostles for the ministry among the Jews. The Apostle thus explains his ministry more fully, for he is not merely a servant of Jesus Christ and an apostle of God, but he is separated before the others to be an apostle to the Gentiles in a unique way.

Again, the words might be understood in the sense of Galatians 1:15,16: "When it pleased God, who separated me from my mother's womb, and called me by his grace, to reveal his Son in me, that I might preach him among the heathen." In that sense the words mean: Paul before others was separated even from his mother's womb to be an apostle to the Gentiles. For this we have an analogy in the Old Testament, for in Jeremiah 1:5 we read: "Before thou camest forth out of the womb I sanctified thee, and I ordained thee a prophet unto the nations." This literally applied to Paul, for having been taken from other occupations and tasks, he was separated, ordained and sanctified for the one office to preach the Gospel. This is the meaning I prefer. Incidentally, he reproves those who, though ordained to the divine ministry and entrusted with the Lord's office, mingle in secular pursuits as if they were men of the world. Paul emphasizes the fact that he was separated not to any work in general, but to the one task of preaching the Gospel. In this sense he writes in I Corinthians 1:17: "Christ sent me not to baptize, but to preach the gospel."

Which he had promised afore (1:2). He adds these words in order that his readers might not think that his Gospel is a reward for our merits or also a figment of human wisdom. The most convincing and persuasive proof (*of the truth*) of the Gospel is the fact that it was witnessed by the Law and the Prophets. The Gospel (*today*) proclaims to us only that which it was to proclaim according to the divine promise. This proves that God's counsel of salvation was foreordained in detail before it was carried into effect. So all glory for this doctrine must be ascribed to God and none to our merits and efforts; for before we ever existed, it was already ordained, according to the testimony in Proverbs 8:23; "I was set up from everlasting, from the beginning, or ever the earth was." It is indeed the Gospel, God's wisdom and God's power (I Cor. 1:24), which has brought forth the Church and accomplished everything which in this passage divine Wisdom says in honor and praise of itself. The same we read in Amos 3:7: "The Lord God will do nothing, but he revealeth his secret unto his servants the prophets." So also in Isaiah 48:5 we are told: "I have even from the beginning declared it to thee; before it came to pass I shewed it thee: lest thou shouldest say, Mine idol hath done them, and my graven image, and my molten image, hath commanded them."

By his prophets in the holy scriptures (1:2). This the Apostle states in contradistinction to God's promise which He predetermined before the foundation of the world. Of this divine eternal promise he writes in Titus 1:2: "In hope of eternal life, which God, that cannot lie, promised before the world began." This eternal promise was made known by the prophets in time and in human speech. It is indeed a wonderful proof of God's grace that He published this eternal promise in human words and that not merely orally, but also in writing. He did all this, in order that when the promise would be fulfilled, men would realize that He was dealing with them in accordance with His predetermined counsel of salvation. From this we see that the Christian religion owes its existence neither to blind chance nor to fate (as some foolish people think), but to the divine predetermined counsel and foreordained purpose, according to which it had to be fulfilled. It is very significant too that the Apostle adds to the words "his prophets" the phrase "in the holy scriptures." The reason for this is clear. Had he merely said "by his prophets," some might maliciously interpret this as signifying such men as then were dead and so had passed away together with their prophecies. But as it is, He points us to the Sacred Scriptures of the prophets which still exist.

Concerning his Son Jesus Christ our Lord, which was made of the seed of David according to the flesh; and declared to be the Son of God with power, according to the spirit of holiness, by the resurrection from the dead (1:3, 4). The meaning of these words, in my opinion, is this: The Content, or Object of the Gospel, or as some put it, the Subject, is Jesus Christ, the Son of God, born of the seed of David, according to the flesh, and now appointed to be King and Lord of all things with power, and this according to the Holy Ghost who raised Him from the dead.

Let us study the words in detail. The Gospel centers in the Son of God, but not merely in the Son of God as such, but inasmuch as He became incarnate of the seed of David, that is to say, inasmuch as He emptied Himself and became a weak man. He who was before all things and created all things, Himself assumed a beginning and was made man. The Gospel, however, treats not only of the humiliation of the Son of God, according to which He emptied Himself, but also of His majesty and sovereignty,

which in His humiliation He received of God according to the
human nature. Just as the Son of God by His humiliation and
self-emptying became the son of David in the weakness of the
flesh, so now conversely He is ordained and appointed to be the
Son of God with omnipotence and glory. And just as He emptied
Himself of His form of God to deep lowliness of the flesh and so
was born into the world, so now He elevated Himself from His
form of a servant to the full deity and ascended unto heaven. It
is necessary at this point carefully to consider the manner in which
the Apostle most peculiarly expresses himself; for he does not say:
"He was *made* the Son of God with power," as he says: "He was
made the seed of David according to the flesh." From the very
moment when Christ was conceived, it was correct to say, because
of the communion of the two natures (*in His person*): "This God
is the son of David;" and: "This man is the Son of God."

But even though He was not made the Son of God and though
He was made the son of man, yet He always was the Son of God
and remains the same forever. That, however, was not yet fully
made known and revealed to men. He had already (*by his incarnation*) received sovereignty over all things and was the Son of
God, yet He did not exercise it. In His state of humiliation He
therefore was not yet regarded as the Son of God. That was
accomplished by the Spirit of Holiness, for the Spirit had not yet
been given Him (*for glorification*) while as yet He was not exalted,
as He Himself says: "He shall glorify me" (John 16:14). The
Holy Spirit firmly established and made known through the
apostles that Jesus Christ is the Son of God, the sovereign Lord
of all things, to whom all creatures are subject and whom God the
Father has appointed to be Lord and Christ (Acts 2:36). That is
what the words "declared to be the Son of God with power" express:
This man, the son of David according to the flesh, is now publicly
made known as the Son of God with power, that is, as the omnipotent Lord of all things, after He had been subjected to all
things in weakness as the son of David. And all this was done
according to the Spirit of Holiness; for, as said before, to Him
is ascribed Christ's glorification. That, however, the Holy Spirit did
only after the resurrection, for which reason the Apostle adds:
"By the resurrection from the dead."

The Apostle uses the expression "spirit of holiness" in place of "Holy Spirit," but that is of no significance, for He is the same Spirit who, according to His divine work, is called either "Holy Spirit" or "Spirit of Holiness." The phrase "with power" must be understood of that divine omnipotence which rules all things according to the word of the prophet: "Whom he hath appointed heir of all things" (cf. Ps. 8:1 ff with Heb. 1:2). The Gospel, then, is the joyous message of Christ, the Son of God, who first humbled Himself and then was glorified through the Holy Spirit. Gospel therefore is not merely what Matthew, Mark, Luke, and John have written, but, as the verse shows, the Word concerning the Son of God, who was made man, suffered, and was glorified.

By whom we have received grace and apostleship, for obedience to the faith among all nations, for his name (1:5). Paul here speaks of "obedience to the faith," and not of obedience to such wisdom as first must be proved by arguments of reason and experience. It is not at all his intention to prove what he says, but he demands of his readers implicit trust in him as one having divine authority. Nor does he want his hearers to argue about the faith, or that which they are to believe. In the Church of Christ no minister is ordained for his own sake, but on account of others, namely, to make them such as obey the Gospel.

Among whom are ye also called of Jesus Christ: to all that be in Rome, beloved of God, called to be saints: Grace to you and peace from God our Father, and the Lord Jesus Christ (1:6, 7). From this verse we learn that (*divine*) love precedes the calling (*of sinners*), just as the calling precedes their sanctification. Paul's hearers were to realize that they were saints, not because of any merit on their part, but because of God's love and call, so that he ascribes all things — (*their whole salvation*) — to God. No one indeed becomes a believer, or a saint, unless he is called by God. But (*let us also remember*): "Many be called, but few chosen" (Matt. 20:16).

First, I thank my God through Jesus Christ for you all, that your faith is spoken of throughout the whole world (1:8). Jesus Christ is our only Mediator, and the true Christian way of praising (*God*) is not simply to praise men, but to praise, primarily and above all, God in them and to ascribe to Him all glory. Again, we can (*rightly*) praise God only through Christ; for as we receive all blessings through Him from God, so we must also through Him acknowledge them all as God's, since Christ alone is worthy to appear before the throne of God and as our Priest to intercede for us. Lastly, we must let those whom we praise know definitely that they are to advance still more (*in their Christian faith*) and become established, in order that they may not become proud. (*With regard to the words*) "your faith is spoken of throughout the whole world," (*let me say that*) Christian love manifests itself in this that it rejoices at every good thing that it sees in others, especially at their spiritual blessings, and thanks God for them. On the other hand, envy manifests itself in this that a person is grieved because of the good which he recognizes in others, and so wishes him evil.

For God is my witness, whom I serve with my spirit in the gospel of his Son, that without ceasing I make mention of you always in my prayers (1:9). Christian prayer is complete only when we intercede for the common good of all and not merely for ourselves; there must be (*fellowship*) prayer. The Apostle in his prayers makes mention of his hearers always and without ceasing. If we are to begin lesser tasks with prayer and intercession before God, then much more must we undertake spiritual matters in this way.

Making request, if by any means now at length I might have a prosperous journey by the will of God to come unto you. For I long to see you, that I may impart unto you some spiritual gift, to the end ye may be established: that is, that I may be comforted together with you by the mutual faith both of you and me (1:10-12). The Apostle longed to see the believers at Rome. The same longing is found in every faithful shepherd who does not desire what the sheep possess, but seeks only the sheep themselves; and this (*desire*) is prompted solely by love. (*Note that he says*): "I long to see you," not the city of Rome nor any other people, as do those who are prompted by curiosity, but only you who believe and so are Christians. (*Paul writes*): "That I may impart unto you some spiritual gift, to the end ye may be established." Carnal curiosity seeks to satisfy its own cravings by seeing others; but he who is spiritual desires the happiness of others, even when he is acting in his own occupation. Here the Apostle teaches very graphically by his own example for what purpose a pastor must visit his parishioners, or why one Christian should visit another.

Now I would not have you ignorant, brethren, that oftentimes I purposed to come unto you, (but was let [hindered] *hitherto,) that I might have some fruit among you also, even as among other Gentiles. I am debtor both to the Greeks, and to the Barbarians; both to the wise, and to the unwise. So, as much as in me is, I am ready to preach the gospel to you that are at Rome also* (1:13-15). Paul here meets two objections which secretly might be raised against him. In the first place, he might be charged with arrogance for extending his apostolic ministry beyond the Greek areas into those where Latin was used, and indeed even beyond these. Others might accuse him of presumption for attempting to instruct those who already were wise and instructed in the faith, and to these belonged the Christians at Rome. In the same way he might be criticized for his boldness in forcing his teachings upon the wise of this world. To these objections he replies: I do this not by chance, but to pay a debt that I owe.

(With the words) "So, as much as in me is, I am ready to preach the gospel to you who are at Rome also," the prologue ends, and the letter properly begins. His introduction was designed to render his readers attentive and willing to listen to him. He gains their attention by extoling his office and the glory of the *(divine)* Word. He makes them willing to listen by promising solely to serve their salvation as their minister and debtor.

For I am not ashamed of the gospel of Christ: for it is the power of God unto salvation to every one that believeth; to the Jew first, and also to the Greek (1:16). The Gospel is a power which saves all who believe it, or, it is the *(divine)* Word which is powerful to rescue all who put their trust in it. This indeed is through God and from God! By "power of God" we must not understand the power according to which God Himself is omnipotent as God, but the power by which He makes *(anyone or anything)* powerful or mighty. As we speak of the "gift of God," so also we speak of "the power of God," that is, of the power which comes from God. We thus read in Acts 1:8: "Ye shall receive power, after that the Holy Ghost is come upon you"; again in Luke 1:35: "The power of the Highest shall overshadow thee."

The Gospel is called the power of God in contradistinction to the power of man. The latter is the (*supposed*) ability by which he, according to his carnal opinion, obtains salvation by his own strength, and performs the things which are of the flesh. But this ability God, by the Cross of Christ, has utterly declared null and void, and He now gives us His own power by which the spiritual — (*the believer*)— is empowered unto salvation. (*Man's own power must be destroyed*); otherwise the power of God will not be in us; for the rich and the mighty do not receive the Gospel, and so also not the power of God, as it is written: "To the poor the gospel is preached" (Luke 7:22).

To this day it remains true that whoever does not believe, will be ashamed of the Gospel and contradict it, at least in his heart and conduct; for he who finds pleasure in that which is of the flesh and of the world, cannot find pleasure in that which is spiritual and of God. So he is not only ashamed of preaching the Gospel, but also personally fights against it and refuses to let it convert him, since he hates the light and loves the darkness. It thus becomes foolishness to him; indeed it appears to him as downright stupidity, according to I Corinthians 2:14: "The natural man receiveth not the things of the Spirit of God: for they are foolishness unto him: neither can he know them, because they are spiritually discerned"; or Romans 8:7: "The carnal mind is enmity against God: for it is not subject to the law of God, neither indeed can be."

So, then, the verdict holds: He who believes the Gospel, must become weak and foolish before men, in order that he might be strong and wise in the power and wisdom of God, as it is written in I Corinthians 1:25 ff.: "The foolishness of God is wiser than men; and the weakness of God is stronger than men . . . . not many wise men after the flesh, not many mighty, not many noble, are called: but God hath chosen the foolish things of the world to confound the wise; and God hath chosen the weak things of the world to confound the things which are mighty."

For therein is the righteousness of God revealed from faith to faith: as it is written, The just shall live by faith (1:17). God's righteousness is that by which we become worthy of His great salvation, or through which alone we are (*accounted*) righteous before Him. Human teachers set forth and inculcate the righteousness of men, that is, who is righteous, or how a person becomes righteous, both in his own eyes and those of others. Only the Gospel reveals the righteousness of God, that is, who is righteous, or how a person becomes righteous before God, namely, alone by faith, which trusts the Word of God. Thus we read in Mark 16:16: "He that believeth and is baptized shall be saved; but he that believeth not shall be damned." The righteousness of God is the cause of our salvation. This righteousness, however, is not that according to which God Himself is righteous as God, but that by which we are justified by Him through faith in the Gospel. It is called the righteousness of God in contradistinction to man's righteousness which comes from works. This human righteousness of works Aristotle clearly describes in the third book of his *Ethics*. According to his view, righteousness follows man's works, and is brought about by them; God's judgment, however, is different, for according to it, righteousness (*justification*) precedes works and good works grow out of it.

The words "from faith to faith" have been interpreted in various ways. Some explain them thus: From the faith of the Fathers of the Old Testament to the faith of the New Testament. This exposition may be accepted, though also it may be contested; for the righteous do not live by faith of past generations, but, as it is written, "The just shall live by (*his*) faith." The Fathers believed the same Gospel that we have; for there is but one faith, even though it may not have been as clear to them as it is to us. The words evidently mean: The righteousness of God comes altogether from faith, but in such a way that there appear constant growth and constant greater clarity, as it is written in II Corinthians 3:18: "We . . . are changed into the same image from glory to glory." The words "from faith to faith" therefore signify that the believer grows in faith more and more, so that he who is justified becomes more and more righteous (*in his life*). This he adds in order that no one might think that he has already apprehended (Phil. 3:13) and so ceases to make progress (*in sanctification*); for that indeed means that he begins to fall behind. St. Augustine explains the words in the eleventh chapter of his book *Concerning the Spirit and the Letter* thus: "From the faith of those who confess it with the mouth to the faith of those who actually obey it."

Why Sinful Man Needs the Gospel of Christ

For the wrath of God is revealed from heaven against all ungodliness and unrighteousness of men, who hold the truth in unrighteousness; because that which may be known of God is manifest in them; for God hath shewed it unto them. For the invisible things of him from the creation of the world are clearly seen, being understood by the things that are made, even his eternal power and Godhead; so that they are without excuse: because that, when they knew God, they glorified him not as God, neither were thankful; but became vain in their imaginations, and their foolish heart was darkened. Professing themselves to be wise, they became fools, and changed the glory of the uncorruptible God into an image made like to corruptible man, and to birds, and four-footed beasts, and creeping things. Wherefore God also gave them up to uncleanness through the lusts of their own hearts, to dishonour their own bodies between themselves: who changed the truth of God into a lie, and worshipped and served the creature more than the Creator, who is blessed for ever. Amen. For this cause God gave them up unto vile affections: for even their women did change the natural use into that which is against nature: and likewise also the men, leaving the natural use of the woman, burned in their lust one toward another; men with men working that which is unseemly, and receiving in themselves that recompence of their error which was meet. And even as they did not like to retain God in their knowledge, God gave them over to a reprobate mind, to do those things which are not convenient; being filled with all unrighteousness, fornication, wickedness, covetousness, maliciousness; full of envy, murder, debate, deceit, malignity; whisperers, backbiters, haters of God, despiteful, proud, boasters, inventors of evil things, disobedient to parents, without understanding, covenantbreakers, without natural affection, implacable, unmerciful: who knowing the judgment of God, that they which commit such things are worthy of death, not only do the same, but have pleasure in them that do them (1:18-32).

For the wrath of God is revealed from heaven against all ungodliness and unrighteousness of men, who hold the truth in unrighteousness (1:18). Here the Apostle begins to show that all men live in sin and folly, in order that they may realize that their wisdom and righteousness (*of works*) are in vain and they need the righteousness of Christ. This he illustrates, first of all, by describing the moral condition of the heathen. The Apostle has in mind primarily the wise and mighty of this world. If they bow (*to the Gospel*), then also their subjects, the common people, will readily accept it. He does this also for the reason that they most bitterly opposed the Gospel and Word of Christ's Cross and incited others against it. He therefore charges them with sin and guilt as if they were the only transgressors, and proclaims to them the wrath of God. To no one else does the Gospel appear so utterly foolish as to the wise and mighty (of this world), because it goes counter to their notions.

(In verse 19) the words "which may be known of God" might best be rendered with an abstract expression as, for example, "the knowledge of God."

God hath showed it unto them (1:19). These words declare that all earthly gifts must be ascribed to God as their Donor; for here the Apostle speaks of the natural knowledge of God, as the explanatory words prove: "The invisible things of Him from the creation of the world are clearly seen." This statement tells us that from the beginning of the world the invisible things of God have always been recognized through the rational perception of the (divine) operations (in the world). All men therefore, in particular all idolators, had a clear knowledge of God, especially of His Godhead and His omnipotence. They proved this by calling the idols which they made "gods," and even "God", and they revered them as eternal and almighty, at least as strong enough to help them. This demonstrates that there was in their hearts a knowledge of a divine sovereign Being. How else could they have ascribed to a stone, or to the deity represented by a stone, divine attributes, had they not been convinced that such qualities really belong to God! Manifestly they knew that God is mighty, invisible, just, immortal and good. But they erred in ascribing to their idols the divine attributes (that belong only to the true God).

From the creation of the world (1:20). This phrase emphasizes the fact that God was known ever since the world came into existence. The invisible things of God could be seen at all times, (they being understood by the things that are made).

In our text the Apostle rebukes not only the Romans (as some think), but the whole heathen world. That is clear from what he says in Romans 3:9: "We have before proved both Jews and Gentiles, that they are all under sin." He therefore excepts no

one, as he expressly speaks of "all." Nevertheless, He judges the
Romans and their wise men much more severely, because they
led the world through their hegemony, dominion and philosophy.
The text teaches us incidentally that ministers of the Gospel must
reprove, first and above all, the rulers and thinkers of the people,
not indeed in their own words coming from an erratic confused
mind, but by means of the Gospel showing them how they act
contrary to the divine Word and so sin. The band of such witnesses
is indeed very small!

Their foolish heart was darkened (1:21). As a person would be
foolish to look for money only to look at it, without trying to get
it into his possession, so the heathen, though they knew God, were
satisfied with and gloried in the mere knowledge of Him. They
left out of mind His worship, in particular, the inward dedication to
God, whom they knew.

Professing themselves to be wise, they became fools (1:22). This
is a golden rule which holds true in all cases (*where men fail in
their duty to God*), for what is true of the special is true also of
the general. In the mouth of another person (*than the inspired
Apostle*) this (*statement*) would, of course, be quite another matter.
Those who really regard themselves as foolish, (*namely, the pious,
humble believers*), are truly wise. Conversely, they who boast of
their being mighty, influential and noble, are weak, deformed
and ignoble before God, even though in the eyes of men they
might boast (*of such gifts*), and that because they glory (*in their
gifts and good qualities*).

*And changed the glory of the uncorruptible God into an image
made like to corruptible man* (1:23). In other words, they did
not honor God (*as they knew Him*), but their own notions (*of
God*). I favor this interpretation, for even the Children of Israel
are charged with showing divine honor to Baal and golden calves,
though, without doubt, they meant to worship the true God under
these forms and images. But that God had forbidden them.

The sin of omitting that which is good leads to the sin of committing what is positively evil. For this reason, the Apostle, after
having shown how the heathen sinned by neglecting the worship
of the true God, now demonstrates how they sinned (*positively*)
by establishing the worship of false gods, or idolatry. The human

mind is so inclined by nature that as it turns from the one, it of necessity becomes addicted to the other. He who rejects the Creator needs must worship the creature.

Also man is "uncorruptible" so far as his soul is concerned. But the heathen dishonored God even to the extent that they failed to make Him like to the soul that is in them. They only made Him like to man's bodily appearance, or the image of his body, according to which he is "corruptible."

And to birds, and four-footed beasts, and creeping things. (1:23). All this is known to those who have read the books of the heathen. The Apostle does not mention the stars, or heavenly bodies, and other similar things, because naturally those who worship the objects made by man, worship also those made by God. In this way the Apostle by implication argues from that which is lesser and more common. There are indeed still many who honor God, not as He demands this, but according to their speculations concerning Him. The proof for this is supplied by the strange superstitious customs (*prevalent today*) which are as stupid as they can be. It certainly means to change the glory of God into an image, or a figment of the mind, when men neglect what He demands and honor Him by works which they have chosen for themselves, thinking that He follows them and their wishes, just as though He were different from the way in which He has revealed Himself in His Word. For this reason God even today gives up many to their vain minds and corrupt hearts.

Notice in the text the steps or stages of (*heathen*) perversion. The first step of their idolatry is ingratitude: they were not thankful. So Satan showed himself ungrateful over against his Creator before he fell. Whoever enjoys God's gifts as though he had not graciously received them, forgetting the Donor, will soon find himself filled with self-complacency. The next step is vanity: they "became vain in their imaginations." In this stage men delight in themselves and in creatures, enjoying what is profitable to them. Thus they become vain in their imaginations, that is, in all their plans, efforts and endeavors. In and through them they seek whatever they desire; nevertheless, all their efforts remain vain since they seek only themselves: their glory, satisfaction and benefit. The third step is blindness; for, deprived of truth and steeped in vanity, man of necessity becomes blind in his whole feeling and thinking, since now he is turned entirely away from God. The fourth step or stage is man's total departure from God, and this is the worst; for when he has lost God there remains nothing else for God to do than to give him up to all manner of shame and vice according to the will of Satan.

In the same way also, man sinks into spiritual idolatry of a finer kind, which today is spread far and wide. Ingratitude and love of vanity (of one's own wisdom, or righteousness, or, as it is commonly said, of one's "good intention") pervert man so thoroughly that he refuses to be reproved, for now he thinks that his conduct is good and pleasing to God. He now imagines he is worshiping a merciful God, whereas in reality he has none; indeed, he worships his own figment of reason more devoutly than the living God. Oh, how great an evil ingratitude is! It produces desire for vain things, and this again produces blindness; and blindness produces idolatry, and idolatry leads to a whole deluge of vices. Conversely, gratitude preserves love for God and so the heart remains attached to Him and is enlightened. Filled with light, he worships only the living God and such true worship is followed immediately by a whole host of virtues.

Wherefore God also gave them up to uncleanness. (1:24). This giving up is not merely by God's permission, but by His will and command, as we clearly see from I Kings 22:22-23, where we are told that God commanded the lying spirit to persuade Ahab to act against His will. The same we learn from II Samuel 16:10 and other passages. To the objection that God prevents what is evil and so cannot give up anyone to what is evil, we reply that this is correct, judged from the viewpoint of divine love. But when God deals with transgressors according to His stern justice, He permits the perverse sinner to break His commandments all the more viciously in order that He might punish him the more severely. Viewed from the standpoint of the sinner who is given up, this is indeed a "permission" on God's part, since He withdraws His saving hand from him and deserts him. But this takes place according to God's righteous judgment, for it is His most severe punishment to give up a sinner to him whom He hates most, (*namely, the Devil*).

From this we must not conclude that God desires sin, even if it does occur according to His (*punitive*) will. On the contrary, it shows that He hates sin exceedingly. God never desires sin as such, but He permits sin to execute His punitive judgment upon those who deserve it. The punishment, however, is not properly the sin itself, but the reprobation which is connected with it.

It is evidently not the intention of the Apostle to say that all idolaters committed all these enormous vices; many no doubt committed only some. Some sinned in one way, and others in another, but God's judgment exerted itself in all of them. Manifestly there were many who were not at all given to such vices (*as here described*), as, for example, some of the Roman consuls; indeed there may have been many who were chaste and virtuous in a high degree. But all of them were idolaters, nevertheless.

Nor must we believe that Paul with his threefold "God gave them up," which here he enumerates in proper order, meant to say that his divine punishment was of necessity executed (*in the same manner*) upon all sinners. Some may have been given up to all three vices, others only to one, and again others to two, just as God in His judgment had decreed. What the Apostle means to show is the fact that all were sinners and in need of the grace of Christ.

To dishonour their own bodies (1:24). Very cautiously and by way of paraphrase the Apostle speaks of the perversions of the heathen, rebuking them with such terms as "uncleanness" and "dishonour." In I Corinthians 6:9,10 he writes (*more explicitly*): "Be not deceived: neither fornicators, nor idolators, nor adulterers, nor effeminate, nor abusers of themselves with mankind . . . shall inherit the kingdom of God." So also in Ephesians 5:3 and II Corinthians 12:21. Since to honor the body (at least in this one respect) means to be chaste and continent, or to use it properly, so the abuse of the body, by changing its natural use, means to dishonor it. The body is disgraced and degraded most viciously not only by adultery and similar violations of chastity, but all the more by the degrading perversions (*that are here named*).

As a rule, when a young man has no longer any spark of reverence for God in his heart, but goes his way unrestrainedly and without any regard for God, it can hardly be assumed that he is still chaste. Of necessity either the flesh or the spirit is alive in him, and so either the flesh or the spirit has the ascendancy. There is no safer way to victory over the lusts of the flesh than to flee from them by devout prayer.

Who is blessed for ever. Amen (1:25). The Apostle evidently adds this blessing because of his Jewish piety; for whenever the Jewish teachers mention God, they supplement it with such terms as the "Holy One," or the "Blessed One," as Caiaphas did when he asked: "Art thou the Christ, the Son of the Blessed?" (Mark 14:61). But alas, most people even today entertain unworthy thoughts of God and assert in a bold, not to say, arrogant way that God is so or so. They do not do Him the honor to admit that the glorious God is supremely exalted over their reason and judgment, but they elevate their own opinions (*of God*) so highly that they have no more difficulty or fear to judge God than they judge the leather of a poor shoemaker. They think that God's righteousness and mercy are just so as they imagine them to be; and although they are without the Spirit who knows even the deep things of God, in their arrogance they boast as though they were full, yes, more than full of Him. So do the heretics, the Jews, and all men of conceited mind, all indeed who are outside divine grace. No one certainly can rightly judge God who is without the Holy Spirit. Without Him men judge and teach falsely, whether it be about His righteousness or His mercy, whether about themselves or others. God's Spirit must bear witness to our own spirit (Rom. 8:16).

They did not like to retain God in their knowledge (1:28). This is the reason why God gave them up into various vices, for vices indeed, (*as the Apostle here shows*), appear in great variety. To all of these, or to some of these, God gave up the heathen, or let us rather say, some of them. Not all were murderers or addicted to all the other transgressions (*which are named here*). God, in punishing, does not give up all sinners in like manner, even though they might sin in like manner. The reason for this is to be sought in His hidden divine judgment as also in the circumstance that one sinner also might do something that is good, while another does no good at all or at least very little. At any rate, God stops every arrogant mouth in order that no one might prescribe to Him any rule according to which He should punish sin or reward virtue. Therefore He permits men to sin in the same way, and yet He has mercy on some and forgives them, while He hardens and condemns others. Similarly He allows some (*outwardly*) to do good and lead a righteous life, and yet He rejects and casts away the one and receives and exalts the other.

Being filled with all unrighteousness (1:29). In Scripture, as the study of Hebrew shows, there is a difference between unrighteousness and iniquity. (*The Latin has iniustitia and iniquitas.*) Unrighteousness — (*lack of conformity with what is right*) — is the sin of unbelief, or the lack of that righteousness which flows from faith, just as, for example, he is righteous who believes; and he is unrighteous who does not believe (cf Rom. 1:17; Mark 16:16). He who does not believe is disobedient; and he who is disobedient is unrighteous. Iniquity — (*violation of what is right*) — is the sin of self-righteousness which men choose for themselves in their own foolish zeal for piety. We might also say: Iniquity consists in this, that man neglects the duty which he is bound to do, and that he does that which, (*contrary to the divine Word*), seems good in his sight. The right conduct, however, shows itself in this, that man puts aside what seems good to him, (*but is contrary to the divine Word*), and does what he should do. In the area of civil righteousness, of course, different rules apply.

Being filled with . . . maliciousness (1:29). Maliciousness is the perverse tendency in man to do evil despite the good which he has received; indeed he abuses even the good things which God gives him in the service of evil. Conversely, goodness is the right disposition in man to do good even when his effort is hindered or checked by some wrong done to him; goodness even makes evil serve that which is good. A person is not good in the Christian sense of the term who does only good so long as he fares well and no resistance is offered to him in any way. Of being good in this Christian sense, those who are good only in a worldly sense are not capable, as we read in Matthew 7:18: "A good tree cannot bring forth evil fruit, neither can a corrupt tree bring forth good fruit."

In similar contrast stand the terms "benevolence" and "malevolence." Benevolence is the heartfelt desire to be obliging and to do good to others. It is of two kinds. Christian, or perfect, benevolence always remains the same, no matter whether it encounters gratitude or ingratitude. The imperfect human, or earthly benevolence continues only so long as it meets with appreciation, but ceases when it encounters ingratitude or any other evil. In Matthew 5:48 we read: "Be ye therefore perfect, even as your Father which is in heaven is perfect"; and in Luke 6:35: "But love ye your enemies, and do good, and lend, hoping for nothing again; and your reward shall be great, and ye shall be children of the Highest: for he is kind unto the unthankful and to the evil." Malevolence, on the contrary, is the perverse, hateful tendency to hurt or harm others. In his total depravity man does injury even to those who are grateful and good, and not merely to the evil. That truly is bestial malevolence. With regard to Christian benevolence it is written in Galatians 5:22: "The fruit of the Spirit is . . .gentleness, goodness."

Being filled with. . .malignity (1:29). Malignity is the perverse tendency willfully to omit what is good and to hinder what is evil. Some act in this way because of envy, but others from an impudence that cries to high heaven. "Whisperers" (1:29) and "backbiters" (1:30) may be distinguished from each other in this way that the backbiters destroy the good reputation of others, while the whisperers destroy concord and create disharmony by secretly carrying tales of one sort to some and of another sort to others.

Romans Two

Content of the second chapter: The Apostle rebukes the sins of the Jews and shows them that are in the same guilt as the heathen; indeed, in a certain sense the Jews are even worse than the Gentiles.

THE JUDGMENT OF GOD AGAINST ALL SINNERS

Therefore thou art inexcusable, O man, whosoever thou art that judgest: for wherein thou judgest another, thou condemnest thyself; for thou that judgest doest the same things. But we are sure that the judgment of God is according to truth against them which commit such things. And thinkest thou this, O man, that judgest them which do such things, and doest the same, that thou shalt escape the judgment of God? Or despisest thou the riches of his goodness and forbearance and longsuffering; not knowing that the goodness of God leadeth thee to repentance? But after thy hardness and impenitent heart treasurest up thou thyself wrath against the day of wrath and revelation of the righteous judgment of God; who will render to every man according to his deeds: to them who by patient continuance in well doing seek for glory and honour and immortality, eternal life: but unto them that are contentious, and do not obey the truth, but obey unrighteousness, indignation and wrath, tribulation and anguish, upon every soul of man that doeth evil, of the Jew first, and also of the Gentile; but glory, honour and peace, to every man that worketh good, to the Jew first and also to the Gentile: for there is no respect of persons with God. For as many as have sinned without law shall also perish without law: and as many as have sinned in the law shall be judged by the law; (for not the hearers of the law are just before God, but the doers of the law shall be justified. For when the Gentiles which have not the law, do by nature the things contained in the law, these, having not the law, are a law unto themselves: which shew the work of the law written in their hearts, their conscience also bearing witness, and their thoughts the mean while accusing or else excusing one another:) in the day when God shall judge the secrets of men by Jesus Christ according to my gospel (2:1-16).

Therefore thou art inexcusable, O man, whosoever thou art that judgest: for wherein thou judgest another, thou condemnest thyself: for thou that judgest doest the same things (2:1). This

51

mistake (*of condemning others though guilty themselves*) is committed by all who are outside of Christ; for, while the righteous (*true believers*) make it a point to accuse themselves in thought, word and deed, the unrighteous (*unbelievers*) make it a point always to accuse and judge others, at least in their hearts. For this (*fact*) there is an explanation. The righteous invariably try to see their own faults and overlook those of others. Again, they are eager to recognize the good things in others and to disregard those of their own. On the other hand, the unrighteous look for good in themselves and for evil in others.

For this reason it is indeed well for the Apostle, after having spoken of those, (*the heathen*), who actually commit the (*gross*) transgressions (*described above*), to show that also such are in the same class (*of transgressions*) as imagine themselves to be better than the former. From their guilt the Apostle infers that also they, (*the Jews*), are in need of Christ and His righteousness, since of necessity all who are outside of Christ commit the same sins, notwithstanding their hypocrisy and show of piety. Their arrogant assertion finds its explanation in the fact that the Apostle enumerates many vices that some (*the Jews*) do not practice; so they accuse others, (*the heathen*), of these transgressions without noticing that they themselves are guilty of different sins, and indeed of such as the Apostle mentions, and of which the former, (*the heathen*), are not guilty.

To illustrate (*by a more general application*): usurious misers usually accuse and condemn the adulterers while they forget their own sins. Adulterers again may treat misers the same way. Just so the haughty may charge others with faults. For this reason it is impossible for such wicked judges to be guiltless, unless they become justified through Christ. This is indeed true of the heathen, yet even in a greater measure of the Jews. The Apostle therefore at the beginning of the chapter stresses the thought that in his accusation he has in mind mainly the Jews. To them we may compare, in a special degree, the heretics and hypocrites as also our modern jurists and priests, and lastly also those who quarrel among themselves and judge one another, while they do not regard themselves as offenders. Indeed they boast of their being right and even invoke God's wrath upon their adversaries; for certainly the Apostle here did not have in mind merely those who lived in Rome at his time.

But we are sure that the judgment of God is according to the truth against them which commit such things. And thinkest thou this, O man, that judgest them which do such things, and doest the same, that thou shalt escape the judgment of God? (2:2,3).

What the Apostle here says (*against the judging Jews*) is certainly true, as later he writes: "There is no respect of persons with God" (v. 11). It would indeed be so (*as the Jews think*) if those could escape God's judgment who do the very things for which they regard others as worthy of damnation. And here is a mistake which most people make. When they see how other sinners are punished, they are glad and say: "Well and good! The punishment is just! That evildoer deserved it!" In reality, however, they should become afraid and confess: "That person was punished yesterday, and tomorrow it may be my turn," according to the proverb: "The puppy is punished to terrify the hound."

Today we may apply the Apostle's words first to those (*rulers*) who without cogent cause inflict exorbitant taxes upon the people, or by changing and devaluating the currency, rob them, while at the same time they accuse their subjects of being greedy and avaricious. Even worse are the blinded ecclesiastical rulers who commit similar, if not greater wrongs as everyone knows. Guilty of excesses, vainglory, pomp, envy, covetousness, gluttony, and other iniquities, they yet regard themselves as beyond judgment. We may apply the passage also to those who judge others, either in their hearts or with their mouths, condemning them even though they themselves are as bad as those whom they judge. Or we may refer it to those who look upon themselves as holy, although they are guilty of other sins than those which they judge, just as though they were righteous for not committing all the wrongs which others do. But to teach and correct such sinners is a most difficult task.

Or despisest thou the riches of his goodness and forbearance and longsuffering; not knowing that the goodness of God leadeth thee to repentance? — (2:4) There are three (*special*) favors which God, as the Apostle here shows, confers upon sinners: goodness, forbearance and longsuffering; and these He bestows in great riches,

that is, in fulness and abundance. The riches of His goodness
consist in the abounding fulness of His temporal and spiritual
benefactions such as the blessings of body and soul, the free use
of His creatures, the services which they render man, the protection
of the holy angels, and the like. The riches of His forbearance
consist in His abundant clemency with which He bears those who
reward His divine blessings with ingratitude and in addition requite
good with evil by committing so many more and greater sins. The
riches of His long-suffering manifest themselves in this that He
postpones His just punishment of such ungrateful sinners for an
incredibly long time, waiting for His goodness to lead them to
repentance.

But so great is the blindness of the wicked that they abuse
to their own harm the very blessings which God bestows upon
them for their good. On the other hand, the light shines in the
righteous and pious so brightly that they use for their good the
very evil which men have intended for their harm. The ungodly
do not realize that the goodness of God should lead them to repentance. The righteous, on the contrary, know that even the severity
of God must redound to their good; for God wounds and again
heals; He slays and again makes alive.

But after thy hardness and impenitent heart, treasurest (thou) *up
unto thyself wrath against the day of wrath and revelation of the
righteous judgment of God* (2:5). The greater God's long-suffering
is, the greater also will be His judgment if His goodness is bestowed
in vain. Therefore the Apostle writes: "After thy hardness and
impenitent heart treasurest (*thou*) up unto thyself wrath." He does
not simply say: "You will receive wrath," but: "You treasure up
a large amount of wrath, or you store up for yourself a full, yes
an overflowing measure of wrath." From this we learn what a
hardened heart really is, namely, a heart that despises God's goodness, forbearance, long-suffering. It receives innumerable blessings
and yet it commits countless sins and never thinks of mending its
evil ways.

*Against the day of wrath and revelation of the righteous judgment
of God* (2:5). The Apostle addresses those (*who harden their
hearts*) much more severely, for it is so much more difficult to
correct those whose mind is perverse, as, for example, those who

(*unjustly*) condemn others. It is impossible for such to repent, unless they are brought to a knowledge of their sinfulness and cease to judge others. They are fools who regard themselves as wise, and sinners who regard themselves as just, as it is written in Proverbs 26:12: "Seest thou a man wise in his own conceit? there is more hope of a fool than of him." Such transgressors are sure that their intentions and actions are good and right, and so they harden themselves more and more and continue in impenitence; for they do not think it proper to repent of something of which they think that it is good, nor will any admonition turn them from their wicked way.

Judgment Day is called a day of wrath and a day of mercy; a day of tribulation and a day of peace; a day of damnation and a day of glory. On that day the wicked will be punished and put to shame, while the righteous will be rewarded and crowned with glory.

(*Luther makes the following general comment on* 2:6-10): Patient continuance is so altogether necessary that no work can be good in which patient continuance is lacking. The world is so utterly perverse and Satan is so heinously wicked that he cannot allow any good work to be done, but he must persecute it. However, in this very way God, in His wonderful wisdom, proves what work is good and pleasing to Him. Here the rule holds: As long as we do good and for our good do not encounter contradiction, hatred, and all manner of disagreeable and disadvantageous things, so we must fear that our good work as yet is not pleasing to God; for just so long it is not yet done with patient continuance. But when our good work is followed by persecution, let us rejoice and firmly believe that it is pleasing to God; indeed, then let us be assured that it comes from God, for whatever is of God is bound to be crucified by the world. As long as it does not bring the cross, that is, as long as it does not bring shame and contempt as we patiently continue in it, it cannot be esteemed as a divine work since even the Son of God was not free from it — (*suffering for the sake of the good He did*) — but left us an example in this. He Himself tells us in Matthew 5:10,12: "Blessed are they which are persecuted for righteousness' sake. . . .Rejoice, and be exceeding glad: for great is your reward in heaven."

Those who complain and are chagrined when they suffer for doing good show by this that their good work is not of God, but something which they have presumed to do moved by self-sufficiency. Such persons do good for their own sake, either seeking honor and glory by it, or trying to avoid slander, defamation, and hatred to which omission of the good might subject them. Their chagrin at suffering shows very clearly that they did not do good for God's sake, in true humility and from love, but for their own sake, in particular, for their good reputation, and so from secret self-love and pride. Those who lovingly and humbly do good for God's sake will say, if praised: "As I have not begun it to be praised, so I will not continue it for the sake of praise." If reproved they say: "As I have not begun it to be criticized, so I will not discontinue it because of my critics." They therefore continue to do good from love to God and are protected against the dangers both of flattery and criticism. In Hebrews 10:36 we read: "For ye have need of patience, that, after ye have done the will of God, ye might receive the promise."

The pagan proverb of Cicero, "Virtue increases in proportion as it is praised," should be treated with scorn in the Church and rejected; for the Apostle declares the opposite to be true when he says in II Corinthians 12:10: "I take pleasure in infirmities, in reproaches, in necessities, in persecutions, in distresses for Christ's sake: for when I am weak, then am I strong." Carnal virtue indeed grows by praise, because it seeks praise, but Christian virtue grows despite criticism and suffering, while it is destroyed by praise if the heart takes pleasure in adulation. Carnal virtue, which increases by praise, turns into wrath and despair if it is criticized.

Who will render to every man according to his deeds. . .glory and honour (2:6, 7). In his commentary on John, Chapter 17, St. Augustine remarks: "A person has glory, in the sense of the ancient classics when his name is mentioned far and wide with approval." In the fifth book of his *City of God* he writes: "Glory exists when men so esteem others that they show how good an opinion they have of them." Honor, according to Aristotle, is the esteem which men show (*certain*) persons in recognition of their ability, or the esteem which people show individuals by word, deed and tangible proof because of their virtues. This, then, is the difference (*between the two terms*): Glory streams forth from a person toward others; honor comes from others and turns to the (*honored*) person; or, glory goes out from a person, and honor comes toward a person.

Unto them that are contentious . . . indignation and wrath (2:8). I take these words to express God's indignant wrath with which he punishes (*the sinner*) both in his body and soul. It is His most severe wrath.

Tribulation and anguish, upon every soul of man that doeth evil (2:9). These terms explain the preceding more fully, and there is an inward relation also between them. I take them to mean that the Apostle has in mind not any kind of tribulation but such tribulation as is joined with anguish. This means that then there is no more way out, not even any hope for a way out; so also in this tribulation there is no more comfort. Christians, it is true, also endure tribulation, but they are consoled in their tribulation, as the Apostle writes in II Corinthians 1:4: "Who comforteth us in all our tribulation." The believer has such comfort because he hopes and trusts in God, but reprobate sinners are tormented in their tribulation by despair. They have nothing in which they might trust or hope, as they cannot hope in God that at last they might be redeemed.

For there is no respect of persons with God. For as many as have sinned without law shall also perish without law; and as many as have sinned in the law shall be judged by the law; (for not the hearers of the law are just before God, but the doers of the law shall be justified) (2:11-13). Here the Apostle anticipates the subterfuges of the Jews and the Gentiles. He had said: "Who will render to every man according to his deeds" (v.6), no matter whether he is a Jew or a Gentile. To this assertion the Jews might reply, indeed, they were minded to reply: "We know the Law and obey it, for we are the chosen people of God through the covenant of the Law made on Mount Sinai." The Gentiles might say: "We did not know the Law, and so we should be excused because of our ignorance of the Law." To both (*objections*) the Apostle answers: "No, indeed!" He first addresses himself to the arrogant Jews who gloried in the Law which they had received and which, as they boasted, they heeded and obeyed. According to their argument,

God therefore should ascribe to them only what is good and charge the heathen with what is evil. They reasoned that since they were the seed of Abraham, they should share his reward with him. So at all times and in every way the Jews tried to make God a respecter of persons.

Similarly the Apostle crushes the pride of the heathen who gloried in the excuse that they had not known the Law and so in their estimation did not deserve any divine wrath. Paul tells them: "Oh, no! They shall perish without law," just as also they are saved without the Law. They were to keep the Law which they had, the Law inscribed in their hearts from creation. Though it was not given to them (*as the revealed law was entrusted to the Jews*), the Law which they knew without tradition was alive in them, although it was not given to them in letters.

By "Law" we must understand in this whole chapter the Law of Moses in its totality, as summed up in the Decalogue, in which love for God and the neighbor is commanded. By the expression "without law" the Apostle means the Law of which he says later: "Which shew the work of the law written in their hearts" (2:15). Although the heathen did not receive the commandments and ordinances of the Mosaic Law, yet they had a spiritual law, which the commandments and ordinances of the Mosaic Law represented in their moral sense. This Law is inscribed in the hearts of all men, Jews as well as Gentiles, and it obligates every person. Of this Law our Lord says in Matthew 7:12: "All things whatsoever ye would that men should do to you, do ye even so to them; for this is the law and the prophets."

The Law gives occasion to sin unless there is the assistance of divine grace, and the heart, mind and will are divinely directed toward keeping the Law. The human will (*by nature*) always goes against the Law; it would rather do the opposite (*of its demands*), if only it could, even if (*outwardly*) man does what the Law commands. Wherever the Law prevails, man is moved (*by it*), to sin more than he is moved to fulfill it. So the poet (*Ovid,* Amores, *III,* 4, 17, 18) says: "We always seek what is forbidden and stretch out our hands, desiring to obtain what is denied us." Again: "The sick person thus desires the water that is forbidden him." Or: "Whatever is allowed, we do not want, but that which is not permitted us, we burn all the more fiercely to possess it." Again: "Whatever follows me, I flee; but whatever flees me, I pursue." St. Augustine writes in the fifth chapter of his book *Concerning the Spirit and the Letter*: "I do not know why it is that what we desire becomes all the more alluring to us if it is forbidden." In the eighth chapter of the same book he says: "Whoever does what the Law commands without the help of divine grace, does it because he fears punishment, and not from love for what is right. Before God therefore that is missing in man's will which appears to him, who sees only the outward performance of the work." Of such nature was the outward obedience of the Jews, of which Christ says in Matthew 5:20: "Except your righteousness shall exceed that of the Pharisees, ye shall in no case enter into the kingdom of heaven." They said, for instance, that wrath in the heart is not sin, but that he only sins who commits (*actual*) murder.

For when the Gentiles, which have not the law, do by nature the things contained in the law, these, having not the law, are a law unto themselves; which shew the work of the law written in their hearts, their conscience also bearing witness, and their thoughts in the meanwhile (interchangeably) *accusing or else excusing one another;* (2:14-15). St. Augustine explains the words "the Gentiles, which have not the law, do by nature the things contained in the law" in two ways. According to his (second) exposition, these words pertain to the (*heathen*) who, though leading a wicked life and not truly and rightly worshiping God, nevertheless perform this or that good work, for which reason they may be rightly said to do some of that which the Law demands, or (*at least*) they understand something of it. Hence it can be said of the heathen only with limitation that they by nature do the things contained in the Law. Understood in this sense, the passage is clear and St. Augustine's explanation may stand; for in that case the Apostle here mentions the heathen because they have observed the Law as little as have the Jews. Hence both are sinners, no matter how much good they may have done: the Jews, because they fulfilled the Law only according to its letter; the heathen, because they fulfilled the Law only in part and not at all according to its spirit. This interpretation I approve since the whole scope of the chapter, as Paul himself shows in 3:9, serves to point out that all men, Jews and Gentiles, are sinners and so in need of divine grace.

But how do the Gentiles show that the work of the Law is written in their hearts? First, so far as others are concerned, by doing what the Law demands. In the second place, so far as they themselves are concerned, now and on the Day of Judgment, by their conscience, which bears witness. This witness is favorable when it concerns good deeds, for in that case their thoughts excuse or defend them. It is a condemning witness, when they do evil works, for then their thoughts accuse them and their conscience torments them. All of this proves that they know the Law by nature, or that they can distinguish between good and evil.

The conscience of every person groans and cries out when a person does what is evil, unless it is altogether misled or altogether dulled by neglect. But it is at peace when a person does what is good, as also Cicero says (*Cato Maior,* 3, 9): "The satisfaction which a person receives from a life well lived brings with it memories that are filled with joy." So, then, their thoughts show that the heathen know what they should do or also not do, in other words how they are to observe the (*divine*) Law.

In the day when God shall judge the secrets of men by Jesus Christ according to my Gospel (2:16). Men will finally be judged by their own thoughts, which either accuse them of guilt or defend them according to the good which they have done; for then not words or works, which might deceive, but their own innermost thoughts witness concerning them publicly, just as these now witness in them, telling them what they are and what they have done.

From our own (*guilty*) conscience certainly only accusing thoughts can come, because our works are vain before God, unless He himself is efficacious in us by His grace. We, of course, may easily excuse ourselves. But that does not mean that we have satisfied God or fully kept His Law. But from whom, then, do we obtain the thoughts that (*truly*) excuse us? Only from Christ and in Christ; for if the conscience of a believer in Christ reproves, accuses and condemns him as an evil-doer, he quickly turns from himself to Christ and says: "He has atoned for my sins. He is just and my Justifier, who died for me. He has made His righteousness my own and my sins His own. But if He has made my sins His own, then I no longer have them but am free from them. And if He has made His righteousness my own, then I am righteous because of His righteousness, for He is God, blessed forever."

So, then, "God is greater than our heart" (I John 3:20). Far greater is He who defends me than that which accuses me, indeed, infinitely greater. God is my Defender, while my heart is my accuser. Oh, what a blessed relation! But so it is, just so! "Who shall lay anything to the charge of God's elect?" (Rom. 8:33ff.) No one! Why? "It is God that justifieth! Who is he that condemneth?" No one! Why? "It is Christ (and He is God!) that died, yea rather, that is risen again, who is even at the right hand of God, who also maketh intercession for us." In short, "If God be for us, who can be against us?"

GOD'S JUDGMENT AGAINST THE JEWS

Behold, thou art called a Jew, and restest in the law, and makest thy boast of God, and knowest his will, and approvest the things that are excellent, being instructed out of the law; and art confident that thou thyself art a guide of the blind, a light of them which are in darkness, an instructor of the foolish, a teacher of babes, which hast the form of knowledge and of the truth in the law. Thou therefore which teachest another, teachest thou not thyself? thou that preachest a man should not steal, dost thou steal? Thou that sayest a man should not commit adultery, dost thou commit adultery? thou that abhorrest idols, dost thou commit sacrilege? thou that makest thy boast of the law, through breaking of the law dishonourest thou God? For the name of God is blasphemed among the Gentiles through you, as it is written. For circumcision verily profiteth, if thou keep the law: but if thou be a breaker of the law, thy circumcision is made uncircumcision. Therefore if the uncircumcision keep the righteousness of the law, shall not his uncircumcision be counted for circumcision? And shall not uncircumcision which is by nature, if it fulfil the law, judge thee, who by the letter and circumcision dost transgress the law? For he is not a Jew, which is one outwardly; neither is that circumcision, which is outward in the flesh: but he is a Jew, which is one inwardly; and circumcision is that of the heart, in the spirit, and not in the letter; whose praise is not of men, but of God (2:17-29).

After the Apostle has shown that all heathen are sinners, he now, in a special and most emphatic way, shows that also the Jews live in sin, above all because they obey the Law only outwardly, that is, according to the letter and not according to the spirit.

Thou therefore which teachest another, teachest thou not thyself? (2:21). But how can the Jew teach when he himself does not know anything (*about rightly keeping the Law*), in particular, when he refuses to be instructed? The Apostle clearly shows by this reproof that he is speaking of the spiritual knowledge and understanding of the Law, regarding which those refuse knowledge who instruct others according to the letter. They do not teach themselves, nor indeed others, that they must do the works commanded by the Law with a willing and sincere heart. So he continues:

Thou that preachest a man should not steal, dost thou steal? Thou sayest a man should not commit adultery, dost thou commit adultery? (2:22). The Apostle here declares that the Jew steals in his will (*thought*) or also secretly, that is, he would steal if he were permitted. But such a wicked will is regarded by God as an accomplished deed. So also the Jew commits adultery inwardly and before God by the sinful lusts of his heart. The words "dost thou steal?" also apply to the rulers and tyrants of this world who seize the possessions of their subjects, not indeed by force or open robbery, but by threatening those who do not yield to them with their disfavor and by refusing to help them when they are in trouble. So they say: "We did not compel them, but they gave us these things of their own free will." Most certainly, they did not force them directly,' but by withdrawing from them their protection, they coerced them. So wicked is the mind of man!

Thou that makest thy boast of the law, through breaking of the law dishonourest thou God? (2:23). The Apostle manifestly wishes this to be taken in the sense of the words: "He is not a Jew, which is one outwardly (v. 28)." He freely admits that the Jew observes the Law outwardly, but not inwardly and willingly. As the Saviour says in Matthew 5:28: "Whosoever looketh on a woman to lust after her hath committed adultery with her already in his heart," so the Apostle understands the charge: You do the same wrong which you judge; for you do the evil, if not (*openly*) before men, at least in your desires and before God. So, then, it is clear that the Apostle here means by "doing," "committing adultery," "stealing," etc., the inward sinful passions of the heart. If any one desires to commit such sins, then in the eyes of God he is already a malefactor in the fullest sense of the term. But they (*such offenders*) neither believe these words, nor do they admit that they are such transgressors. For this reason, the Apostle, to make it clear that he is speaking of the spiritual keeping of the Law, continues.

Circumcision verily profiteth, if thou keep the law (2:25). **To** the objection of the Jews that they keep the Law, the Apostle replies: Indeed, you do, but only outwardly. Yours is a circumcision of the flesh and not of the spirit, as he explains in the following: "Neither is that circumcision, which is outward in the flesh" (v. 28). With these words he rejects all righteousness that is merely of the letter as insufficient; and this again proves that he had accused the Jews because of the inward sins of their (*evil*) hearts.

But now someone might say: "Such (*demanded*) circumcision of the spirit can be accomplished only by grace; for human nature, as shown above, is inclined to all evil, incapable of doing good, full of hatred against the Law which compels man to be good and checks what is evil, and so he cannot love it. Man therefore remains captive continually in his wicked lusts, which resist the Law. He remains immersed in evil desires, even if outwardly from fear of punishment, or from love for an earthly advantage he obeys (*the Law*) ever so well. In this (*evil state*) he continues until he receives help from God." To this I reply: Just that is the objective of the Apostle and his Lord, to humble the proud and to bring them to a full knowledge of their evil condition; to teach them that they need (*divine*) grace; to destroy their own righteousness, so that in deep humility they seek after Christ, confess their sins and so accept grace and be saved.

Therefore if the circumcision keep the righteousness of the law, shall not uncircumcision be counted for circumcision? (2:26). Here the Apostle speaks of the heathen who believe in Christ, and he puts them in opposition to the Jews who boast of their righteousness. Otherwise (*without faith in Christ*) they would not keep the Law rightly. Only he is a genuine Jew who is one inwardly (v. 29), that is, who believes in Christ.

For he is not a Jew, which is one outwardly; neither is that circumcision, which is outward in the flesh: but he is a Jew, which is one inwardly; and circumcision is that of the heart, in the spirit, and not in the letter; whose praise is not of men, but of God (2:28, 29). With these words the Apostle clinches the charge that the Jews are sinners; in fact, with them he motivates all he has said above. At the same time he meets the objection (*of the Jews*): "We keep the Law, for we are Jews that have received the circumcision." To this the Apostle replies: "That is not keeping the Law at all, for the Law is spiritual." The Jews kept the Law only outwardly and according to the letter. St. Augustine says: "The circumcision of the heart, is according to Paul, the cleansed will (*of man*), that is, the will which has been purified from all illicit desires. This is brought about not by the letter, which demands and threatens, but by the Spirit who helps and heals. For this reason the praise of such is not of man, but of God, who grants by His grace that for which they are praised. The Psalmist therefore says: 'My soul shall make her boast in the Lord!' (Ps. 34:2)."

The Apostle here teaches what our Lord says of the work-righteous in Matthew 23:5: "But all their works they do for to be seen of men." The praise of outward righteousness, however, comes from men; but it is rebuked by God. The praise of inward (*spiritual*) righteousness, however, comes from God; but it is rejected and persecuted by men. Spiritual righteousness (*which is by faith in Christ*) seems foolish, yes, and unjust to men; but the outward righteousness (*of the flesh*) is regarded by God as stupid, indeed as a twofold unrighteousness, (*that is, unrighteousness in itself and unrighteousness because it demands a merit*).

Romans Three

Content of the third chapter: The Apostle shows that the Jews indeed have an advantage over the heathen, but that both Jews and heathen are in need of Christ's grace.

The Law Does Not Save But Merely Declares Man Guilty Before God.

What advantage then hath the Jew? or what profit is there of circumcision? Much every way: chiefly, because that unto them were committed the oracles of God. For what if some did not believe? shall their unbelief make the faith of God without effect? God forbid: yea, let God be true, but every man a liar: as it is written, That thou mightest be justified in thy sayings and mightest overcome when thou art judged. But if our unrighteousness commend the righteousness of God, what shall we say? Is God unrighteous who taketh vengeance? (I speak as a man) God forbid: for then how shall God judge the world? For if the truth of God hath more abounded through my lie unto his glory; why yet am I also judged as a sinner? And not rather, (as we be slanderously reported, and as some affirm that we say,) let us do evil, that good may come? whose damnation is just. What then? are we better than they? No, in no wise: for we have before proved both Jews and Gentiles, that they are all under sin; as it is written, There is none righteous, no, not one: there is none that understandeth, there is none that seeketh after God. They are all gone out of the way, they are together become unprofitable: there is none that doeth good, no, not one. Their throat is an open sepulchre; with their tongues they have used deceit; the poison of asps is under their lips: whose mouth is full of cursing and bitterness: their feet are swift to shed blood: destruction and misery are in their ways: and the way of peace have they not known: there is no fear of God before their eyes. Now we know that what things soever the law saith, it saith to them who are under the law: that every mouth may be stopped, and all the world may become guilty before God. Therefore by the deeds of the law there

65

shall no flesh be justified in his sight: for by the law is the knowledge of sin (3:1-20).

What advantage then hath the Jew? or what profit is there of circumcision? Much in every way: chiefly, because that unto them were committed the oracles of God. For what if some did not believe? shall their unbelief make the faith of God without effect? God forbid: yea, let God be true, but every man a liar; as it is written, That thou mightest be justified in thy sayings, and mightest overcome when thou art judged (3:1-4). Since the Apostle has condemned those who are Jews after the flesh, and the circumcision which is outward in the flesh (2:28), it might have seemed as though he regarded circumcision as altogether worthless and its command to the Jews as purposeless. But that is by no means the case, and so he shows in this chapter what purpose circumcision and the Jews in general serve.

The advantage of the Jews over the heathen consisted above all in this that "to them were committed the oracles of God." That is to say, circumcision was of value to the Jews because they believed the divine promise *(connected with it)* and so they awaited its fulfillment. To the heathen God had given no such gospel promise, and it was sheer mercy on His part when in the fulness of the time He was pleased graciously to put them on the same level as the Jews. But to the Jews God showed Himself not only as merciful, but also as faithful, because he actually granted to them the mercies which He had promised them *(in Christ)*. For this reason truth *(faithfulness)* and mercy are often placed side by side in Scripture as in Romans 5:8, 9: "Now I say that Jesus Christ was a minister of the circumcision for the *truth* of God, to confirm the promises made unto the fathers: and that the Gentiles might glorify God for his *mercy*."

For what if some did not believe? (3:3) God did not give His promise in such a way, nor was His promise so believed by the Jews, that they had to obtain the promised inheritance whether they wanted it or not. Some did not believe and so did not receive the promise. The fault was solely theirs who did not desire to obtain the fulfillment of the promise. But that did not keep God from being true *(faithful)*. If they, the heirs of the circumcision, did not wish to receive the promise, though God had given it to them as such, then no one can charge God with faithlessness. To the Jews He fulfilled His promise in such a way that not all, but indeed some, namely the elect, received the promise, for God cannot lie. So God is justified in His sayings or promises.

There is a difference between the two statements: "God is justified" and "God is justified in His sayings or works"; for God cannot be justified by any man, since He Himself is Righteousness, indeed, the Eternal Law, Judgment and Truth. But God is justified in His sayings when His Word is recognized and accepted by us as just and truthful. This takes place when we believe in His Word (Gospel). Conversely, God is judged in His sayings if men regard His Word as false and fallacious. So God is justified in His sayings even by His enemies, for His Word is victorious over all. For some He, (Christ), is set for a rising, for others, a fall, namely those for whom He is a sign which is spoken against (Luke 2:34). Such persons judge Him indeed, but their judging is in vain. If God is judged in His sayings, it is really we (the believers) who are justified; if He is judged and condemned, it is they (the unbelievers) who are judged and condemned according to Mark 16:16: "He that believeth not shall be damned."

That in this connection the expression "faith of God" (v. 3) is to be taken in the sense of faithfulness or trustworthiness, is clear from Paul's argument: Because God is faithful, unbelief cannot make His trustworthiness without effect. God, who has given His promises and fulfilled them, if not to all men, at least to the heirs of promise, is not a liar; but all those are liars who do not believe (the divine Gospel promise).

But if our unrighteousness commend the righteousness of God, what shall we say? Is God unrighteous who taketh vengeance? (I speak as a man) God forbid; for then how shall God judge the world? For if the truth of God hath more abounded through my lie unto his glory; why yet am I also judged as a sinner? And not rather, (as we be slanderously reported, and as some affirm that we say,) Let us do evil, that good may come? whose damnation is just (3:5-8).

Here the Apostle digresses from his subject till verse 9, where he resumes it by asking: "What then? are we better than they?"

There are some who say that God's righteousness is placed in its true light by punishing our unrighteousness, for it is only then that His righteousness becomes manifest by His punishment of the unrighteous. That is correct, but it has nothing to do with the subject which the Apostle here treats, for he speaks of the righteousness of God by which He Himself is the Righteous, (*that is, God's essential righteousness, or justice*). He rather denies the assertion that God's righteousness is manifested by our unrighteousness. It is not our unrighteousness (*as such*) which God always hates and which is opposed to His majesty, but rather the acknowledgment and confession of our unrighteousness that commends His righteousness, for by these it becomes obvious how necessary and beneficial His righteousness is. God's righteousness humbles us, casts us down before His feet and causes us to long for His righteousness; for as soon as we receive it (*through faith in Christ*), we glorify God as its (*generous*) Giver and we praise and love Him.

Our righteousness (*it may be said*) commends God's righteousness in three ways. First, when God punishes the unrighteous, He thereby shows that He is righteous, and His righteousness manifests itself by His punishment of our unrighteousness. Secondly, by way of comparison, for the greater God's righteousness shines forth, the more wicked appears our unrighteousness. Lastly, God's righteousness is commended by His work in us; that is to say, since we cannot be justified by our own merit, we must appeal to Him to make us righteous. If we confess that we have no power over our sins (*to cleanse ourselves of our sins*), He justifies us through faith in His Word, (*the Gospel promise*). Through such faith He justifies us, that is, He declares us as righteous (*for Christ's sake*). This is the faith-righteousness and a truly divine righteousness, which He works (*in us*).

Nevertheless, the Apostle does not say that our righteousness commends God's righteousness; on the contrary, he denies this. But he puts the question (3:5) in the sense of those who thought that they might draw this conclusion. (*Of these he says*): "Whose damnation is just" (3:8). This passage shows clearly that the Apostle in this chapter does not direct himself against such as boast of their sins, but rather of such as think themselves righteous and trust in their own works to save them. These he tries to induce to praise and glorify the grace of God; but divine grace is magnified only after the sin which is to be forgiven has first been recognized and acknowledged as exceedingly great.

They are all under sin (3:9). So, then, though the Jews have an advantage over the Gentiles, as has already been shown, nevertheless before God they are not better, but like the heathen they are under sin. The Gentiles, on the other hand, despite the statement of the Apostle that they "by nature do the things contained in the law," have only a partial, or legal (*outward*) righteousness, not however, that true righteousness which is perfect, everlasting, and altogether divine, and which we may obtain only through faith in Christ.

The expression "all are under sin" must be taken in a spiritual sense; that is to say, not as men appear in their own eyes or in those of others, but as they stand before God. They all are under sin, those who are manifest transgressors in the eyes of men, as well as those who appear righteous in their own sight and before others. Those who perform outwardly good works do them from fear of punishment or love of gain and glory, or otherwise from pleasure in a certain object, but not from a willing and ready mind. In this way man exercises himself continually in good works outwardly, but inwardly he is totally immersed in sinful desires and evil lusts, which are opposed to good works. Such outward good works are doubly evil; first, because they do not flow from a good will and so are sinful (*in themselves*), and again, because with incredible arrogance they are upheld and defended as good. If the will of men is not sanctified by the grace of God, which He has promised and imparts to those who believe in Christ, so that freely and joyously and solely to please God in doing His will they do the works demanded by the Law, with full freedom from fear of punishment and selfish love for the act, they always are under sin.

There is none righteous (3:10). The corruption (*of which the Apostle here speaks*) is so very deep that it is not fully understood even by such as are spiritual (*believers*). For this reason the truly righteous pray fervently and entreat God for divine grace, not only because they know that their will is evil, but also because they can never fully comprehend the unspeakable depth of their depravity. So they humble themselves and earnestly ask God to sanctify them perfectly, which, however, takes place only in death. So it is that we all offend "in many things" (Jas. 3:2); and: "If we say that we have no sin, we deceive ourselves, and the truth is not in us" (I John 1:8). Indeed, how does a person know, or how can he know, even though he should imagine that he does good and avoids evil, whether it is really so, since only God can decide this? It is in fact a most dangerous arrogance for men to imagine that they have such a will (*that does the good and omits the evil*). Man (*by nature*) selfishly seeks only what is to his advantage; he can love only himself above all things; and that is the sum and substance of all transgression. Such (*self-sufficient*) persons seek only to please themselves and secure applause, even when they follow piety and virtue.

There is none that understandeth (3:11). The wisdom of God (*the Gospel*) is hidden and therefore it is unknown to the world. So Christ can be known only through divine revelation. Those therefore who are wise only in earthly things — as are all who do not believe, and so know as little of God as of eternal life — are without insight and understanding, foolish and blind, even though they regard themselves as, wise. By this fact, however, they prove themselves to be fools. Theirs is not the divine wisdom which is hidden (I Cor. 2:7), but a wisdom that may be discovered by human means.

There is none that seeketh after God (3:11). That is true both of those that do not at all care for God and of those who seek after Him, or rather who imagine themselves to seek after God. They do not seek after God as He desires to be sought and found, namely, not by human wisdom and searching, but by faith and in humility. The Apostle first says that there is none that understandeth, and that there is none that seeketh after God, for the understanding goes before the willing and doing. The true seeking after God, which moves man to dedication and obedience, follows upon the right understanding (*of God*). The understanding which is without the seeking after God, is dead, just as faith without works is dead and neither quickens nor justifies. The understanding, of which the Apostle here speaks, is nothing else than the faith itself or the spiritual apprehension of things which cannot be seen, but must be believed. It is the understanding of that which man cannot know of himself, as we read in John 14:6: "No man cometh unto the Father, but by me." Of Peter (*who had this understanding*), Christ said in Matthew 16:17: "Flesh and blood hath not revealed it unto thee, but my Father which is in heaven." The inward desire or seeking after God is true love for God, which moves believers to long for and love that which this (*spiritual*) understanding makes known to them. In this life we never reach such perfection that we fully possess God, but we must continuously seek after Him; indeed, we must seek Him evermore, as the Psalmist says in Psalm 105:4: "Seek the Lord . . . seek his face evermore." Those who do not make progress in seeking after God, are bound to retrogress; indeed, those who do not seek, will lose that which they already have obtained. We must never stand still in seeking after God.

They are all gone out of the way, they are together become unprofitable (3:12). The "all" here refers to those who have not yet become children of God through faith, or who have not yet been born again "of water and of the Spirit" (John 3:5). Of these some go out of the way to the left, namely, those who serve mammon, honor, pleasure and the glory of this world. The others go out of the way to the right, namely, those who hold to their own righteousness, virtue and wisdom. Neither of them cares for God's righteousness nor obeys Him, but all fight the divine truth in its present humble form with spiritual deceit.

The term "together" must be taken in the sense that *all* have become unprofitable, that is, vain and chasing after things that do not benefit. Those who seek after unprofitable things, themselves become unprofitable and vain through their association with vanities; and indeed, they deserve nothing better. They may be said to be unprofitable also from the viewpoint that they profit neither God nor men; but the first interpretation is preferable, since the Apostle here means to point out that they have fallen from the truth and righteousness of God and are going their own wicked way. Here, then, we have a climax: *None is righteous: none understandeth; none seeketh after God; none doeth good.* Even if such transgressors do good outwardly, they do not do it with sincerity, for they do not seek God in it, but only their own glory, gain, or, to say the least, freedom from punishment. On the other hand, those who (*in true faith*) seek after God, do good from a thankful and joyful heart, solely for God's sake, and not to gain any spiritual or temporal good on earth. But that is the work of divine grace, and not of nature.

Their throat is an open sepulchre (3:13). In the next three verses the Apostle shows how such (*unrighteous persons*) sin also against others. As they themselves have turned away from God, so they seek to draw to themselves and away from God other people. As the sepulcher takes the dead, so their throat or doctrine devours those who already are so completely dead that there is no more hope that they might be reclaimed from damnation, unless by a special act of His power God should intervene. Their throat is an "open" sepulcher, because they devour and mislead many, as we read in II Timothy 2:17: "Their word will eat as doth a canker." Such (*wicked deceivers*) devour also righteous persons. But as they cannot pervert their faith, they destroy them in their bodies (*by persecution*). Their throat therefore is truly an open sepulcher. They devour ever so many by teaching false and deceitful doctrine; and they proclaim their false doctrine in such a way that it appears to be holy, full of salvation, and coming from God. Those who permit themselves to be deceived by them, believe that they are listening to God and to a teaching proceeding out of the mouth of God. Every word of theirs flatters the hearts of those who take pleasure in their wisdom and righteousness, so that by word and deed they say: "Prophesy not unto us right things; speak unto us smooth things; prophesy deceits" (Isa. 30:10). They abhor the message of the Cross (*the Gospel of Christ*) and desire to hear only what flatters their vanity.

Oh, what a terrible word (*of condemnation*)! They destroy those who listen to their doctrine, for the "poison of asps is under their lips." The asp is a serpent, and its poison is sure to kill. So also they (*who are misled by such false prophets*) cannot be restored to spiritual life. Only, these most pitiable persons do not recognize the poison nor the death of their soul, as the words "under their lips" suggest. Death lurks in secret, while the words of their false teachers seemingly offer them life and truth.

Whose mouth is full of cursing and bitterness (3:14). (*Here we learn how such*) false teachers act toward those who do not obey, but rather resist them, yes, and who try to teach them the divine truth in order to save them from destruction. Oh, how sinfully they reward them! Against them their mouth is full of cursing. They curse them by reviling them before men, by execrating and defaming them, and by denouncing them with every kind of foul language. Nor do they do this listlessly, but with great zeal, for their mouth is "full" of cursing, that is, they curse with the greatest vehemence. So also their mouth is full of "bitterness," that is, full of hateful backbiting. They vilify the righteous not only in their hearing; but when they are together by themselves, they drag them into the gutter by evil-speaking that is most scurrilous.

Their feet are swift to shed blood (3:15). Also this is a most graphic description. They (*the wicked teachers*), cannot always accomplish what they set out to do, but they are always waiting for a chance to execute their ungodly designs. If they cannot defeat the messengers of truth by vilification and defamation, they finally take steps to remove them by murder, in order that their evil teaching may not be destroyed. This way the Jews followed with great tenacity as we learn from the Book of Acts. But even today every enemy of the divine truth acts in the same way to uphold his false doctrine; for indeed, he has a "good intention" and acts from "love to God."

Destruction and misery are in their ways (3:16). Here the Apostle describes the fate of such wicked teachers. They are pursued by destruction, that is, they are cast down, crushed and debased both in body and soul as we learn from the Jews; for "they are like the chaff which the wind driveth away" (Ps. 1:4). Again, they reap misery, or wretchedness. As Christians always succeed, so they (*who oppose Christ*) in the end never succeed, no matter what they may undertake. Also this we learn from the Jews, for while they progress in their wickedness, they are brought low by many misfortunes.

The way of peace have they not known (3:17). Why do they not know the way of peace? Because it is hidden, for (*this*) peace is spiritual and concealed beneath much tribulation. No one indeed regards it as peace when he sees how a Christian day by day is exposed to suffering with loss of his good name, reputation and even his life, so that as long as he lives he must count, not peace but cross and suffering his own. Yet under this tribulation their is concealed peace which only that person knows who believes and has experienced it. But the wicked do not want to believe, and they abhor the experience (*of faith*). Behind it all is their pride which renders them impervious (*to the peace of God*). The wicked do not understand the way of peace, because they are conceited; and they are conceited, because they do not fear God. If they would fear God, they would know that it is alone by Christ's righteousness and truth that they can escape judgment. Praise and glory to God to all eternity for having granted all this to us in and through Christ, in order that we might be truly justified by Him and so escape His judgment.

There is no fear of God before their eyes (3:18). Where there is no fear of God, there men become proud and presumptuous; but where the fear of God prevails, there men become humble and pious. Nevertheless, the wicked imagine that they possess the fear of God, and that in the highest degree. They boast of having all virtues, in particular, righteousness and insight. They boast above all, to be seeking after God, and of fearing God and doing every good work which the Apostle denies to them. If we do not accept the words of the Holy Spirit in Psalm 14:3 (*quoted in v.* 12) in true faith, then no one is righteous before God. Again, no one who is truly righteous can believe this (*that he is truly righteous*) to be possible by his own power. We must therefore always believe that what is here said is the divine truth concerning all men, and that it pertains to each and every one of us, for by nature we are unrighteous and without the fear of God. Hence, we must deeply humble ourselves and confess our depravity and ignorance before God, so that we may be found worthy to be justified by Him.

The law saith (3:19). Here the Apostle meets the subterfuge of those (*the Jews*) who say: "What he said does not apply to us since we are righteous, (*that is, obedient to the Law*)." But most certainly it does! And this (*their subterfuge*) clearly proves that Psalm 14:3, quoted in Romans 3:12, must be understood as referring mainly to the Jews; for the heathen did not have the revealed Law, so that the Psalmist here does not speak of them, at least not primarily.

That every mouth may be stopped, and all the world may become guilty before God (3:19). The Law declares all men to be unrighteous, in order that through this very judgment all may confess themselves to be unrighteous, no longer regard themselves righteous and no longer boast of their righteousness, but acknowledge themselves guilty before God. To praise and glorify God means for us to be silent *(before Him)*, not to extol ourselves, *(our good works)*, but believe that we are lost sinners.

Here the question arises: How can a person be justified without the works of the Law, or how can it be that justification does not flow from our works? For St. James writes: "We see how that by works a man is justified, and not by faith only" (Jas. 2:24). So also St. Paul: "Faith . . . worketh by love" (Gal. 5:6); and: "The doers of the law shall be justified" (Rom. 2:13). To this we reply: As the Apostle distinguishes between the law and faith, the letter and grace, so also he distinguishes between the works resulting from these. He calls those deeds "works of the Law" that are done without faith and divine grace, merely because of the law, moved either by fear of punishment or the alluring hope of reward. But works of faith he calls those deeds which are done in the spirit of *(Christian)* liberty and flow from love to God. These can be done only by such as are justified by faith. Justification, however, is not in any way promoted by the works of the Law, but they rather hinder it, because they keep a person from regarding himself as unrighteous and so in need of justification. When James and Paul say that a man is justified by works, they argue against the false opinion of those who think that *(for justification)* a faith suffices that is without works. Paul does not say that true faith exists without its proper works, for without these there is no true faith. But what he says is that it is faith alone that justifies, regardless of works. Justification therefore does not presuppose the works of the Law, but rather a living faith, which performs its proper works, as we read in Galatians 5:6.

By the law is the knowledge of sin (3:20). Such knowledge of sin is obtained in two ways. First, by meditation *(of the Law)*, as we read in Romans 7:7: "I had not know lust except the law had said, Thou shalt not covet." Secondly, by experience, namely, by trying to fulfill the Law, or we may say, through the Law as we assume to fulfill its obligations. Then the Law will become to us an occasion to sin, for then the perverted will of man, inclined to evil, but urged by the Law to do good, becomes all the more unwilling and disinclined to do what is good. It hates to be drawn away from what it loves; and what it loves is sin, as we learn from Genesis 8:21. But just so, man, forced by the Law and obeying it unwillingly, sees how deeply sin and evil are rooted in his soul. He would never notice this, if he did not have the Law and would not try to follow it. The Apostle here only mentions this thought, since he intends to treat it more fully in Chapters 5 and 7. Here he merely meets the objection that the Law would be useless if its works would not justify.

CHRIST'S RIGHTEOUSNESS BY FAITH
SAVES AND ESTABLISHES THE LAW

But now the righteousness of God without the law is manifested, being witnessed by the law and the prophets; even the righteousness of God which is by faith of Jesus Christ unto all and upon all them that believe: for there is no difference: for all have sinned, and come short of the glory of God; being justified freely by his grace through the redemption that is in Christ Jesus: whom God hath set forth to be a propitiation through faith in his blood, to declare his righteousness for the remission of sins that are past, through the forbearance of God; to declare, I say, at this time his righteousness: that he might be just, and the justifier of him which believeth in Jesus. Where is boasting then? It is excluded. By what law? of works? Nay: but by the law of faith. Therefore we conclude that a man is justified by faith without the deeds of the law. Is he the God of the Jews only? is he not also of the Gentiles? Yes, of the Gentiles also: seeing it is one God, which shall justify the circumcision by faith, and uncircumcision through faith. Do we then make void the law through faith? God forbid: yea, we establish the law (3:21-31).

But now the righteousness of God without the Law is manifested (3:21). St. Augustine writes in the ninth chapter of his book *Concerning the Spirit and the Letter*: "He does not speak of the righteousness of God, by which God is righteous, but of that with which He clothes a person when He justifies the ungodly." Again in the eleventh chapter he comments: "But now the righteousness of God without the law is manifested; that is, God imparts it to the believer by the Spirit of grace without the work of the Law, or without the help of the Law. Through the Law God opens man's eyes so that he sees his helplessness and by faith takes refuge to His mercy and so is healed." The Apostle therefore does not describe the righteousness of God, by which He is essentially righteous, but the righteousness (*by which a sinner is justified*), which they can obtain only by faith in Christ.

Being witnessed by the law and the prophets (3:21). An example for this we have in Habakkuk 2:4: "The just shall live by his faith." St. Augustine says in the thirteenth chapter of his book *Concerning the Spirit and the Letter*: "What the Law of works commands with threatening, that the Law of faith accomplishes through faith." In the nineteenth chapter he remarks: "The Law was given, in order that we might seek after grace. Grace was given, in order that we might fulfill the Law. It was not the fault of the Law that it was not fulfilled, but the fault was man's carnal mind. This guilt the Law must make manifest, in order that we may be healed by divine grace."

Even the righteousness of God which is by faith of Jesus Christ (3:22). This is a most important addition, and is directed against the rebellious mind of arrogant objectors who say: "Very well, then, we know of ourselves that we are unrighteous; we also know that we are inclined to evil and that inwardly we are enemies of God. We believe therefore that we must be justified before God, but this we desire to achieve by our prayers, repentance and confession. We do not want Christ, for God can give us His righteousness even without Christ." To this the Apostle replies: Such a wicked demand God neither will nor can fulfill, for Christ is God; righteousness for justification is given us only through faith in Jesus Christ. So God has willed it, and so God is pleased to do, and this He will never change. And who is there to resist His will? Now, however, if that is true then there is no greater arrogance than not to desire to be justified by faith in Christ.

For all have sinned, and come short of the glory of God (3:23). Men are altogether without any virtue in which they may glory (*before God*). They have no righteousness at all of which to boast before God, as we read in I Corinthians 1:29 "No flesh should glory in his presence." In Romans 4:2 the Apostle says: "If Abraham were justified by works, he hath whereof to glory; but not before

God." So also they (*the self-righteous Jews*) may have cause to glory in their works before men. But they have no glory before God. The real glory before God is righteousness, wisdom and spiritual strength, and all these come from God and are given to us freely by His grace. In these we glory, both in God and with respect to God, (*He being the Donor*).

Being justified freely by his grace through the redemption that is in Christ Jesus (3:24). God does not justify us freely by His grace in such a way that He did not demand any atonement to be made (*for our sins*), for He gave Jesus Christ into death for us, in order that He might atone for our sins. So now He justifies freely by His grace those who have been redeemed by His Son, (*as he adds: "Through the redemption that is in Christ Jesus"*).

Whom God hath set forth to be a propitiation through faith in his blood (3:25). This is a perplexing and difficult text that must be explained and understood as follows: God from eternity has ordained and set forth Christ as the propitiation for our sins, but that only for those who believe in Him. Christ wanted to become a propitiation for us only through His blood, that is, He first had to make amends for us through the shedding of His blood. And all this God did "*to declare his righteousness*," that is, to make it known that all men are sinners and in need of His righteousness. The very fact that Christ suffered for us, and through His suffering became a propitiation for us, proves that we are (*by nature*) unrighteous, and that we for whom He became a propitiation, must obtain our righteousness solely from God, now that forgiveness for our sins has been secured by Christ's atonement. By the fact that God forgives our sins (*only*) through Christ's propitiation and so justifieth us by faith, He shows how necessary is His righteousness (*for all*). There is no one whose sins are not forgiven (*in Christ*).

Of sins that are past (3:25). That is, the sins which preceded the demonstration of His righteousness (*through Christ's propitiation*). These were committed before the world knew that those who are justified are justified alone through (*faith in*) Christ.

Through the forbearance of God (3:25). Had God not patiently borne the sinners, there never could have been any remission of sins, nor any proof of His righteousness. God bears sinners so patiently to forgive them. He forgives them to show forth His righteousness and the justification of sinners which they receive through faith in His, (Christ's) blood, (*as the Apostle adds: "That He might be just, and the justifier of him which believeth in Jesus"*).

There are some who explain the words "for the remission of sins that are past, through the forbearance of God," thus: God showed His righteousness to the Fathers of the Old Covenant. He forgave them their sins through His forbearance, that is, in view of the promised atonement to be made by Christ. But I prefer the explanation: God reveals Himself through the remission of sins that are past as the One who justifies all men. His gracious remission of sins proves Him to be the God who is just and who alone has power to justify. With these words he also gives the answer to foolish objectors: Well, then, God has fulfilled the Law; hence, from now on He will no longer impute sin. Nor will He regard that as sin which He regarded as sin in the past. Hence, we may sin as we please, for what used to be sin, is no longer sin.

Where is the boasting then? It is excluded. (3:27). The Law of works of necessity puffs up and increases vainglory, for he who regards himself as just by fulfilling the Law, doubtlessly has something of which he might arrogantly boast. The Jews thus regard themselves as righteous, because they outwardly obey the Law. Therefore they do not seek to be justified (*by grace through faith in Christ*). They do not want Christ's righteousness, because they fully believe that they are already in possession of righteousness. Those who are of the Law say to God, as he speaks in the Law: "We have done what thou hast commanded us." On the other hand, those who are of faith say: "We cannot do it, nor have we done it; but grant us grace that we may do what Thou hast commanded us." While therefore they who are of the Law are arrogant and boastful, they who are of faith are humble and despise their own righteousness.

So throughout life (*God's*) believing, spiritual people pray with their hearts, their lips and their whole conduct that they might be justified (*by grace*) and kept in faith till the end. They also pray that they may never regard themselves as having apprehended and so cease (*in their striving after sanctification*). They finally pray that they may never regard any work of theirs as one by which they have obtained the righteousness (*of life*). While their life remains burdened with sin, they are always seeking after the perfect righteousness (*of life*) which, so to speak, keeps waiting outside.

Therefore we conclude that a man is justified by faith (3:28). The words "we conclude" must not be taken in the sense "we think," as though there were attached to the righteousness of faith any doubt, for such doubt would be wicked. The expression rather means: We believe most assuredly and firmly; indeed, we know; or, we are persuaded (*by the divine Word*) to believe that sinners are justified by faith.

When the Apostle says that we are justified "without the deeds of the law," he does not speak of the works of faith and grace; for he who does such works, does not believe that he is justified by doing these works. (*While doing such works of faith*), the believer seeks to be justified (*by faith*). What the Apostle means by "deeds of the law" are works in which the self-righteous trust as if, by doing them, they were justified and so were righteous on account of their works. In other words, while doing good, they do not seek after righteousness, but they merely wish to boast that they have already obtained righteousness through their works.

Seeing it is one God, which shall justify . . . by faith (3:30). Christ takes away all our sins, provided we (*believers*) do not take pleasure in them. But (*by faith*) they no longer are our sins, but His; and in exchange His righteousness is ours.

We establish the law (3:31). The Law is made void if its validity and authority are denied, so that it is no longer obligatory and men may transgress it. The carnally minded might have accused the Apostle of making void the Law, since he said that sinners are not justified by the Law, but that the righteousness of God is manifested and imparted without the Law. On the other hand, the Law is established and confirmed when its demands or injunctions are heeded. In this sense the Apostle says: "We establish the Law"; that is: We say that it is obeyed and fulfilled through faith. But you who teach that the works of the Law justify without faith, make the Law void; for you do not obey it; indeed, you teach that its fulfillment is not necessary: The Law is established *in us* when we fulfill it willingly and truly. But this no one can do without faith. They destroy God's covenant (*of the Law*) who are without the divine grace that is granted to those who believe in Christ.

Romans Four

Content of the fourth chapter: The Apostle shows from the example of Abraham that faith is necessary for salvation and that the Old Testament (*Mosaic*) Law was not sufficient for salvation.

ABRAHAM JUSTIFIED BY FAITH

What shall we say then that Abraham our father, as pertaining to the flesh, hath found? For if Abraham were justified by works, he hath whereof to glory; but not before God. For what saith the scripture? Abraham believed God, and it was counted to him for righteousness. Now to him that worketh is the reward not reckoned of grace, but of debt. But to him that worketh not, but believeth on him that justifieth the ungodly, his faith is counted for righteousness. Even as David also describeth the blessedness of the man, unto whom God imputeth righteousness without works, saying, Blessed are they whose iniquities are forgiven, and whose sins are covered. Blessed is the man to whom the Lord will not impute sin. Cometh this blessedness then upon the circumcision only, or upon the uncircumcision also? for we say that faith was reckoned to Abraham for righteousness. How was it then reckoned? when he was in circumcision, or in uncircumcision? Not in circumcision, but in uncircumcision. And he received the sign of circumcision, a seal of the righteousness of the faith which he had yet being uncircumcised: that he might be the father of all them that believe, though they be not circumcised; that righteousness might be imputed unto them also: and the father of circumcision to them who are not of the circumcision only, but who also walk in the steps of that faith of our father Abraham, which he had being yet uncircumcised. (4:1-12).

What shall we say then that Abraham . . . hath found? (4:1). Here the chapter refutes the unbelieving, arrogant Jews who tried to be justified by works. They labored under the delusion that their father Abraham was pictured to them as an example of work-righteousness. He therefore shows that Abraham was justified solely by faith without works.

Our father, as pertaining to the flesh (4:1). Inasmuch as Abraham was their (*the Jews'*) father according to the flesh, he "found" nothing, just as also we find nothing (*according to the flesh*); but only so do we find as Abraham becomes our father by faith.

Abraham believed God (4:3). This must be understood in the sense that Abraham was always ready to believe God. He steadfastly believed God. This fact we learn from Genesis chapters 12 and 13, where we are told that Abraham believed God who called and commanded him to leave his country and go into a strange land. Again he believed God when, according to Genesis 22:1ff., he was commanded to slay his son Isaac, and so forth. Whatever he did, he did by faith as the Apostle declares in Hebrews 11:8-10. So also what is stated in our text (v.3) is said of Abraham's faith in general, and not merely with regard to the one promise recorded in Genesis 15:4-6. To believe God means to trust Him always and everywhere.

To him that worketh is the reward not reckoned of grace, but of debt (4:4). The Apostle here explains the quoted passage (*Gen.* 15:4-6) to conclude and prove from it that justification is by faith and not by works. This he does first of all by explaining the meaning of the words "it was *counted unto him* for righteousness." These words explain that God receives (*sinners*) by grace and not because of their works.

To him that worketh not, but believeth in him that justifieth the ungodly (4:5). He who works properly receives a reward; but he receives the reward of debt, and not of grace. On the other hand, to him who does not rely on his works nor regards them as (*necessary for salvation*), righteousness is given freely by faith, which relies on God.

Even as David also describeth the blessedness of the man (4:6). This statement must be joined to the preceding as follows: "His faith is counted for righteousness," in which sense also David acknowledges that salvation is granted only to those to whom God counts their faith for righteousness, without works. The phrase "without works," however, applies only to such works of which the doer believes that by them he merits righteousness; in other words, that God regards him as righteous because of his works. That indeed is not true, for God does not accept the person on account of his works, but He accepts the works on account of the (*believing*) person. He first accepts the person who believes in Him and then the works flowing from faith. The former, (*the work-righteous*), finally regard themselves no longer as sinners; the latter, (*the believers*), always acknowledge themselves to be sinners.

Blessed are they whose iniquities are forgiven (4:7). Believers inwardly are always sinners; therefore they are always justified from without. The hypocrites, (*the work-righteous*), on the other hand, are always righteous inwardly; therefore they are always sinners from without. By "inwardly" I mean, as we appear in our own judgment and opinion; by "from without," as we appear before God and His judgment. We are righteous "outside ourselves" when our righteousness does not flow from our works; but is ours alone by divine imputation. Such imputation, however, is not merited by us, nor does it lie with our power, as the prophet says in Hosea 13:9: "O Israel, thou hast destroyed thyself; but in me is thine help." Of ourselves we are always wicked, as the Psalmist says in Psalm 51:3: "My sin is ever before me." But they, (*the work-righteous*), say: "My righteousness is ever before me, and blessed are they who do works of righteousness."

The text says: "Blessed are they whose iniquities are forgiven"; that is to say: Blessed are they who by grace are freed from the burden of iniquity, namely, of the actual sins which they have committed. That, however, is not sufficient, unless also their "sins are covered," that is, unless the radical evil which is in them, (*original sin*), is not charged to them as sin. That is covered when, though still existing, it is not regarded, considered and imputed by God; as we read: "Blessed is the man to whom the Lord will not impute sin."

Cometh this blessedness then upon the circumcision only . . . How was it then reckoned? when he was in circumcision, or in uncircumcision? (4:9, 10). This is a strong argument against the foolish Jews. If their father Abraham, of whom they boast so much, was not justified by circumcision, or by the works of the Law, but before the circumcision and before the giving of the

Law, and so was justified by faith, why do they who are his children (*desire to*) obtain righteousness by circumcision or the works of the Law, without faith? By this they prove themselves to be children of the circumcision, rather than (*spiritual*) children of Abraham.

He received the sign of circumcision, a seal of the righteousness of the faith (4:11). If the objection is raised that God later commanded circumcision and that indeed for justification, the Apostle replies: No, indeed; circumcision was not instituted for justification, but as a sign of the justification which already had taken place by faith. So today those who are justified by faith are commanded to do good, to circumcise without ceasing their perverse desires and to crucify their flesh with its wicked affections and lusts. By doing this they prove, as by signs, that they have faith and have been justified (*by faith*).

And the father of circumcision to them who are not of the circumcision only, but who also walk in the steps of that faith of our father Abraham (4:12). These words tell us that Abraham was justified before he was circumcised. Afterwards he received circumcision as a seal (*of his justification*). All this God did in order that we may know that throughout the world all those who followed Abraham's faith shall be his children. In this way (*by faith*) also the Jews will become his children, namely, if besides the circumcision of the flesh, they receive also the circumcision of the heart. According to the flesh they already are his children, but they must become also his spiritual children, in order that they may be Abraham's children not only according to the flesh, but also according to the spirit.

THE FIRM FAITH OF ABRAHAM

For the promise, that he should be the heir of the world, was not to Abraham, or to his seed, through the law, but through the righteousness of faith. For if they which are of the law be heirs, faith is made void, and the promise made of none effect: because the law worketh wrath: for where no law is, there is no transgression. Therefore it is of faith, that it might be by grace; to the end the promise might be sure to all the seed; not to that only which is of the law, but to that also which is of the faith of Abraham; who is father of us all, (As it is written, I have made thee a father of many nations,) before him whom he believed, even God, who quickeneth the dead and calleth those things which be not as though they were. Who against hope believed in hope, that he might become the father of many nations, according to that which was spoken, So shall thy seed be. And being not weak in faith, he considered not his own body now dead, when he was about a hundred years old, neither yet the deadness of Sarah's womb: he staggered not at the promise of God through unbelief; but was strong in faith, giving glory to God; and being fully persuaded that, what he had promised, he was able also to perform. And therefore it was imputed to him for righteousness. Now it was not written for his sake alone, that it was imputed to him; but for us also, to whom it shall be imputed, if we believe on him that raised up Jesus our Lord from the dead; who was delivered for our offences, and was raised again for our justification (4:13-25).

The promise . . . was not . . . through the law (4:13). Here again the Apostle shows that righteousness does not come from the Law, but from faith; for the Law and faith result in the very opposites: the Law in divine wrath and the loss of the promise; faith, however, in grace and the reception of the promise.

For if they which are of the law be heirs, faith is made void (4:14). Here the Apostle shows in another way that faith is made void by those who trust in their being the seed according to the flesh; for if that would suffice to make us righteous and worthy of the promise that we are children according to the flesh, then faith would not be necessary. He who is able to be justified by (*his descent according to*) the flesh and the Law, is not in need of faith, as they (*the Jews*) believe. But now the very opposite is the case: through (*trust in*) the carnal descent and the works of the Law they are damned. (*We are justified only*) "through the righteousness of faith" (v. 13). Also the (*believing*) heathen follow Abraham, as children follow their dear father, for also their seed has been promised to him.

The promise made of none effect (4:14). (*That is true*), for faith and the promise belong together. If the promise is abrogated, then also faith ceases. Without the promise faith is of none effect; and again, where there is no faith, there the promise fails.

The law worketh wrath. (4:15). This is properly the effect of the Law: it works wrath. That is to say, if it continues to stand (as it needs must stand), and is not obeyed, then those to whom it is given suffer God's wrath. Yet the Law is not evil, but those are evil to whom it has been given (*and who do not obey it*).

Where no law is, there is no transgression (4:15). It is properly the transgression that worketh wrath, but the transgression would not work wrath, were it not for the Law. And the Law gives occasion to sin.

Therefore it is of faith, that it might be by grace (4:16). It is the spiritual descent, received by faith, which makes us righteous and worthy of the promise. That suffices and does not need the other, (*that is, any descent according to the flesh*).

I have made thee a father of many nations (4:17). This the Jews understand in a carnal sense, just as though the descendants of Abraham would take possession of the whole world as their forefathers captured Canaan. But here the Apostle speaks of the spiritual inheritance which is received by faith, He means to say that the whole world, (*not merely Jews, but also Gentiles*), will follow Abraham's faith, confess him as their spiritual father and receive his Seed (*Christ*) as their Lord.

Before him (God) whom he believed (4:17). When God gives a promise and there is no one to believe His divine promise, then He will neither give any more promises nor fulfill them (*that are given*). Faith therefore confirms the promise, and the promise requires faith on the part of him to whom it is given. The Apostle says very aptly: If they believe that the promise of the inheritance is not bound to faith, then there is no other promise that is given them (*as of salvation by works or by the Law*). Abraham did not believe God in order that he might become the father of many nations, but he believed God as the One who is true and faithful.

Who quickeneth the dead, and calleth those things which be not as though they were (4:17). These words are an incentive that move us to faith. Abraham might have argued: "Behold, the inheritance which has been promised to me can be given to me neither now while I live, nor after my death; for my own body now is dead, and if my descendants will obtain the inheritance, then it is not I, but they who will have possession of it. Again, if the inheritance is given to me while I live, then it is not my descendants that will have it." Thus it always appears as if the promises of God contradict one another; and indeed, judged by human wisdom, they are impossible.

Who against hope believed in hope (4:18). Faith is something arduous and difficult. First, it is directed to what a person does not see (Heb. 11:1); indeed, to the very opposite of what one perceives. It seems utterly impossible. Then regarding the divine promise there arises the anguished thought in one's heart that God might change His counsel and do something else. The first pertains to God's power; the second, to His veracity. But behind the divine promise stands God's immutability both as regards His essence and His actions.

But was strong in faith, giving glory to God (4:20). We read in Numbers 23:19: "God is not a man, that he should lie; neither the son of man, that he should repent: hath he said, and shall he not do it? or hath he spoken, and shall he not make it good?" Man often breaks his promise (because he does not have the power to fulfill it, or because he is unstable), even if such breach of promise goes counter to his will. Man often cannot do what he has promised, because something intervenes which prevents it, since it lies beyond his power. But that cannot happen to God. He who believes God, glorifies God; conversely, he who does not believe God, refuses to give glory to Him, as we read in I John 5:10: "He that believeth not God hath made him a liar; because he believeth not the record that God gave of His Son." He who believes God, recognizes Him as true and faithful, and himself as a liar; for he mistrusts his own thinking as false, and trusts the Word of God as being true, though it absolutely contradicts his own reasoning. St. Augustine says that God is glorified through faith, hope and love. According to a common saying, God is directly insulted by three sins: unbelief, despair and hatred.

Who was delivered for our offences (4:25). Christ's death is the death of sin, and His resurrection is the raising up of righteousness. For by His death Christ has atoned for our sins, and through His resurrection He has procured for us righteousness. Christ's death does not merely signify, but has effected the remission of our sins. Christ's resurrection is not merely the pledge of our righteousness, but also its cause.

Romans Five

Content of the fifth chapter: The Apostle shows the power of faith as it proves itself in the justification of believers; for from Adam to Christ death exercised its destructive power. St. Paul speaks in this chapter with great joy and exceeding exultation. In the whole Bible there is hardly another chapter which can equal this triumphant text. The Apostle here most clearly describes God's grace and mercy and shows of what nature it is and how abundantly it has been poured out upon us.

The Abundant Blessings of Justification by Faith

Therefore being justified by faith, we have peace with God through our Lord Jesus Christ: by whom also we have access by faith into this grace wherein we stand, and rejoice in hope of the glory of God. And not only so, but we glory in tribulations also: knowing that tribulation worketh patience; and patience, experience; and experience, hope: And hope maketh not ashamed; because the love of God is shed abroad in our hearts by the Holy Ghost which is given unto us. For when we were yet without strength, in due time Christ died for the ungodly. For scarcely for a righteous man will one die: yet peradventure for a good man some would even dare to die. But God commendeth his love toward us, in that, while we were yet sinners, Christ died for us. Much more then, being now justified by his blood, we shall be saved from wrath through him. For if, when we were enemies, we were reconciled to God by the death of his Son, much more, being reconciled, we shall be saved by his life. And not only so, but we also joy in God through our Lord Jesus Christ, by whom we have now received the atonement. Wherefore, as by one man sin entered into the world, and death by sin; and so death passed upon all men for that all have sinned (5:1-12).

We have peace (5:1). Since God now has justified us by faith, and not by works, we have peace with Him both in heart and conscience, though not with man and with the flesh, nor with the world and the Devil. Believers rather have all the more trials.

Through our Lord Jesus Christ (5:1). That is, through our Mediator, and not through ourselves, we are justified by faith. Through Christ as our Mediator we also have access to God, as also by faith we love Him, know Him and take delight in Him. Without faith there is no access through Christ to God's gracious remission of sin and justification. In this we now stand through our firm profession of faith.

With "peace" the Apostle here means that peace of which all prophets speak, namely, spiritual peace, as he indicates this by the phrase "peace with God." This peace consists properly in an appeased conscience and in confidence in God, just as conversely the lack of peace means spiritual anxiety, a disturbed conscience and mistrust over against God. Because of this peace Christ is called the Prince of Peace (Isa. 9:6). In Ephesians 2:14 we are told: "He is our peace, who hath made both one"; and again in Ephesians 2:17: "(He) came and preached peace to you which were afar off, and to them that were nigh." So this expression must not be interpreted as signifying earthly peace, for Christ says in Matthew 10:34: "Think not that I am come to send peace on earth: I came not to send peace, but a sword." In John 16:33 Jesus says: "In me ye might have peace. In the world ye shall have tribulation." Therefore the words in Psalm 72:7: "In his days shall the righteous flourish; and abundance of peace so long as the moon endureth," must not be explained as signifying such earthly peace as the world enjoyed under Caesar Augustus, as many believe, but "peace with God," or spiritual peace.

In these words the Apostle sets forth a most apt antithesis (*in four ways*): first, he who is justified by faith has peace with God, but tribulation in the world, because his life is spiritual. Secondly, the unrighteous have peace with the world, but anguish and tribulation with God, because their life is carnal. Thirdly, as God the Holy Spirit is eternal, so also the peace of the righteous and the tribulation of the unrighteous will be everlasting. Lastly, as the flesh is temporal, so also the tribulation of the righteous and the peace of the unrighteous will be temporary.

By whom also we have access by faith (5:2). Very instructively the Apostle here connects "through our Lord Jesus Christ" and "by faith." He first directs himself against the arrogance of those who believe that they have access to God without Christ, just as though their mere believing would suffice for salvation. They want to have access to God by faith, yet not through Christ, but past Christ, just as though they had no need of Christ. Their desire to have access to God without Christ, by their bare faith, means to reject the salvation of Christ. Such a faith is not true, but counterfeit. By their sham faith they do not have access to God, but they rather depart from God.

Again, the Apostle directs himself against those who are secure through Christ, but without faith, just as though they could be saved through Christ, yet without faith. Both must be together: "by faith" and "through our Lord Jesus Christ," so that by faith in Christ we accomplish and endure all things. Yet despite all this we should acknowledge ourselves unprofitable servants and should be sure that we have access to God solely through Christ. In all works of faith our main concern must be that we become worthy of Christ and His favor which gives us His righteousness.

We glory in tribulations also (5:3). From this verse appears the distinction between a twofold wrath of God, a twofold divine mercy and a twofold tribulation; for there is a tribulation which comes to us from severity (*divine wrath*), and another which comes from divine goodness. The tribulation which comes from divine love can work only that which is good (*for us*) as it is here described, even though it accidentally results in something else. This is the fault not of the tribulation, but of the weakness of him who endures the tribulation. In that case he fails to understand the nature, power and operation (*purpose*) of tribulation and judges it only according to its outward appearance. He thinks wrongly about it, though it should be reverenced as the very Cross of Christ.

Knowing that tribulation worketh patience (5:3). He who has faith indeed has all the excellent things (*which are mentioned in the text*), but in a hidden way. Through tribulation they are tried and purified to the highest degree. Whatever (*virtues*) tribulation finds in us, it develops more fully. If anyone is carnal, weak, blind, wicked, irascible, haughty, and so forth, tribulation will make him more carnal, weak, blind, wicked and irritable. On the other hand, if one is spiritual, strong, wise, pious, gentle and humble, he will become more spiritual, powerful, wise, pious, gentle and humble, as the Psalmist says in Psalm 4:1: "Thou hast enlarged me when I was in distress."

Those speak foolishly who ascribe their anger or their impatience to such as offend them or to tribulation. Tribulation does not make people impatient, but proves that they are impatient. So everyone may learn from tribulation how his heart is constituted.

Those are ignorant, childish and indeed hypocritical who outwardly venerate the relics of the holy Cross, yet flee and detest tribulation and affliction. Holy Scripture calls tribulation the cross of Christ in a special sense, as in Matthew 10:38: "He that taketh not his cross, and followeth after me, is not worthy of me."

Let everyone be sure that he is no Christian but a Turk and an enemy of Christ who refuses to bear this cross; for here the Apostle speaks of all (*believers*) when he says: "We glory in tribulations." And in Acts 14:22 we read: "We must through much tribulation enter into the kingdom of God." "Must" does not mean that tribulation comes by chance, or that it is a matter of choice for us, or that we may take it or leave it. In many Scripture passages our Lord is called a "Saviour" and a "Helper in need," and this means that all who do not desire to endure tribulation, rob Him of his titles and names of honor. To such people our Lord will never become a Saviour, because they do not admit that they are under condemnation. To them God is never mighty, wise and gracious, because they do not desire to honor Him as creatures that are weak, foolish and subject to punishment.

Experience (worketh) *hope* (5:4). Experience must here be understood in a good sense as the object of tribulation, or the good which tribulation is to effect. God accepts no one as righteous whom He has not first tried. But He tries us through the fire of affliction, as we read in Psalm 11:5: "The Lord trieth the righteous." God tries us in this way, in order that we may know whether we really love God for His own sake. We thus read in Psalm 139:23, 24: "Search me, O God, and know my heart: try me, and know my thoughts: and see if there be any wicked way in me, and lead me in the way everlasting." If God would not try us by tribulation, it would be impossible for us to be saved.

Hope maketh not ashamed (5:5). Tribulation takes from man everything (*in which he trusts*) and leaves him naked and destitute. It also prevents him from seeking help and salvation in his own temporal and spiritual good works. Finally, it causes him to despair of every creature, to look away from himself, and, apart from himself and everything else, to seek help alone from God (*the Creator*), as the Psalmist says in Psalm 3:3: "But thou, O Lord, art a shield for me; my glory, and the lifter up of mine head." That is what "hope" means, and through the experience (*of tribulation*) such hope is confirmed in us. On the other hand, the wicked, who trust in their virtues and do not endure tribulation with patience, and so do not allow themselves to be tried by it, never discover that we must put our trust alone in God. Therefore when the last trial (*affliction*) will come and all their virtues and merits will disappear, then, when they sink into a hopeless eternity, they will cry out to the mountains: "Fall on us" (Luke 23:30). Their assumed hope was no hope at all, but only a perverse, arrogant trust in their own works and righteousness.

Because the love of God is shed abroad in our hearts 5:5. Hope maketh not ashamed, because the love of God, that is, the love which is of God and works in us an unshakable adherence to Him, is shed abroad in our hearts. This love we receive by grace and not on account of our merits; and it makes us willing to endure tribulation. If men are unwilling and of an unstable mind, they do not endure it by the Holy Ghost. St. Augustine remarks on this passage: "Step by step he, (*the Apostle*), leads us toward love, which, as he says, we have as a gift from the Holy Spirit. He shows us thereby that we must ascribe all that we might claim for ourselves to God who by grace grants us His Holy Spirit."

We must understand these words as an added motivation or instruction of the Holy Spirit, showing why we can glory in tribulation, though this is impossible by our own strength. It is not the effect of our own power, but it comes from the divine love which is given us by the Holy Ghost.

Let us note: 1. It *is shed abroad,* hence not born in us or originated by us. 2. It is by *the Holy Ghost,* therefore it is not acquired by our virtuous efforts as we may acquire good habits which lie on a merely moral plane. 3. *In our hearts,* that is, it is in the innermost core of our being, not merely on the surface, as foam is swimming on the top of the water. Such (*superficial*) love is that of the hypocrites who imagine and pretend to love. 4. *Which is given unto us*, that is, which is not merited, for we deserve the very opposite. 5. It is called *love* (*caritas*) in contradistinction to the inert and lower form of love with which we love creatures. It is a precious and worthy love, by which we most highly esteem that which we love, as we esteem God above all things, or as we love Him with highest esteem. He who loves God merely for the sake of His gifts or the sake of any advantage, loves Him with the lowest form of love, that is, with sinful desire. Such (*earthly*) love means to use God, but not to delight in God. 6. *Of God*, because only God is so loved. The neighbor is loved for God's sake, that is, because God wills this.

In due time Christ died for the ungodly 5:6. He died at that time when we were still weak, that is, when we were neither righteous nor sanctified, but helpless and lost, (*that is, ungodly, v. 6*). In 5:10 the Apostle says: "When we were enemies, we were reconciled to God." (*So also v. 8:* "*While we were yet sinners, Christ died for us.*")

Much more, being reconciled, we shall be saved by his life (5:10). The resurrection and life of Jesus Christ is a cause, that is, an efficacious means of our spiritual resurrection and spiritual life; for it causes us to believe and to rise (*from sin*), as we read in 10:9: "If thou shalt confess with thy mouth the Lord Jesus, and shalt believe in thine heart that God hath raised him from the dead, thou shalt be saved." In Christ's death we die unto spiritual life, as we read in 6:3,4: "So many of us as were baptized into Jesus Christ, were baptized into his death (that) we also should walk in newness of life."

Wherefore, as by one man sin entered into the world, and death by sin (5:12). (*Here the Apostle shows*) that by one man righteousness has come into the world. But this he discusses after a digression which he interposes. The words "and death by sin" show clearly that he is speaking of original sin; for if death comes by sin, then also the little children have sinned who die. So this must not be understood in the sense of actual sin. That the Apostle is here speaking not of actual sin, but of original sin, is proved also by the following:

1. He says: "By one man." Of this statement St. Augustine writes against the Pelagians in the first chapter of his book *Concerning the Deserved Punishment of Sins and their Forgiveness*: "So, then, the Apostle making mention of that sin and of death, which passed from one to all by propagation, represents him as the originator from whom the propagation of the human race had its beginning."

2. He says: "By one." Actual sin comes into the world through many, because through each person his own peculiar sin is put into the world.

3. He says: "Sin entered into the world." Actual sin really does not enter into the world, but the (*actual*) sins of every person burden the head of the transgressor. The word "world" here does not signify heaven and earth, but the human beings that live in the world, as the Apostle says in Romans 3:6: "For then how shall God judge the world?" In 5:19 he explains the term by the words: "By one man's disobedience many were made sinners."

4. He says: "And death by sin." Certainly the death of men does not come merely from their personal sins, since also such die as have not committed actual sins. Therefore the Apostle here does not mean any special (*actual*) sins.

5. He says: "And so death passed upon all men." With regard to (*a person's*) own actual sin, this is true: If death follows it, it comes alone to him who commits the sin, as the Law says in Deuteronomy 24:16: "Every man shall be put to death for his own sin."

6. The Apostle speaks of "sin," speaking of the one (*original*) sin in the singular. If he wanted this to be understood of actual sins, he would have had to speak in the plural as in 5:16: "Of many offences."

7. He says: "For that all have sinned." One's own (*actual*) sin is not that of another so that by it all men have sinned, but every person commits his own (*actual*) sins.

8. He says: "For until the law sin was in the world." That is to say, the punishment of (*actual*) sin was recognized, but not (*original*) sin. Actual sin existed also before Moses and was

charged to the sinner, for it was punished. But original sin was unknown until Moses (*by his Law*) made it known.

9. He says. "(They) had not sinned after the similitude of Adam's transgression." All who commit transgressions like that of Adam, sin by actual transgression and not by a similar, imitated sin as Pelagius explained this.

10. He says that through (*original*) sin Adam became the figure of Him that was to come, but that does not take place through every individual actual sin, for otherwise every sinner would be the figure of Him that was to come. But now only Adam is the figure of Christ, because this one sin of his has come upon all.

But what, then, is original sin? According to the Apostle it is not only the lack of a good quality in the will, nor merely the loss of man's righteousness and ability (*to do good*). It is rather the loss of all his powers of body and soul, of his whole outward and inward perfections. In addition to this, it is his inclination to all that is evil, his aversion against that which is good, his antipathy against (*spiritual*) light and wisdom, his love for error and darkness, his flight from and his loathing of good works, and his seeking after that which is sinful. Thus we read in Psalm 14:3: "They are all gone aside, they are all together become filthy; there is none that doeth good, no, not one"; and in Genesis 8:21: "The imagination of man's heart is evil from his youth." Actual sins essentially consist in this that they come from out of us, as the Lord says in Matthew 15:19: "Out of the heart proceed evil thoughts, murders, adulteries, fornications, thefts, false witness, blasphemies." But original enters into us; we do not commit it, but we suffer it. We are sinners because we are the sons of a sinner. A sinner can beget only a sinner, who is like him.

ADAM'S IMPUTED TRANSGRESSION; CHRIST'S IMPUTED RIGHTEOUSNESS

(*For until the law sin was in the world: but sin is not imputed when there is no law. Nevertheless death reigned from Adam to Moses, even over them that had not sinned after the similitude of Adam's transgression, who is the figure of him that was to come. But not as the offence, so also is the free gift. For if through the offence of one many be dead, much more the grace of God, and the gift by grace, which is by one man, Jesus Christ, hath abounded unto many. And not as it was by one that sinned, so is the gift; for the judgment was by one to condemnation, but the free gift is of many offences unto justification. For if by one man's offence death reigned by one; much more they which receive abundance of grace and of the gift of righteousness shall reign in life by one, Jesus Christ.) Therefore as by the offence of one judgment came upon all men to condemnation; even so by the righteousness of one the free gift came upon all men unto justification of life. For as by one man's disobedience many were made sinners, so by the obedience of one shall many be made righteous. Moreover the law entered, that the offence might abound. But where sin abounded, grace did much more abound; that as sin hath reigned unto death, even so might grace reign through righteousness unto eternal life by Jesus Christ our Lord* (5:13-21).

Until the law sin was in the world (5:13). St Augustine explains this in the tenth chapter of his book *Concerning the Deserved Punishment of Sins and their Forgiveness* as follows: "Sin could not be taken away through the Law, neither through the natural nor the revealed Law; for no one could be justified by the works of the Law." In another book he refers the phrase "until the law" to the whole duration of the Law till its end, which is Christ. (*Luther himself prefers this explanation.*) Sin was not recognized until the law came, which produced sin inasmuch as by the Law there came knowledge of sin.

Nevertheless death reigned from Adam to Moses (5:14). That is to say, sin's punishment, namely death, was well known to all men by experience, but not the cause of death, namely, sin. We must not understand the words in such a way that death reigned only to Moses, for Moses also died, and all men continue to die till the end of the world. But to Moses death reigned in the sense that men did not know why death ruled so mightily.

That had not sinned after the similitude of Adam's transgression (5:14). St. Augustine explains this statement as follows: (*Death reigned over them*) "that had not yet sinned through their own personal volition as he (*Adam*)." That is, all had sinned, not (*merely*) by actual sin, but because of the one and the same guilt (*of Adam*). (*Luther, in his exposition of the whole passage, stresses the fact that the Apostle here speaks of the imputation of Adam's guilt to all his descendants.*)

Who is the figure of him that was to come (5:14). How is Adam a figure of Christ? As Adam became a cause of death to his descendants, though they did not eat of the forbidden tree, so Christ has become a Dispenser of righteousness to those who are of Him, though they have not earned any righteousness; for through the Cross He has secured (*righteousness*) for all men. The figure of Adam's transgression is in us, for we die just as though we had sinned as he did. The figure of Christ is in us, for we live just as though we had fulfilled all righteousness as He did.

But not as the offence, so also is the free gift (5:15). Original sin is by Adam's transgression. This sin we bear as his children and we are guilty on account of it, for with his nature Adam also transfers his sin to all. As he himself became sinful and evil through that sin, so he begets only sinners and evildoers, namely, such as are inclined to all evil and resist that which is good.

Much more the grace of God, and the gift by grace, which is by one man, Jesus Christ, hath abounded unto many (5:17). As is the sin of the one, so is the grace of the other. As the sin of the one becomes known through our condemnation without any actual sin of our own, so the grace of the other is made known by this that His righteousness is granted to us without our merit.

And not as it was by one that sinned, so is the gift (5:17). The free gift (*of justification*) is granted not only against the one sin of the one sinner; in other words, the gift of grace frees us not only from that one condemnation, which is ours because of (*Adam's*) one transgression.

For if by one man's offence death reigned by one; much more they . . . shall reign in life by one, Jesus Christ (5:17). The Apostle repeats the same thought in ever new and different words to magnify the abounding grace of God.

As by the offence of one judgment came upon all men to condemnation (5:18). Here the Apostle says "all"; first, because as all who are begotten of Adam are born again through (*faith in*) Christ; and secondly, because as there is no carnal begetting except through Adam, so also there is no spiritual begetting except through Christ.

As by one man's disobedience many were made sinners, so by the obedience of one shall many be made righteous (5:19). Here the Apostle speaks of "many" and not of "all," to show that in the preceding verse his emphasis is not on the number of the sinners or the righteous, but upon the power of sin and grace. If sin proved itself so powerful that a single transgression has perverted many, or rather all, then divine grace is much more powerful; for the one act of grace, (*Christ's atonement*) can save many, indeed, all men, of many sins, if they only would desire it.

St. Chrysostom says with reference to this: "If a Jew should ask you, how it is possible that through the power of the one Christ the world is saved, then ask him how it is possible that through the one disobedient Adam the whole world was damned."

In verse 15 the Apostle connects the "grace of God" with the "gift of grace" as though they were distinct from each other. He does this to stress the fact that we do not receive the grace of God by merit, but as a free gift which the Father has given to Christ, in order that He might impart it to men, according to Ephesians 4:8: "When he ascended on high . . . (he) gave gifts unto men." But really the "grace of God" and the "gift by grace" are one and the same thing, namely, the righteousness which God bestows upon us by grace through Christ.

The law entered, that the offence might abound (5:20). The statement "the law entered" shows that sin remained, indeed, that it was increased (*by the Law*); for the Law followed sin, in order to make it abound by commanding the opposite of man's sinful desires, and by forbidding his (*sinful*) passions. The words "that the offence might abound" do not denote purpose, but result. The sense (*of the verse*) is: Through the transgression of the Law there came the knowledge of original sin. Thus St. Augustine in his *Propositions from the Epistle to the Romans* says: "With these words he shows clearly that the Jews did not understand for what purpose the Law was given; for it was not given to make *sinners* alive — it is (*divine*) grace alone which by faith makes alive — but to show with what strong chains of sin those are bound and held captive who arrogantly assert that the Law is to be kept by their own power." The human race therefore did not receive help and healing from the Law, but only an increase of its sickness (*of sin*).

Romans Six

Content of the sixth chapter: The Apostle shows that we must not continue in sin, but live in holiness.

BELIEVERS IN CHRIST ARE DEAD TO SIN

What shall we say then? Shall we continue in sin, that grace may abound? God forbid. How shall we, that are dead to sin, live any longer therein? Know ye not, that so many of us as were baptized into Jesus Christ, were baptized into his death? Therefore we are buried with him by baptism into death; that like as Christ was raised up from the dead by the glory of the Father, even so we also should walk in newness of life. For if we have been planted together in the likeness of his death, we shall be also in the likeness of his resurrection: knowing this, that our old man is crucified with him, that the body of sin might be destroyed, that henceforth we should not serve sin. For he that is dead is freed from sin. Now if we be dead with Christ, we believe that we shall also live with him: knowing that Christ being raised from the dead dieth no more; death hath no more dominion over him. For in that he died, he died unto sin once: but in that he liveth, he liveth unto God. Likewise reckon ye also yourselves to be dead indeed unto sin, but alive unto God through Jesus Christ our Lord (6:1-11).

Shall we continue in sin, that grace may abound? (6:1) Since some misunderstood the words of the Apostle: "Where sin abounded, grace did much more abound" (5:20), they were offended at what he said, as we learned already in 3:8: "Let us do evil, that good may come." The Apostle did not say this to excuse sin, but to glorify divine grace. St. Augustine therefore rightly says in the seventh chapter of his book *Of the Spirit and the Letter*: "The Apostle Paul received pardon instead of condemnation, grace instead of punishment. Hence it is meet and right that, above all, he should raise his voice to champion and contend for grace. Nor did he concern himself about the deep and exceedingly difficult problem regarding the misinterpretations of those who were incapable of appreciating his doctrine and perverted his most rational words in a wrong sense." However, in this chapter the Apostle treats the mystery of the death and resurrection of Jesus Christ.

How shall we, that are dead to sin, live any longer therein? (6:2) St. Augustine says: "It is the work of (*divine*) grace that we are dead to sin"; and commenting on this passage he writes: "From this passage on the Apostle describes only such persons as have been placed under grace, where, according to their new man, they already serve the Law of God, though in their flesh they might serve the Law of sin ever so much." Then, explaining this two-fold servitude of the Law and sin, he continues: "He, (*the believer according to the new man*), does not obey the allurements of sin; no matter how greatly his passions may incite and provoke him, he does not yield to them." Hence when we do not yield to our perverse lusts, we are under grace, and sin no longer reigns in our body. He, however, whom sin holds in its power, is still under the Law, and not under grace, no matter how greatly he may resist sin.

From this we clearly see what the words of the Apostle mean. All such statements as: 1. "We are dead to sin," 2. "We live unto God," etc., signify that we do not yield to our sinful passions and sin, even though sin continues in us. Nevertheless, sin remains in us until the end of our life, as we read in Galatians 5:17: "The flesh lusteth against the Spirit, and the Spirit against the flesh: and these are contrary the one to the other." Therefore all apostles and saints confess that sin and the sinful passions remain in us till the body is turned into ashes, and a new (*glorified*) body is raised up which is free from passion and sin. So we read in II Peter 3:13: "We, according to his promise, look for new heavens and a new earth, wherein dwelleth righteousness." But to hate the body of sin and to resist it, is not an easy, but a most difficult task.

Know ye not, that so many of us as were baptized into Jesus Christ were baptized unto his death? (6:3) There is a twofold death, namely, the natural, or temporal, and the everlasting death.

Temporal death is the separation of body and soul, and is merely an image of everlasting death. This everlasting death also is two-fold. The one is good and glorious; it is death unto sin, or the death of death, by which the soul is saved and separated from sin, as also the body is freed from corruption. By this death we are bound by grace and glory to the living God. This is the death which Scripture has in mind first of all; for God has decreed to destroy through Christ what Satan brought into the world through Adam, namely, sin and death. Thus God brings about the death of death, as we read in Hosea 13:14: "I will redeem them from death: O death, I will be thy plagues." The other death is also everlasting, but absolutely destructive, for it is the death of the damned. Here man perishes while sin lives and remains forever and ever throughout eternity. That is the worst death of the sinner.

We are not found in a state of perfection as soon as we have been baptized into Jesus Christ and His death. Having been baptized into His death, we merely strive to obtain (*the blessings of*) this death and to reach our goal of glory. Just so, when we are baptized into everlasting life and the kingdom of heaven, we do not at once fully possess its full wealth (*of blessings*). We have merely taken the first steps to seek after eternal life. Baptism has been instituted that it should lead us to the blessings (*of this death*) and through such death to eternal life. Therefore it is necessary that we should be baptized into Jesus Christ and His death.

We are buried with him by baptism into death (6:4). As the dead and buried Christ appeared in the eyes of the Jews, so also the spiritual person, (*that is, one who is buried with Christ by baptism into death*) must appear in his own eyes and the eyes of others. As Christ after His death no longer took notice of what took place outside (*the grave*), so also the spiritual person, though with his senses he is present in all (*earthly*) things, must be totally separated from and dead in his heart to all (*temporal*) things. This he does when with all his spiritual strength he despises what belongs to this earthly life; indeed, when he loathes everything which in this life is of prominence, gladly continues (*in faith*), and glories in this that he is a dead body, or, as the Apostle says in I Corinthians 4:13: "The offscouring of all things."

If we have been planted together in the likeness of his death, we shall be also in the likeness of his resurrection (6:5). Here the Apostle states the same truth taught in John 12:24: "Except a corn of wheat fall into the ground and die, it abideth alone: but if it die, it bringeth forth much fruit." He speaks of the *likeness* of His death and resurrection to show that here he is not thinking of the bodily death and resurrection, but of the spiritual death and resurrection (*which takes place in and through baptism*).

Our old man is crucified with him (6:6). (*We speak of*) the "old man" inasmuch as it, (*our nature,*) is begotten of Adam. Properly, the expression does not refer to our nature, but to its corruption. The nature (*in itself*) is good, but the corruption of it is evil. A person is said to be an "old man" not merely inasmuch as he does the works of the flesh, but also, and that with far greater right, inasmuch as (*outwardly*) he acts righteously, seeks after wisdom, exercises himself in all manner of spiritual gifts, and even loves and honors God. The reason for this is that he, (*the old man, or corrupt natural man*), in all these things enjoys the gifts of God, and so merely uses God. From the sin of such misuse he can be raised only by the grace of God. (*Luther here has in mind the eternal keeping of the Law, which is without Christ, and so without true love for God; of this the Apostle speaks in Rom. 2:14, 15.*)

That the body of sin might be destroyed (6:6). That is done through the continuous progress of the new (*spiritual*) life. This destruction must therefore be understood in a spiritual sense. In a literal sense the body is being destroyed also in those whose old man is not crucified, whether they want this or not. The Apostle explains this (*spiritual*) destruction by adding: "Henceforth we should not serve sin." In Colossians 3:5 he explains it by the words: "Mortify your members which are upon the earth; fornication, uncleanness, inordinate affection, etc." The carnal nature has the seed of the Devil and endeavors to bring forth sin and bear sinful fruit. The spiritual nature, (*the new man*), has the seed of God and seeks to bring forth righteousness and the fruits of righteousness.

Knowing that Christ being raised from the dead dieth no more (6:9). He does not say: "He will live," but: He "dieth no more."

This negative formulation is more emphatic and meaningful. It stresses the eternity of Christ's life.

In that he died, he died unto sin once; but in that he liveth, he liveth unto God (6:10). Because Christ is eternal, so also is our spiritual life; for Christ is our life and through faith He shines into our hearts the rays of grace which abide forever. In verse 8 he expresses the thought thus: "If we be dead with Christ, we believe that we shall also live with him." Our spiritual life is a matter not of experience, but of faith. No one knows or experiences the fact that he lives spiritually or is justified, but he believes and hopes this. We live unto God, that is, in our spiritual and new life to eternity.

Reckon ye also yourselves to be dead indeed unto sin, but alive unto God through Jesus Christ our Lord (6:11). He (*who is dead unto sin*) has Christ for his own Lord, who dieth no more; therefore also he will die no more, but will live with Christ through all eternity. Only he lives unto God who is eternal and spiritual; for God is the eternal Spirit. Therefore only he is acceptable to Him who is spiritual and eternal.

As Servants of Christ Believers Should Live in Holiness

Let not sin therefore reign in your mortal body, that ye should obey it in the lusts thereof. Neither yield ye your members as instruments of unrighteousness unto sin: but yield yourselves unto God, as those that are alive from the dead, and your members as instruments of righteousness unto God. For sin shall not have dominion over you: for ye are not under the law, but under grace. What then? shall we sin, because we are not under the law, but under grace? God forbid. Know ye not, that to whom ye yield yourselves servants to obey, his servants ye are to whom ye obey; whether of sin unto death, or of obedience unto righteousness? But God be thanked, that ye were the servants of sin, but ye have obeyed from the heart that form of doctrine which was delivered you. Being then made free from sin, ye became the servants of righteousness. I speak after the manner of men because of the infirmity of your flesh; for as ye have yielded your members servants of uncleanness and to iniquity unto iniquity; even so now yield your members servants to righteousness unto holiness. For when ye were the servants of sin, ye were free from righteousness. What fruit had ye then in those things whereof ye are now ashamed? for the end of those things is death. But now being made free from sin, and become servants to God, ye have your fruit unto holiness, and the end everlasting life. For the wages of sin is death; but the gift of God is eternal life through Jesus Christ our Lord (6:12-23).

Let not sin . . . reign in your mortal body (6:12). This (*mortal body*) the Apostle stresses in contradistinction to our mystical body, which is the Church of Christ. This is an immortal body, just as also the Head is immortal.

Sin shall not have dominion over you (6:14). This is understood not only of lusting after earthly goods and temporal possessions, but also of aversion to temporal affliction and adversity. He who has Christ by faith does not desire the things of this world, no matter how greatly they may allure him. Nor does he sinfully desire even this earthly life. Nor is he afraid of any tribulation, not even death, no matter how much terror it may hold for him. He stands on a firm rock, and neither seeks after what is pleasant, nor flees from what is adverse. This does not mean that he is unaffected by the temptation to become timid in facing terror, to yield to his passions, and be misled by allurements which infatuate the heart. He is susceptible to both pleasure and displeasure. But he ultimately refuses to yield to passions and allurements, even though he may resist and gain the victory with the utmost exertion and anguish, as we read in I Peter 4:18: "The righteous scarcely (is) saved." With the Lord's permission he may be tried and tempted to the extreme of his endurance as gold is tried in fire.

He who fears death more than Christ and loves life more than Christ, does not yet possess Christ by faith. Sin still has dominion over him and he is under the Law, as Christ explains this in John 12:25: "He that loveth his life shall lose it"; in Matthew 10:37: "He that loveth father and mother more than me is not worthy of me"; and in Matthew 10:38: "He that taketh not his cross, and followeth me, is not worthy of me." It is not easy to overcome sin, and if the Lord were not with us, "God is faithful, who will not suffer you to be tempted above that ye are able" (I Cor. 10:13), the flood would swallow us up. While He permits the wicked to be tempted and to fall, He is faithful to all who stand in the faith and call upon Him.

If sin tempts us and fails to rule over us, it is forced to serve the saints (*believers*), since "all things work together for good to them that love God" (Rom. 8:28). Thus (*the temptation to*) impurity by its attack renders the (*believer's*) soul all the more chaste. Pride makes it all the more humble. Indolence makes it all the more industrious. Avarice makes it all the more generous. Anger makes it all the more gentle. Gluttony makes it all the more obedient. In this way temptation turns out to be a great blessing. Sin indeed rules in our mortal body if we yield to it; but we must resist it and make it our servant (*for good as was just shown*).

Ye are not under the law, but under grace (6:14). Believers are not under the Law, but under grace, because they have fulfilled it through faith in Christ, whose fulfillment of the Law and righteousness is ours. This is freely given us by God's grace, because He has mercy upon us. In John 8:34 Christ says: "Whosoever committeth sin is the servant of sin." Therefore sin is his master. Those, however, who are under the Law, are of necessity also under sin, for no one can fulfill the Law who is outside (*divine*) grace, at least not in his heart. The Apostle here meets the objection: How can anyone resist the onslaught of sin and passion? To this he replies: Sin shall not have dominion over you nor triumph over you, no matter how fiercely it may tempt and assail you, provided you do not yield to it. But he who is without faith in Christ is always dominated by sin, even when he does good (*before men*). From this tyrannical dominion of the Law and sin no one can be freed except by Christ, as the Apostle writes in I Corinthians 15:57: "But thanks be to God, which giveth us the victory through our Lord Jesus Christ." So also St. John says in I John 5:4: "This is the victory that overcometh the world, even our faith."

Ye have obeyed from the heart that form of doctrine which was delivered you (6:17). The Apostle means to say: From the form (*teaching*) of error (*justification by works*) you were led to the form (*teaching*) of the Gospel (*justification by faith*). The wisdom of the flesh (*conceited reason asserting work-righteousness*) — is enmity against the Word of God (*the Gospel*). But the Word of God is unchangeable and invincible. Therefore it is necessary that the wisdom of the flesh — (*perverted reason*) — be changed, give up its form, and that man accept the form of the Word. This takes place when through faith it (*reason*) is taken captive and overcome, and the believer confesses that the Word is true and reason false. This is the special mark by which the believer, or saint is known.

I speak after the manner of men because of the infirmity of your flesh (6:19). (*The Apostle means to say*): In the preceding verses I said with great severity that sin must not have dominion over you. But since you are still weak in your struggle against the flesh, see to it that you do not live in sin without any anxiety or in security. If you have no heroic measure of virtue, then at least strive after that standard that is demanded of all believers. In this passage the Apostle sums up what he treats at greater length in I Corinthians 7:1ff. That is to say: Live virtuously, in order that sin might not rule in you to the destruction of your faith and righteousness.

Ye have yielded your members servants to uncleanness and iniquity (6:19). We must not surrender our members to sinful passions so that they, by obeying sin, become instruments of unrighteousness. In this way believers become unbelievers, for they do the works of unrighteousness. We must obey God, in order that our members may become instruments of righteousness in a life of enduring faith.

Yield your members servants to righteousness unto holiness (6:19). The Apostle when here speaking of holiness has in mind the chastity of the body, in particular, that purity which comes from the Spirit of faith, who sanctifies us both inwardly and outwardly. Otherwise it would be a pagan chastity and not holy chastity, or (*true*) holiness, since the soul remains defiled. First the soul must become pure through faith, so that the sanctified mind purifies also the body for God's sake. Of this our Lord speaks in Matthew 23:26: "Thou blind Pharisee, cleanse first that which is within the cup and platter, that the outside of them may be clean also."

What fruit had ye then in those things whereof ye are now ashamed? (6:21). As long as passion burns like glowing fire, it appears as though it were something good and were bearing good fruit, namely, satisfaction and delight. But when sin is finished, it appears to him who becomes conscious of what he did and repents, as most detestable and as something (*disgraceful*) which makes him blush with shame.

Romans Seven

Content of the seventh chapter: The Apostle speaks of the passing of the old Law of death and of the reaction of the carnal nature to the Law.

FREED FROM THE LAW, BELIEVERS SHOULD SERVE CHRIST IN HOLINESS

Know ye not, brethren, (for I speak to them that know the law,) how that the law hath dominion over a man as long as he liveth? For the woman which hath an husband is bound by the law to her husband so long as he liveth; but if the husband be dead, she is loosed from the law of her husband. So then if, while her husband liveth, she be married to another man, she shall be called an adulteress: but if her husband be dead, she is free from that law; so that she is no adulteress, though she be married to another man. Wherefore, my brethren, ye also are become dead to the law by the body of Christ; that ye should be married to another, even to him who is raised from the dead, that we should bring forth fruit unto God. For when we were in the flesh, the motions of sins which were by the law, did work in our members to bring forth fruit unto death. But now we are delivered from the law, that being dead wherein we were held; that we should serve in newness of spirit, and not in the oldness of the letter. What shall we say then? Is the law sin? God forbid, Nay, I had not known sin, but by the law: for I had not known lust except the law had said, Thou shalt not covet. But sin taking occasion by the commandment, wrought in me all manner of concupiscence. For without the law sin was dead. For I was alive without the law once: but when the commandment came, sin revived, and I died. And the commandment which was ordained to life, I found to be unto death. For sin, taking occasion by the command-ment, deceived me, and by it slew me. Wherefore the law is holy, and the commandment holy, and just, and good. Was then that which is good made death unto me? God forbid. But sin, that it might appear sin, working death in me by that which is good; that sin by the commandment might become exceeding sinful. For we know that the law is spiritual: but I am carnal, sold under sin. For that which I do I allow not: for what I would, that do I not; but what I hate, that do I. If then I do that which I would not, I consent unto the law that it is good. Now then it is no more I that do it, but sin that dwelleth in me. For I know that in me (that is, in my flesh) dwelleth no good thing: for to will is present with me; but how to perform that which is good I find not. For the good that I would I do not: but the evil which I would not, that I do. Now if I do that I would not, it is no more I that do it, but sin that dwelleth in me. I find then a law, that, when I would do good, evil is present with me. For I delight in the law of God after the inward man: but I see another law in my members, warring against the law of my mind, and bringing me into captivity to the law of sin which is in my members. O wretched man that I am! who shall deliver me from the body of this death? I thank God through Jesus Christ our Lord. So then with the mind I myself serve the law of God; but with the flesh the law of sin (7:1-25).

Know ye not . . . how that the law hath dominion over a man as long as he liveth? (7:1) The Apostle here confirms and describes more fully what he has said in the preceding chapter about the dying of the old man and the vivification of the new man; to this end he uses the analogy of the temporal or human law. Above all, he wishes to make clear what he says in 4:15: "The law worketh wrath: for where no law is, there is no transgression." He speaks of the Law as it refers to man's heart and will, and not merely to his external works. To understand the Apostle's propositions the reader must grasp his basic premise.

Sin and wrath come from the Law. Hence, no one dies to the Law who does not die to sin; and whoever dies to sin, dies also to the Law. As soon as a person is free from sin, he also is free from the servitude of the Law. So, then, when sin has dominion over us, then also the Law has dominion over us, and vice versa.

However, unless first the inward dying (*to sin*) takes place, sin remains and has dominion, and with it the Law which rules through sin. Therefore those act with amazing folly who (*merely*) imitate the works of the saints as do the monks. They are foolish, for they desire merely to do the same works without concerning themselves about their spirit. For this reason we must ask God for divine grace, so that we may become new in spirit, willing and doing all good works with a joyous, ready heart and a free and manly mind, and not moved by servile fear or by some childish desire. But this alone the Holy Spirit works (*in us*).

The woman which hath a husband is bound by the law to her husband so long as he liveth (7:2). The Apostle here emphasizes the thought that there is no freedom from the Law, unless death takes place. Just so, no one is free from the Law of the letter, unless he is buried with Christ by baptism into death, as he said in the preceding chapter.

Ye also are become dead to the law by the body of Christ (7:4). It is a strange and profound teaching which the Apostle sets forth in this chapter. He means to show that there are two men (*in the believer*), the old and the new, corresponding to Adam and Christ. But no one recognizes the old man, unless he first understands and consents to the Law. But if the Law is recognized, then also the old man, so to speak, becomes alive. So, then, we are subject through the Law to the old man and to sin, that is, we now realize this subjection. Without the Law we would not know that sin has dominion over us. But if the old man is dead, then we also are dead to the Law. It can no longer subject us to sin, but has lost its power over us.

When we were in the flesh, the motions (passions) of sins, which were by the law, did work in our members to bring forth fruit unto death (7:5). The Apostle here refers to the Law of Moses. Through this Law the old man was made alive; for this, while leading to the knowledge of sin, increases sin all the more as long as (*divine*) grace is lacking. The old man, revealed and made manifest by the Law, now does what the corrupt nature desires, as we read in 7:13: "Sin by the commandment (becomes) exceeding sinful." By divine grace, however, the old man dies and the Law can no longer bring him forth and make him manifest. In this way we die to the condemnation and dominion of the Law, though not to the Law itself, or absolutely, for we have the law, even when we are no longer under the Law.

But now we are delivered from the law (7:6). We are delivered from the Law in the sense that by faith in Christ we obey the Law, and by grace freely and willingly do what the Law demands of us. For this we need (*divine*) love which seeks what is God's and which is given to all who in true faith ask for it in the name of

Christ. Though we often sin and are not perfectly willing, we have made a beginning and move forward, for (*by faith*) we are justified and made free. But we must always be afraid of being under the Law. So we must continue in faith and constantly pray for love. For who is sure whether he does not act from fear of punishment or from love for his own advantage? Or who can know whether in his prayers and pious works he, in a very subtle way, does not seek after rest and reward rather than after doing God's will?

We should serve in newness of spirit, and not in the oldness of the letter (7:6). By "letter" the Apostle means all doctrine which prescribes what belongs to a virtuous life. If that is understood and impressed upon the memory without the Spirit of grace, then it is an empty letter and the death of the soul. So also St. Augustine says in the fourth chapter of his book *Concerning the Spirit and the Letter*: "The doctrine through which we receive the commandment to lead an abstinent, virtuous life, is the letter. This kills unless there is with it the Spirit, which makes alive." Not the most learned who read much and write many books are the best Christians. (*Luther has in mind above all the medieval moralists.*) But those are the best (*Christians*) who with ready willingness do what they, (*the learned*), teach from books. But the willing doers can do those things only if through the Holy Spirit they possess love. For this reason we must fear for our time, in which, thanks to the publication of many books, people indeed become very learned men, but also very unlearned Christians.

If people ask why the Gospel is called the Word of the Spirit, or the spiritual doctrine, or the Word of grace, or the publication of what the Word of the Old Testament predicted, or the hidden wisdom and the like, we reply: Solely for the reason that it teaches where and whence we can obtain grace and love. The Gospel offers Jesus Christ, whom the Law (*the Old Testament Scriptures*) promised. The Law commands us to have love and hear Jesus Christ, but the Gospel offers and imparts both to us. The Law is not kept by man's own power, but solely through Christ who pours the Holy Spirit into our hearts. Hence, those do not understand the Gospel who interpret it as anything else than a good news.

I had not known lust, except the law had said, Thou shalt not covet. But sin, taking occasion by the commandment, wrought in me all manner of concupiscence (7:7, 8). In the righteous who love the Law, the Law does not work concupiscence (*lust*), nor does it give any cause for sin, nor does sin take occasion by the commandment (*to sin all the more*); for in them sin is no longer present as a dominating power, indeed, it is truly dead. As an analogy I might refer to the heat in lime. No one knows that lime has heat until he pours water upon it. Then the heat has occasion to show itself. The water did not create the heat in the lime, but it has made it manifest. It is similar with the will of man and the Law. Sin is indeed in man, but no one knows it until man learns to know the Law. Then he burns all the more (*with the fires of sin*) though this is not the fault of the Law. But it is by grace that the fire of sin is extinguished.

I was alive without the law once: but when the commandment came, sin revived (7:9). So it is with the work-righteous and the proud unbelievers. Because they do not know the Law of God, which is directed against them, it is impossible for them to know their sin. Therefore also they are not amenable to instruction. If they would know the Law, they would also know their sin; and sin to which they are now dead would become alive in them.

And I died. And the commandment, which was ordained to life, I found to be unto death (7:9, 10). (*The Apostle means to say*): This I recognized in the spirit, or according to my spiritual nature, or as a new man. And in this lies the cause of everything else, of my whole spiritual distress: I was dead, though I was alive. But through the knowledge of the Law, or rather through the Spirit's revelation, I recognized that the commandment worked death in me. Here the Apostle speaks for his own person and in the name of all saints (*believers*) of the deep darkness of our minds, on account of which even the most holy and wise men do not have a perfect knowledge of the Law. So David writes in Psalm 19:12: "Who can understand his errors? cleanse thou me from secret faults." and again in Psalm 25:7: "Remember not the sins of my youth, nor my transgressions." It is only by faith that we can say with the Psalmist in Psalm 51:3: "I acknowledge my transgressions: and my sin is ever before me"; and in verse 6: "In the hidden part thou shalt make me to know wisdom." Such are the most hidden depths of the Law that with our natural knowledge we can never fully know it. But now it is revealed (*to us by the Holy Spirit*), in order that we may come to faith. Whoever therefore does not desire to confess any more of his sins than those which he knows and recalls, will confess but few of his transgressions. He cannot truthfully say with the Psalmist in Psalm 32:5: "I acknowledged my sin unto thee, and mine iniquity have I not hid."

There are some, and among them St. Augustine, who denied that the Apostle here speaks of his own person, and indeed of himself as being spiritual and not as carnal. But the whole passage shows very clearly a strong hatred against the flesh and a sincere love for the Law and all that is good. No carnal man ever does this. He rather hates the Law and follows his flesh and evil lusts. The spiritual man fights against his flesh and deplores that he cannot do what (*as a new man*) he desires to do. The carnal does not fight at all, but readily yields to sin. In I Corinthians 9:27 the Apostle writes: "I keep under my body, and bring it unto subjection: lest that by any means, when I have preached to others, I myself should be a castaway."

Again in 7:14 the Apostle says: "I am carnal, sold under sin." That is the proof of a spiritual and wise man. He knows that he is carnal, and he is displeased with himself; indeed, he hates himself and praises the Law of God, which he recognizes because he is spiritual. But the proof of a foolish, carnal man is this, that he regards himself as spiritual and is pleased with himself.

So also the Apostle says in 7:15: "That which I do, I allow not" (*I do not approve*). The Apostle means to say: As a spiritual man I recognize only what is good, and yet I do what I do not desire, namely, that which is evil, not indeed willfully and maliciously. But while I choose the good, I do the opposite. The carnal man, however, knows what is evil, and he does it intentionally, willfully and by choice.

In the same verse the Apostle says: "What I would, that do I not; but what I hate, that I do." (*This the Apostle says as a spiritual man*), for of the carnal man Scripture says in Psalm 36:4: "He abhorreth not evil."

In verse 16 the Apostle writes: "I consent unto the law that it is good." The Law desires what is good, and so does the Apostle.

Hence both agree to the good. But the carnal man is always against the Law; and if it were possible, he would rather have no Law at all. He never desires what is good, but only what is evil. Even when he does what is good (*externally*), he finds no pleasure in it. He does it merely because he is driven to it by fear, or with a servile mind; if he could do the opposite with impunity, he would rather do it.

In verse 20 the Apostle says: "It is no more I that do it, but sin that dwelleth in me." It is not the Apostle (*as a spiritual, or a new man*) who sins, because he does not consent to the sinful passions of his flesh. And yet he says: "The good that I would, I do not; but the evil which I would not, that I do." The one and the same person is both flesh and spirit. So both are true: he does, and yet he does not. What he does according to the flesh, he does in his whole person. But inasmuch as he resists the evil, it is not the whole person who sins, but only a part of the person (*his corrupt nature*).

In verse 18 (*the Apostle clarifies this by saying*): "I know that in me (that is, in my flesh,) dwelleth no good thing." Here the Apostle ascribes the flesh to himself as a part of himself, just as he says: "I am carnal." He is carnal and evil on account of his carnal nature. The words "I will" and "I hate" refer to his spiritual nature; but the words "I do" and "I am carnal" refer to his fleshly nature. Because the total person consists of flesh and spirit, the Apostle ascribes to the whole person both things, which contradict each other and stem from parts of his being that are contradictory. This cannot be said of a person who is carnal (*unconverted*), for his whole person is totally carnal. There is nothing in him of the Spirit of God. In verse 18 the Apostle likewise says: "To will is present with me; but how to perform that which is good I find not." This "to will" is the readiness of the spirit and flows from love, as we read (*of the spiritual man*) in Psalm 1:2: "His delight is in the law of the Lord."

In 7:21 the Apostle says: "I find a law, that, when I would do good, evil is present with me." He means to say: When I desire and am ready to do according to the divine Law, then I find in me a law (*principle, or power*) which is contrary to me — (*my desire to obey the Law*). This cannot be said of a carnal person.

In 7:22 the Apostle says: "I delight in the law of God after the inward man." Here the Apostle says that he has an inward man, and this is none other than his "spiritual man," or "spiritual nature." And his delight in the Law flows out of the love, worked by the Holy Spirit, for without Him we can love neither the Law nor what is righteous. To this he adds in verse 23: "I see another law in my members, warring against the law of my mind." The "law of my mind" is love, which is the spiritual law or the spiritual nature; for it is most properly this that fights against the sinful lust, or the "law in my members" (*the corruption of the flesh*), as the Apostle says in Galatians 5:17: "The flesh lusteth against the Spirit, and the Spirit against the flesh." That is to say, the evil desires war against the good desires. So there are two active laws (*principles, or powers*) that struggle in man for life and death. The Apostle thus speaks of himself as a warrior (*divided*) between two laws. But he is not defeated (*by the evil lusts*), as long as he does not surrender to them, which the carnal man does. Indeed the Apostle here shows that he (*as a spiritual man*) serves only one Law, while he resists the other.

In 7:24 the Apostle says: "O wretched man that I am! who shall deliver me from the body of this death?" This the Apostle does not say of bodily death, which he rather desires. St. Augustine explains this correctly in the second chapter of his Book *Against Julian*: "To be delivered from the body of this death means that the body which now is one of death, might become a body of life by having this (*spiritual*) death die in (*temporal*) death; and this is the end of the struggle." So here he does not speak of natural, or temporal death. This (*prayer*) shows still more clearly than the preceding (*words*) that the Apostle here speaks as a spiritual man; for he prays, is worried, and longs for the final redemption. No one regards himself as a miserable man who is not spiritual. In Philippians, 1:23 the Apostle expresses the same thought in the words: "I (have) a desire to depart, and to be with Christ."

In 7:25 the Apostle writes: "With the mind I myself serve the law of God; but with the flesh the law of sin." This is the clearest passage of all, and from it we learn that one and the same (*believing*) person serves at the same time the Law of God and the Law of sin. *He is at the same time justified and yet a sinner (simul iustus est et peccat*); for he does not say: "My mind serves the Law of God"; nor does he say: "My flesh serves the Law of sin"; but he says: "I myself." That is, the whole man, one and the same person, is in this twofold servitude. For this reason he thanks God that he serves the Law of God and he pleads for mercy for serving the Law of sin. But no one can say of a carnal (*unconverted*) person that he serves the Law of God. The Apostle means to say: You see, it is just so as I said before: The saints (*believers*) are at the same time sinners while they are righteous. They are righteous, because they believe in Christ, whose righteousness covers them and is imputed to them. But they are sinners, inasmuch as they do not fulfill the Law, and still have sinful lusts. They are like sick people who are being treated by a physician. They are really sick, but hope and are beginning to get, or be made, well. They are about to regain their health. Such patients would suffer the greatest harm by arrogantly claiming to be well, for they would suffer a relapse that is worse (*than their first illness*).

The Apostle, therefore, fully realizing this fact, directs himself in the second chapter against those who regard themselves as righteous and judge others as evildoers, while they themselves do what is evil. He may not have known anything of their actual external works, but of one thing he was sure, namely, that as long as such persons are without (*divine*) grace, they go counter to the Law in their hearts. If already a spiritual (*converted*) man does not do what he should, though he desires to do good, how much more will the carnal (*unconverted*) man, who does not even desire good, but does it only under coercion, refuse to serve the Law of God?

(*In this whole passage Luther shows by twelve different proofs, based on Paul's words, that the Apostle here, does not speak of himself as one who is still carnal, or unconverted, but as of one who is already spiritual, or converted, yet deeply laments the struggle of the old man in himself against the new man. Here, as in Galatians 5:17ff., the Apostle argues against the error of perfectionism. After the Apostle has clarified this point, he briefly explains in his further exposition of the chapter a number of important points for greater emphasis.*)

Without the law sin was dead (7:8). The Law begins to be alive and sin is revived then when a person begins to understand the

Law. Then the sinful lust comes out into the open and shows itself. Then a man burns all the more with evil yearning for what he desires, and he hates the Law with yet greater hatred.

It is no more I that do it, but sin that dwelleth in me (7:17). Oh, how the false philosophy of Aristotle has deceived our theologians (*the medieval Scholastics*)! They teach that sin is entirely destroyed by baptism or repentance, and so regard it as absurd that the Apostle should here confess: "Sin . . . dwelleth in me." As a converted, or spiritual man, they say, he could no longer have any sin in him; therefore, they argue, he here speaks of himself as a carnal (*or unconverted man*). But sin remains in the spiritual man, in order that he might exercise himself in grace, put off his pride and check his arrogance. He who confesses his sins should not believe that he can thereby shake off the burden (*of sin*) and quietly live on (*in sin*). But he should know that when he puts off the burden (*of sin*), he enters the warfare for God and takes up a new burden for God against the Devil and his own remaining faults. The Apostle here calls evil lust sin; for while in the words of St. Augustine, sin is forgiven in baptism, so far as condemnation is concerned, it remains in us as a reality (*as an actual corruption*) moving us to sin.

How to perform that which is good I find not (7:18). In the third chapter of his book *Against Julian* St. Augustine writes: "Recall what the Apostle writes to the Galatians (and so to persons that were baptized) in Galatians 5:16: 'Walk in the Spirit, and ye shall not fulfill the lust of the flesh.'" The Spirit, (*that is, the spiritual man*), does a good work by not yielding to the evil lust; but he does not perform that which is good inasmuch as he himself cannot destroy the evil lusts. Vain and injurious are the speculations (*of the Scholastics*) who teach from Aristotle that our virtues and faults adhere to the soul merely as whitewash to the wall. By this teaching they fully destroy the distinction between spirit and flesh — (*the new man and the old man in the believer*).

Romans Eight

Content of the eighth chapter: The Apostle shows that we must firmly adhere to the Law of Christ, because His Law is one of life and spirit.

The Blessedness of God's Dear Children in Christ

There is therefore now no condemnation to them which are in Christ Jesus, who walk not after the flesh but after the Spirit. For the law of the Spirit of life in Christ Jesus hath made me free from the law of sin and death. For what the law could not do, in that it was weak through the flesh, God sending his own Son in the likeness of sinful flesh, and for sin, condemned sin in the flesh: that the righteousness of the law might be fulfilled in us, who walk not after the flesh, but after the Spirit. For they that are after the flesh do mind the things of the flesh; but they that are after the Spirit the things of the Spirit. For to be carnally minded is death; but to be spiritually minded is life and peace. Because the carnal mind is enmity against God: for it is not subject to the law of God, neither indeed can be. So then they that are in the flesh cannot please God. But ye are not in the flesh, but in the Spirit, if so be that the Spirit of God dwell in you. Now if any man have not the Spirit of Christ, he is none of his. And if Christ be in you, the body is dead because of sin; but the Spirit is life because of righteousness. But if the Spirit of him that raised up Jesus from the dead dwell in you, he that raised up Christ from the dead shall also quicken your mortal bodies by his Spirit that dwelleth in you. Therefore, brethren, we are debtors, not to the flesh, to live after the flesh. For if ye live after the flesh, ye shall die: but if ye through the Spirit do mortify the deeds of the body, ye shall live. For as many as are led by the Spirit of God, they are the sons of God. For ye have not received the spirit of bondage again to fear; but ye have received the Spirit of adoption, whereby we cry, Abba, Father. The Spirit itself beareth witness with our spirit, that we are the children of God: and if children, then heirs; heirs of God, and joint-heirs with Christ; if so be that we suffer with him, that we may also be glorified together (8:1-17).

What the law could not do (God did). (8:3). (*In view of salvation by grace*) where, then, is man's free will (*in spiritual things*)? What will those reply who assert that by our natural powers we can awaken in us acts of love for God, so that we love God above all things? The Apostle says that it was impossible for the Law to condemn (*to remove*) sin, since it was weak through the flesh. As I said before it is absolutely impossible for us to fulfill the Law by our own power. It is true, the Natural Law is known to all men and reason advises us to do what seems best. (*But it urges us to do*) what is best not according to the will of God, but according to our own thoughts. It really suggests to do what is good in a bad sense; for reason seeks itself and its own benefit, and not that which is God's. That faith alone does by (*true*) love. If faith does not enlighten man and love does not make him free, then he is incapable of willing anything that is good. He can do only what is evil (*before God*), even when he does that which is good (*in his own sight*).

It has been said that human nature knows and wills what is good in general, but that it errs and does not will what is good in special cases. It is better, however, to say that human nature knows and wills what is good in special cases, but that in general it does not know and will what is good. The reason for this is that it knows only what it regards as good, honorable, useful and not what is good in the sight of God and the neighbor. Therefore it knows and wills the good only as it is connected with man's own interests. The divine Law therefore demands what we (*by nature*) cannot do; as St. Augustine says in the sixteenth chapter of his book *Concerning Grace and Free Will*: "It is faith alone which by prayer and supplication accomplishes what the Law commands."

In vain some seek to exalt the light of nature and regard it as equal to the light of grace. In reality the light of nature is total darkness and the very opposite of divine grace. Divine grace (*working in man*) places nothing above God. In all things it sees only Him, desires only Him, and strives only after Him. Everything else that intervenes between itself and God, it ignores, as though it did not exist. It is directed only toward God. (*Corrupt*) human nature, however, only seeks, desires and strives after itself. Whatever intervenes, even God Himself, it ignores as though

He did not exist. It is directed only toward itself. Such is the froward and wicked heart, of which Psalm 104:4 speaks.

It was weak through the flesh (8:3). It was weak, inasmuch as it was not fulfilled (*by man*). It becomes strong only through the spirit of faith, which alone can do what the Law fails to do. The power of faith confirms and establishes the Law, as we read in 3:31: "We establish the law," (*namely, by faith*). St. Augustine comments on this statement as follows: "The Law proved itself weak, because it did not accomplish what it commanded. This was not the fault of the Law, but that of the flesh, that is, of men, who, seeking earthly possessions, did not love the righteousness of the Law, but preferred temporal advantages to it." Only the will that is perfected and made obedient by love does or omits things according to God's will. It does not concern itself about anything else, nor does it fear any evil; it only seeks to do God's will. Of this (*corrupt*) human nature is incapable; only divine grace, granted through faith in Christ by the Holy Spirit (*is capable of this*).

The expression "the Law was weak" must be understood not so much of the (*external*) performance as rather of the heart, or the inward motives; for men indeed observed the Law so far as outward obedience is concerned, but inwardly, or in their hearts, they hated it, as we read in Psalm 28:3: "The workers of iniquity . . . speak peace to their neighbors, but mischief is in their hearts." We must therefore first of all learn from the perfectly clear Law our inability (*to obey it truly and according to God's will*). Then we shall see that Christ is absolutely necessary as the Giver of the Holy Spirit and of grace.

And for sin, condemned sin in the flesh (8:3). That is, on account of the punishment of sin which He bore for us, or through the merit of His (*bearing our*) sin, which was not in His flesh, but which He took upon Himself, so far as our punishment in the flesh was concerned, (*God destroyed the power of sin that was ours*). Through His death Christ brought it about that we no longer need fear death. Through His death He secured for us (*the grace*) that the Holy Spirit is given us, and that the wisdom of the flesh — (*trust in works*) — is removed from us. It is not our work, but God's gift, that we now hate ourselves — (*our carnal wisdom*) — and our sinful lusts and follow after love. But that the Law was weak through the flesh, was not the fault of the Law, but that of the foolishness and vanity of those who put their trust in it (*to save them*); for the Law in itself is good.

They that are after the Spirit (do mind) *the things of the Spirit* (8:5). Those who are born again by God the Holy Spirit to be new creatures, are always mindful of the things of the Spirit, namely, the uncreated (*spiritual*) blessings, or God Himself. The term "spirit" here must be taken for the inner (*spiritual, or new*) man, as the contrast between "flesh" and "spirit" shows. So the Apostle says in verse 10: "The Spirit is life because of righteousness." But there is no inward (*spiritual*) man, unless there is the Holy Spirit. In Galatians 5:19ff. (*we have a commentary on this passage in the words*): "Now the works of the flesh are . . . Adultery, fornication, uncleanness, lasciviousness," etc. Again: "The fruit of the Spirit is love, joy, peace, longsuffering, gentleness, goodness, faith, meekness, temperance" (*Gal.* 5:22, 23). The inner (*spiritual*) man is like the good tree which bears good fruit; and the flesh is like the corrupt tree which brings forth evil fruit (Matt. 7:17). It is more fitting to say that the Holy Spirit creates the good tree (*in us*) than to say that He Himself is the good tree.

The carnal mind is enmity against God. (8:7). (*That is the case*) because the carnal mind is not of God, but of the Devil.

Ye are not in the flesh, but in the Spirit (8:9). (*That is*): You do not live according to the old man, his wisdom and hatred of God. But you are in the spirit, that is, you live according to the new man, or according to the wisdom of the Holy Spirit and in friendship with God.

If so be that the Spirit of God dwell in you (8:9). That is: If the Holy Spirit dwells in you, who by His indwelling makes us new creatures. St. Augustine remarks on verse 8: "He is called an enemy of God who does not obey His Law, and this because of the wisdom of his flesh, which seeks after earthly gifts and fears temporal evils." Under "evils" we understand such things as sin, death and the like. He who is spiritually wise does not fear these evils. But he who is wise according to the flesh is dreadfully afraid of death and (*the punishment of*) sin. Those who have the wisdom of the Spirit delight in God's will and gladly heed it, for they have become like Him. So if they know that it is God's will that Judgment Day should come, which fills all (*carnal*) men with fear as it manifests the divine wrath, yet they are not afraid of it, but await it with joy, and they desire that it would come soon. Where this (*new*) mind rules, there is neither sorrow nor fear, but only an eager longing for what (*heavenly blessings*) we desire and grateful acceptance of what we seek (*when it is granted*). After the Lord had described the terrors of Judgment Day, he added in Luke 21:28: "When these things begin to come to pass, then look up, and lift up your heads; for your redemption draweth nigh."

He that raised up Christ from the dead shall also quicken your mortal bodies (8:11). In verse 10 the Apostle said: "The body is dead." Here he speaks of "mortal bodies." St. Augustine remarks on this: "Because in the coming (*final*) glorification the body will no longer die, but also will be incapable of dying, he does not say that He will quicken your dead bodies, but your mortal bodies, for then (*in glory*) the bodies will be not merely beyond death, but incapable of death."

If ye through the Spirit do mortify the deeds of the body, ye shall live (8:13). "Through the Spirit," that is, through the love (*for God*) in the inner man, (*created by the Spirit*). The "deeds of the body" are not properly man's evil works, but his sinful lusts, or passions.

As many as are led by the Spirit of God, they are the sons of God (8:14). To be "led by the Spirit of God" means to despise and renounce everything that is not of God, even oneself, and "to reject the pleasures of this world which are impure and covered with filth." It means freely to forsake all (*earthly*) things and to face and welcome the sufferings of the Christian life. But this is not the work of our corrupt nature, but the work of God the Holy Spirit in us.

Ye have not received the spirit of bondage again to fear (8:15). The Apostle here contrasts the "spirit of bondage" with the "spirit of sonship." But he speaks of the "Spirit of adoption" to show in what way we become God's children, and to exalt the grace of God. We are not children of God by nature (as alone in Christ), nor by descent, nor because of our merits (as the Jews boasted), but alone because of our gracious adoption by God as children (*in Christ*). The term "bondage" here must be understood of the bondage of sin, as we read in John 8:34: "Whosoever committeth sin is the servant of sin." Of the bondage of sin the Law cannot free us. It can only force us, through the fear of the impending Judgment, to do its demands (*outwardly*). Therefore it does not destroy the works (*passions*) of the flesh, but rather increases them. It intensifies the hatred of the Law and the desire to transgress it.

The Spirit of adoption, whereby we cry, Abba, Father (8:15). (*The Apostle means to say*): You have become free from fear and have received the Spirit of adoption by which you trust in God. This trust he shows very clearly by the words: "Whereby we cry, Abba, Father." This is the cry of a heart which is full of childlike trust and knows not fear. That the cry is not one of the mouth but of the heart, is clear from Galatians 4:6, 7: "Because ye are sons, God hath sent forth the Spirit of his Son into your hearts, crying, Abba, Father. Wherefore thou art no more a servant, but a son; and if a son, then an heir of God through Christ."

The Spirit itself beareth witness with our spirit, that we are the children of God (8:16). Whoever believes with a firm faith and hope that he is a child of God, *is* a child of God, for that (*to believe*) no one can do without the Holy Spirit. This witness of the Spirit is the filial trust of our heart in God. St. Bernard (*of Clairvaux*) in the first chapter of his *Sermon on the Feast of the Annunciation of the Blessed Mary* comments on this verse: "I believe that this witness consists of three things. First, believe that you can have forgiveness of sins only through the gracious favor of God. Secondly, do not call a single work your own, unless He has given it to you. Finally, believe that you cannot earn eternal salvation by any good works; for also this salvation is given to you out of pure grace." This, however, does not quite suffice, but it — (*the witness of the Holy Ghost*) — must be regarded as the beginning and, so to speak, as the foundation of faith. This is His witness: "Your sins are forgiven you!" Thus man — and this is the meaning of the Apostle — is justified solely by faith.

THE BELIEVERS' CERTAINTY OF SALVATION BY FAITH

For I reckon that the sufferings of this present time are not worthy to be compared with the glory which shall be revealed in us. For the earnest expectation of the creature waiteth for the manifestation of the sons of God. For the creature was made subject to vanity, not willingly, but by reason of him who hath subjected the same in hope, because the creature itself also shall be delivered from the bondage of corruption into, the glorious liberty of the children of God. For we know that the whole creation groaneth and travaileth in pain together until now. And not only they, but ourselves also, which have the firstfruits of the Spirit, even we ourselves groan within ourselves, waiting for the adoption, to wit, the redemption of our body. For we are saved by hope: but hope that is seen is not hope: for what a man seeth, why doth he yet hope for? But if we hope for that we see not, then do we with patience wait for it. Likewise the Spirit also helpeth our infirmities: for we know not what we should pray for as we ought: but the Spirit itself maketh intercession for us with groanings which cannot be uttered. And he that searcheth the hearts knoweth what is the mind of the Spirit, because he maketh intercession for the saints according to the will of God. And we know that all things work together for good to them that love God, to them who are the called according to his purpose. For whom he did foreknow, he also did predestinate to be conformed to the image of his Son, that he might be the firstborn among many brethren. Moreover whom he did predestinate, them he also called: and whom he called, them he also justified: and whom he justified, them he also glorified (8:18-30).

The sufferings of this time are not worthy to be compared with the glory which shall be revealed in us (8:18). The sufferings are worthy or unworthy, not according to our (*natural reckoning*). Our judgment is true and right only as we regard them, (*the sufferings of this present time*), as what they really are, (*judged by God's Word*). That, however, is not the way the proud (*unbelievers*) judge.

The earnest expectation of the creature waiteth for the manifestation of the sons of God (8:19). The Apostle speaks of the creature as if it were alive and capable of feeling and sorrow, because it is forced to serve the wicked despite their misuse (*of the creature*) and their ingratitude to God; for it exists that through and in it God may be glorified by His saints. That is the final blessing for which it waits.

The Apostle thinks and argues quite differently of these matters than do the philosophers. They view the present state of things so exclusively that they speculate only about the essence and attributes (*of created things*). But the Apostle turns our attention from the consideration of the creature in its present condition and directs us to its future state. Speaking of the earnest expectation of the creature, he urges us to explore not what the creature is, but what it expects. But oh, how many foolish opinions befog our philosophy! When shall we become reasonable and perceive that we are wasting precious time by such worthless studies, putting aside things that are of so much greater value. To us the word of Seneca may be applied: "We fail to know what is necessary, because we study unnecessary things: indeed, we do not know what is good for us, because we study merely what injures us."

I therefore admonish you to do away with these studies as soon as you can. It is high time that we devote ourselves to other studies and know Christ, "and him crucified" (I Cor. 2:2). We shall be the best philosophers and best students of nature when we learn of the Apostle to regard nature as one that waits, groans and travails, or as one that abominates what now is and desires what is to be, and is not yet. The Apostle is right when in Colossians 2:8 he warns against (a false) philosophy: "Beware lest any man spoil you through philosophy and vain deceit, after the tradition of men."

For the creature was made subject to vanity (8:20). By "creature" most exegetes here understand man, since he is a part of creation. But it is better to refer "vanity" to man, as Psalm 39:6 says expressly and correctly: "Every man walketh in a vain shew." It is true, if it were not for the old man (*the corrupt nature*) there would be no vanity; for all that God made was very good (Gen. 1:31). So it is good to this day (*inasmuch as it is a creature of God*), for the Apostle writes in I Timothy 4:4 "Every creature of God is good"; and in Titus 1:15: "Unto the pure all things are pure." The creature therefore is vain, evil and guilty without its fault, or from without, namely, inasmuch as (*sinful*) man in his false evaluation, or his (*sinful*) love, or his wrong enjoyment (*of it*) regards it more highly than is fitting.

Thus man, who is able to think of God and find enjoyment in Him, so far as his mind or reasoning is concerned, arrogantly believes that he can find peace and enjoyment in the created things. This is done by every person who is born of Adam and lives without the Holy Spirit. Through him every creature becomes vain against its will as we read in Ecclesiastes 1:2: "Vanity of vanities . . . all is vanity." Thus all things are vanity to (*sinful*) man, as is here said. All creatures are good in themselves, and those who acknowledge God, also acknowledge His creatures not as vanity, but according to truth. They use all things, but do not misuse them, as the Apostle writes in Titus 1:15: "Unto the pure all things are pure; but unto them that are defiled and unbelieving is nothing pure."

The creature itself also shall be delivered (8:21). (*What the Apostle here writes*) is the same as we read in Matthew 24:35: "Heaven and earth shall pass away." But this is to be understood not with reference to its existence in general, but with reference to its "bondage of corruption." Let the learned explain this passage as they understand it. I take it to mean not that the creature will cease to exist absolutely, but that it will no longer be subject to vanity, for it will appear in glory. In Psalm 102:26 we read: "As a vesture shalt thou change them, and they will be changed." As Christ passed through His "passover," that is, as He was changed into the glory of immortality, so all saints are described as such as "pass over," that is, are changed into glory. We read in II Peter 3:13: "We . . . look for a new heaven and a new earth;" and in Isaiah 65:17: "I create new heavens and a new earth: and the former shall not be remembered, nor come into mind."

From the bondage of corruption into the glorious liberty of children of God (8:21). Here the Apostle contrasts the creature's "bondage of corruption" with it's "glorious liberty,"; for now the creature serves, to its own harm, the wicked, for it is subject to their abuse. But then, delivered from corruption, it will serve the children of God in glory.

The whole creation groaneth and travaileth in pain together until now (8:22). It "travaileth," that is, it strives anxiously after the end of its corruption, in order to be born into glory. As a woman in travail has sorrow, but forgets her anguish after she is delivered of the child, (*so also the whole creation*). Note from this how great a supplication rises to God perpetually for the righteous against the unrighteous; for the whole creation prays for its own deliverance and that of the godly, while at the same time it cries out against the ungodly. With it also we (*believers*) pray and cry out, and with us the Holy Spirit.

And not only they, but we ourselves also, which have the firstfruits of the Spirit, even we ourselves groan within ourselves, waiting for the adoption, to wit, the redemption of the body (8:23). Those who have the spirit of fear do not understand this. They rather are horrified by it and wish that it would never take place. Thus the Apostle in this passage declares two things. First, the creature will be delivered from its (*present*) vanity after the wicked are condemned and removed, and the old man is destroyed. This deliverance takes place from day to day in (*God's*) saints. Secondly, then the creature will no longer be subject to vanity and corruption.

Hope that is seen is not hope (8:24). Theologically, this must be understood in its literal meaning, for it (*hope*) denotes an expectation that is most intense. Hope which grows out of the ardent longing for that which is greatly desired, makes love ever greater by the very distance that separates it. Through such high-tensioned hope there is created, so to speak, a unity between the one who hopes and that which he hopes for; as St. Augustine says: "The soul is at home much more where its object of love is, than in the body which it animates.

Likewise the Spirit also helpeth our infirmities (8:26). Even the pious person cannot by his own strength desire the glory of heaven as ardently (*as he would*). Therefore the Holy Spirit intercedes for us with ineffable groanings of which we ourselves are incapable. Even when we pray for eternal glory, in particular, that it may come to us soon, or that it may come to us in a special way, we do not know what we pray for, for it might turn out for our harm if it would be given to us speedily or in this or that way. This is even much more the case when we pray for earthly blessings.

The Spirit itself maketh intercession for us with groanings which cannot be uttered (8:26). These are prayers which no man can describe by words, and which no one can understand except God alone. The groanings are so great that only God can rightly regard and appreciate them: as we read in Psalm 38:9: "All my desire is before thee; and my groaning is not hid from thee." It is not an evil sign, but indeed the very best, if upon our petitions the very opposite happens to us. Conversely, it is not a good sign if everything is granted to us for which we pray.

The reason for this is the following: God's counsel and will tower high above our own counsel and will, as we read in Isaiah 55:8, 9: "My thoughts are not your thoughts, neither are your ways my ways, saith the Lord. For as the heavens are higher than the earth, so are my ways higher than your ways, and my thoughts than your thoughts." Hence, when we ask anything of God and He begins to hear us, He so often goes counter to our petitions that we imagine He is more angry with us now than before we prayed, and that He intends not to grant us our requests at all. All this God does, because it is His way first to destroy and annihilate what is in us — (*our own wisdom and will*) — before He gives us His gifts; for so we read in I Samuel 2:6: "The Lord killeth, and maketh alive: he bringeth down to the grave, and bringeth up." Through this most gracious counsel He makes us fit for His gifts and works. Only then are we qualified for His works and counsels when our own plans have been demolished and our own works are destroyed and we have become purely passive in our relation to Him.

The proud (*unbelievers*) desire to be like God. They want to place their thoughts not under God, but next to His, just as though they were perfect (*as God is*). But that is much less possible than for the clay to tell the potter into what shape he should form it. So we read in Isaiah 64:8: "O Lord, Thou art our Father; we are the clay, and thou our potter; and we all are the work of thy hand." But those who have the Holy Spirit do not despair but have faith when they see that the very opposite of what they asked for happens to them. The work of God must remain hidden in any other form than that which contradicts our thinking and understanding. Thus God permitted St. Augustine to fall deeper and deeper into error, despite the prayers of his mother, in order to grant her much more in the end than she had asked. This He does with all His saints.

We know that all things work together for good to them that love God, to them who are the called according to his purpose (8:28). The Greek text has the singular "works together" (*sunergei*), which is more fitting, since the reference is to the Holy Ghost; for this is the (*Apostle's*) meaning: We must not be surprised that the Holy Spirit intercedes for us, since He works together with God's saints in all they do. That is the true exposition of the statement: "He maketh intercession for the saints." In this (*intercession*) He works together with us, as He works together with us in all other things. (*Luther here follows the Greek reading:*

Panta sunergei ho Theos: *in all things God works together with us for good.*) The Apostle here says without any qualification: "Who are the called according to his purpose." There is only this one purpose, namely, the purpose of God, which those recognize who recognize God. There is no other purpose (*in God*), nor is there carried out any other purpose than the one divine purpose (*of salvation*).

This passage is the foundation on which rests everything that the Apostle says to the end of the chapter; for he means to show that to the elect who are loved of God and who love God, the Holy Spirit makes all things work for good even though they are evil (*in themselves, e.g., sickness, persecution, etc.*) He here takes up the doctrine of predestination or election. This doctrine is not so incomprehensible as many think, but it is rather full of sweet comfort for the elect and for all who have the Holy Spirit. But it is most bitter and hard for (*those who adhere to*) the wisdom of the flesh. There is no other reason why the many tribulations and evils cannot separate the saints from the love of God than that they are the called "according to His purpose." Hence God makes all things work together for good to them, and to them only. If there would not be this divine purpose, but our salvation would rest upon our will or work, it would be based upon chance. How easily in that case could one single evil hinder or destroy it! But when the Apostle says: "Who shall lay anything to the charge of God's elect?" "Who is he that condemneth?" "Who shall separate us from the love of Christ?" (8:33, 34, 35), he shows that the elect are not saved by chance, but by God's purpose and will. Indeed for this reason, God allows the elect to encounter so many evil things as are here named, namely, to point out that they are saved not by their merit, but by His election, His unchangeable and firm purpose (*of salvation in Christ*). They are saved despite their many rapacious and fierce foes and the vain efforts (*to lead them into perdition*).

What then is there to our own righteousness? to our good works? to the freedom of the will? to chance in the things that occur? That (*denial of all these things*) is what we must preach, (*as does the Apostle*), for that means to preach rightly. That means to destroy the wisdom of the flesh. So far the Apostle has destroyed merely the hands, feet, and tongue of the wisdom of the flesh; now he wipes it out utterly. Now he makes us see that it amounts to nothing, and that our salvation altogether lies in His hands. God absolutely recognizes no chance; it is only men who speak of chance. Not a single leaf falls from the tree without the will of the Father. All things are essentially in His hands, and so are also our times.

There are yet three thoughts that should be considered in connection with the subject (*of divine predestination*). First, there are the proofs of God's unchangeable election, gathered from the words of Scripture and His (*divine*) works. The Apostle says: "Who are the called according to his purpose." "Purpose" here stands for God's predestination, or His free election, or His (*eternal*) counsel (*regarding the salvation of individual persons*). Later, in chapter 9, the Apostle illustrates God's eternal election by referring to Isaac and Ishmael, Jacob and Esau (v. 8f.). As he clearly shows, the difference between these men rests solely upon divine predestination. Lastly, for God's eternal election the Apostle quotes two passages: "I will have mercy on whom I will have mercy" (9:15); and: "Therefore hath he mercy on whom he will have mercy, and whom he will he hardeneth" (9:18). Similar passages are found elsewhere in Chapters 9 and 10.

There are passages treating of God's eternal election also in other books of Scripture. Thus we read in John 13:18: "I speak not of you all: I know whom I have chosen"; and in John 10:27-29: "My sheep hear my voice, and I know them, and they follow me: and I give unto them eternal life; and they shall never perish, neither shall any man pluck them out of my hand. My Father, which gave them me, is greater than all; and no man is able to pluck them out of my Father's hand"; and in II Timothy 2:19: "The foundation of God standeth sure, having this seal, the Lord knoweth them that are his."

A further proof for God's eternal purpose of election we find in His works. First, in the works which God did to Ishmael and Esau, Pharaoh and the Egyptians, as they are reported in this chapter and the following. Again, in the divine acts by which He gives over His saints to so many evil and rapacious enemies and yet does not permit them to lose their salvation. This clearly proves that His election stands firm and so cannot be hindered by any creature. Then also this act of God proves the divine election that He permits many to commit great sins and yet they are brought to repentance and are saved (*David: II Samuel* 12:13). while others who in the beginning lead a pious life and do many good works are not saved (*Saul: I Samuel* 13:13). Compare for this also Judas and the thief on the cross (Matt. 26:14; Luke 23:41).

The second thought (*that we should consider in connection with God's eternal election*) is that all objections to predestination proceed from the wisdom of the flesh (*human reason*). Hence, whoever does not deny himself and does not learn to keep his thoughts in subjection to the divine will, never will find an answer to his questions. And that rightly so, for the foolish wisdom of the flesh exalts itself above God and judges His will, just as though this were of little importance. It should rather let itself be judged by God. For this reason the Apostle refutes all objections with two brief statements. First, he checks our arrogance by asking: "O man, who art thou that thou repliest against God?" (Rom. 9:20) Then he defends the divine election by asking: "Hath not the potter power over the clay?" (v. 21)

The first and most flimsy objection against divine election is this, that man has been given a free will by which he can earn for himself either merit or demerit. To this I reply: Man's free will without divine grace has not the least ability to secure righteousness, but is totally corrupt.

The second objection is this: "Who will have all men to be saved" (I Tim. 2:4); that is, God gave His Son into death for us, as He has created us for life eternal. Again: All things exist on account of man; but he himself exists for God's sake to enjoy God. But these and other objections are just as vain as is the first; for all these statements are realized properly in the elect, as the Apostle writes in II Timothy 2:10: "I endure all things for the elect's sakes, that they may also obtain the salvation which is in Christ Jesus with eternal glory."

A third objection reads: Where there is no sin, there God does not condemn. But whoever is a sinner of necessity is condemned unjustly. To this I reply: We all are sinners of necessity and so under condemnation, but no one is a sinner by coercion, or against his will.

A fourth objection is this: God hardens the will of man so that he desires to transgress the divine Law all the more. Hence, God is the cause why men sin and are condemned. This is the strongest and most weighty objection. But the Apostle meets it by saying that so it is God's will, and that if God so wills He does not act unjustly, for all things belong to Him as the clay belongs to the potter. He thus establishes His law in order that the elect may obey it, but the reprobates may be caught in it, and so He may show both His wrath and His mercy. Here indeed the wisdom of the flesh objects saying: "It is cruel and regrettable that God seeks His glorification in my misery." Ah, it is the voice of the flesh that says: "My, my!" Strike out this "my, my" and say instead: "Glory be to Thee, O Lord!" Then you will be saved. The wisdom of the flesh seeks its own glory and is more afraid of suffering than of desecrating God. Hence it follows its own will rather than the divine will. We must think differently of God than we do of men; for He owes us nothing. That is what the Apostle teaches at the close of the eleventh chapter: "Who hath first given to him, and it shall be recompensed unto him again?" (11:35)

The third thought (*that we could consider in connection with God's eternal election*) is that this doctrine is indeed most bitter to the wisdom of the flesh, which revolts against it and even becomes guilty of blasphemy on this point. But it is fully defeated when we learn to know that our salvation rests in no wise upon ourselves and our conduct, but is founded solely upon what is outside us, namely, on God's election. Those who have the wisdom of the Spirit become ineffably happy through the doctrine, as the Apostle himself illustrates this. To them, (*His elect*), Christ says: "Fear not, little flock; for it is your Father's good pleasure to give you the kingdom" (Luke 12:32). So also God says in Isaiah 35:4: "Say to them that are of a fearful heart, Be strong, fear not: behold, your God will come with vengeance, even God with a recompence; he will come and save you." Everywhere in Scripture those are praised and encouraged who listen to God's Word with trembling. As they despair of themselves, the Word of God performs its work in them. If we anxiously tremble at God's Word and are terrified by it, this is indeed a good sign.

If one fears that he is not elected or is otherwise troubled about his election, he should be thankful that he has such fear; for then he should surely know that God cannot lie when in Psalm 51:17 He says: "The sacrifices of God are a broken spirit: a broken and a contrite heart, O God, thou wilt not despise." Thus he should cheerfully cast himself on the faithfulness of God who gives this promise, and turn away from the foreknowledge of the threatening God. Then he will be saved as one that is elected. It is not the characteristic of reprobates to tremble at the secret counsel of God; but that is the characteristic of the elect. The reprobates despise it, or at least pay no attention to it, or else they declare in the arrogance of their despair: "Well, if I am damned, all right, then I am damned."

With reference to the elect we might distinguish between three classes. First, there are those who are satisfied with God's will, as it is, and do not murmur against God, but rather believe that they are elected. They do not want to be damned. Secondly, there are those who submit to God's will and are satisfied with it in their hearts. At least they desire to be satisfied, if God does not wish to save, but reject them. Thirdly, there are those who really are ready to be condemned if God should will this. These are cleansed most of all of their own will and carnal wisdom. And these experience the truth of Canticles 8:6: "Set me as a seal upon thine heart, as a seal upon thine arm: for love is strong as death." Such love is always joined with cross and tribulation, for without it the soul becomes lax, and does not seek after God, nor thirst after God, who is the Fountain of Life.

For whom he did foreknow, he did also predestinate to be conformed to the image of his Son, that he might be the firstborn among many brethren (8:29). (Christ is) the Head, the Firstborn, the Archetype, and the Image of all things according to His human nature; for according to His divine nature He is the Only-begotten and as such has no brethren. The word "many" here has great emphasis. It must not be taken in the sense as though Christ were the Firstborn, not of all but only of many. He is the Firstborn among brethren who indeed are very numerous. Just so the word is used in Romans 5:15: "If through the offence of one many be dead."

Whom he did predestinate, them he also called: and whom he called, them he also justified: and whom he justified, them he also glorified (8:30). The climax at which the Apostle here arrives ("*them he also glorified*") refers to those whom God "did predestinate to be conformed to the image of his Son" (v. 29).

THE BELIEVER'S TRIUMPHANT FAITH

What shall we then say to these things? If God be for us, who can be against us? He that spared not his own Son, but delivered him up for us all, how shall he not with him also freely give us all things? Who shall lay any thing to the charge of God's elect? It is God that justifieth. Who is he that condemneth? It is Christ that died, yea rather, that is risen again, who is even at the right hand of God, who also maketh intercession for us. Who shall separate us from the love of Christ? shall tribulation, or distress, or persecution, or famine, or nakedness, or peril, or sword? As it is written, For thy sake we are killed all the day long; we are accounted as sheep for the slaughter. Nay, in all these things we are more than conquerors through him that loved us. For I am persuaded that neither death, nor life, nor angels, nor principalities, nor powers, nor things present, nor things to come. Nor height, nor depth, nor any other creature, shall be able to separate us from the love of God, which is in Christ Jesus our Lord (8:31-39).

If God be for us, who can be against us? (8:31) If God be for us, who is the Judge of all and whose omnipotence calls into being all things, no one can be against us, since everything that He has created must be subject to the Creator. So also the converse is true! If God be against us no one can be for us.

Who shall separate us from the love of Christ? (8:35) Faber Who can accuse us whom God has predestinated? Absolutely no one! For it is God who justifies us, that is, who declares us to be righteous and so intercedes for us. So also no one can condemn us, for Christ is our Mediator and Bishop who died for us, yea rather, that is risen again, and so was not swallowed up by death, but rather swallowed up death. He is in glory now at the right hand of God, and He as our High Priest makes intercession for us.

Who shall lay anything to the charge of God's elect? (8:33) Stapulensis wanted this to be understood of the active love of

Christ, and not at all of His passive love, (*that is, of the love which Christ has for us, and not of the love which we have for Christ*). But St. Augustine in the seventeenth chapter of his book *Concerning Grace and Free Will* writes in opposition to this interpretation: "This love, that is, this will, glowing red-hot with love for God, the Apostle glorifies when he says: 'Who shall separate us from the love of Christ?'" Both interpretations are acceptable, for if our love (*for Christ*) is invincible, it is so because of the love of God (*for and in us*) and not because of our own strength. It is God who loves us (*first*) and then He imparts love to us.

In all these things we are more than conquerors through him that loved us (8:37). It is Christ's love that makes us triumphant through our love to Him. We did not love Him first, but He first loved us, and He still loves us first. It is not because we love, that He loves; but He loves, therefore we love, as we learn from I John 4:10.

I am persuaded, that neither death, nor life . . . shall be able to separate us from the love of God (8:38, 39). The Apostle here speaks for himself and all the elect. Concerning himself he was sure that he was a "chosen vessel" (Acts 9:15) by a special revelation. Regarding the elect we also are sure (*through faith in Christ Jesus, as Luther shows in his exposition of verses* 31 *and* 34).

Romans Nine

Content of the ninth chapter: The Apostle sorrows over the hardening of the Jews and shows that the Jews have not been cheated out of the promises of the Fathers. He reminds them of the call of the heathen.

ELECTION IS BY GRACE ACCORDING TO THE PROMISE IN CHRIST

I say the truth in Christ, I lie not, my conscience also bearing me witness in the Holy Ghost, that I have great heaviness and continual sorrow in my heart. For I could wish that myself were accursed from Christ for my brethren, my kinsmen according to the flesh: who are Israelites; to whom pertaineth the adoption, and the glory, and the covenants, and the giving of the law, and the service of God, and the promises; whose are the fathers, and of whom as concerning the flesh Christ came, who is over all, God blessed for ever. Amen. Not as though the word of God hath taken none effect. For they are not all Israel, which are of Israel: neither, because they are the seed of Abraham, are they all children: but, in Isaac shall thy seed be called. That is, They which are the children of the flesh, these are not the children of God: but the children of the promise are counted for the seed. For this is the word of promise, At this time will I come, and Sarah shall have a son. And not only this; but when Rebecca also had conceived by one, even by our father Isaac; (for the children being not yet born, neither having done any good or evil, that the purpose of God according to election might stand, not of works, but of him that calleth;) *it was said unto her, The elder shall serve the younger. As it is written, Jacob have I loved, but Esau have I hated. What shall we say then? Is there unrighteousness with God? God forbid. For he saith to Moses, I will have mercy on whom I will have mercy, and I will have compassion on whom I will have compassion. So then it is not of him that willeth, nor of him that runneth, but of God that sheweth mercy. For the scripture saith unto Pharaoh, Even for this same purpose have I raised thee*

*up, that I might show my power in thee, and that my name might be
declared throughout all the earth. Therefore hath he mercy on whom he
will have mercy, and whom he will he hardeneth.* (9:1-18).

I say the truth in Christ, I lie not (9:1). Whoever laughs at his
neighbor's loss and delights in it, while saying that he loves him,
adds to this envy a lie.

I have . . . continual sorrow in my heart (9:2) Love is not only
pure joy, and delight, but also great and deep heaviness of heart
and sorrow. But love too is full of joy and sweetness even in bitter
sorrow, because it regards the misery and injury of others as its own.
So also Christ was glowing with burning love in His last and
greatest agony. According to St. Hilary, it was Christ's greatest
joy that He endured the greatest woe. Thus God "giveth strength
and power unto his people" (Ps. 68:35). While they experience
the greatest sorrow, their hearts overflow with joy.

*I could wish that myself were accursed from Christ for my
brethren.* (9:3) The Apostle begins this chapter with a strong
affirmation and oath, moved to this by an irrepressible urgency.
With these words he desires to win their confidence; for he was
regarded by the Jews as one who was not at all interested in their
salvation; indeed, as one who above all others persecuted them
and destroyed their salvation. The blindness of the Jews caused
him to give expression to his sorrow of heart and to treat the
doctrine of predestination. Their stubbornness practically confirmed
what he knew long before, namely, that not the (*work-*) righteousness of him that runneth, but the gracious purpose of the merciful
God is the cause of man's salvation.

*My brethren, my kinsmen according to the flesh: who are
Israelites; to whom pertaineth the adoption* (9:3-4). All this shows
that God's predestination and sure election is the cause of man's
salvation and not the righteousness of the human will. For since
those were rejected who had all these blessings, and others were
saved who were without them, it is evident that (*God's*) election
saves and not (*man's*) righteousness. The whole arrangement of
the text demonstrates that the Apostle here speaks out of his deep
interest in their salvation and out of his great zeal to bring Christ
to them. He desires for the Jews the greatest salvation, and he is
willing to lose his own salvation if only they would gain theirs.

He says the same thing in II Corinthians 12:15: "I will very gladly spend and be spent for you."

For those who truly love God with a love that comes from the Holy Spirit these words are most wonderful. Such (*consecrated and loving Christians*) never seek what is their own, but they are willing to suffer hell and damnation, in order that God's will might be accomplished (*in the salvation of others*). So also Christ was condemned and forsaken more than all His saints. He did not suffer lightly, as some say, but really and truly He dedicated Himself to God the Father for eternal damnation to save us. In this (*His love*) His saints must imitate Him; and the greater their love, the more willingly and readily will they be able to do it.

Those who shudder and avoid this meaning (*of love*) do not at all know what it means "to love." For "to love" means to hate oneself and to condemn oneself, according to Christ's saying in John 12:25: "He that hateth his life in this world shall keep it unto life eternal." Whoever loves himself in that way, loves himself most truly, for he loves himself in God, or according to His will. So our "life is hid with Christ in God" (Colossians 3:3); and so also our spiritual wisdom and righteousness is hid with Christ in God.

They are not all Israel, which are of Israel (9:6). This does not mean that "the Word of God hath taken none effect." The sense is the same as in 3:3: "For what if some did not believe? shall their unbelief make the faith of God without effect?" The promise was meant for them, (*for all Israel*), but it was not granted to them, because they would not receive it. Nevertheless, it was given to others of the same blood. But it was not given to them merely because they were of the same blood, but because they were (*born*) of the Spirit.

Neither, because they are the seed of Abraham, are they all children (9:7). This is said against the arrogance of the Jews and to extol (*divine*) grace. It destroys the proud trust of everyone in his own righteousness and good works. The Jews wanted to be regarded as heirs of the kingdom, because they were children of Abraham. The Apostle convicts them with an unanswerable argument; for if their arrogant assumption were true, then also Ishmael and the children of Keturah would rightly be heirs of Abraham and have the same dignity as Isaac. But Genesis, Chapter 25, shows that the very opposite is the case. This leads to the irrefutable conclusion that it is not the flesh—(*carnal descent*)—which makes us children of God and heirs of salvation, but God's election to salvation. Only when man's carnal pride is put down, can he be born again by the grace of God of the Holy Spirit.

When Rebecca also had conceived by one, even by our father Isaac (9:10). The meaning of this statement is the following: Carnal descent is of so little benefit for our adoption by God as His children that even Rebecca, that virtuous woman, who was the only wife of saintly Isaac, the father of all the children of Israel, received the promise of God for only one of her sons, so that he alone, and not the other, should be the future lord and heir of the promise. It did not help Esau that he descended from so good a father and from so good a mother and that he was conceived and born according to the flesh in wedlock so undefiled; indeed, it did not benefit him at all that he was the first-born. How much less will it benefit the unbelieving Jews who are born so long afterwards, that they are the sons of patriarchs according to the flesh, if they continue in unbelief, that is, if they are not elected by God.

For the children being not yet born . . . that the purpose of God according to the election might stand, not of works, but of him that calleth (9:11). This is written and quoted in order that divine grace might be magnified and the arrogant boasting of human merit might be utterly destroyed. Very aptly he says: "Neither having done any good or evil"; and not: "Neither being good or evil"; for without doubt both sons were evil by the corruption of original sin. So far as their merit was concerned, they were equal to each other in birth and rank; both belonged to the same corrupt mass (*of humanity*).

Is their unrighteousness with God? God forbid (9:14). The Apostle gives no other reason for his statement that there is no unrighteousness with God than this: "I will have mercy on whom I will have mercy" (9:15). That means: I will have mercy on whom I intended to have mercy, or whom I predestinated for mercy. This is a hard saying for the proud and prudent. But it is sweet to the lowly and humble who despair of themselves. For that very reason the Lord has mercy on them. Indeed, there is no other reason for God's justice, nor can there be any other than His own will. Why, then, should man complain that God acts unjustly, when this is impossible? Or, could it be possible that God is not God? So, since God's will is our supreme good, why should we not desire that His will be done? Since God can in no wise do evil, why should it not be our greatest concern that His will be done? If anyone replies: "But for me His will is evil," that is not true. God's will is evil for no one. But it is evil for (*wicked*) men who do not make His will theirs, nor do it. If they would will what God wills, even though that should mean their rejection and condemnation, there would be no evil for them; for then they would will what God wills, and they would patiently bear what God wills.

I will have compassion on whom I will have compassion (9:15). That means: I will give grace, in time and life, to him concerning whom I purposed from eternity to show mercy. On him will I have compassion and forgive his sin in time and life whom I forgave and pardoned from all eternity. In doing this, God is not unjust, for so He willed and was pleased to do from eternity, and His will is not bound by any law or obligation. (*God's*) free will, which is subject to no one, cannot be unjust. Indeed, it is impossible that it should be unjust. God's will would be unjust only if it would transgress some law, (*and that means that God would go counter to Himself*).

This statement seems hard and cruel, but it is full of sweet comfort, because God has taken upon Himself all our help and salvation, in order that He alone might wholly be the Author of our salvation. So also we read in 11:32: "God hath concluded them all in unbelief, (*not with cruel intention, but*) that he might have mercy upon all"; that is, in order that He might show mercy to all, which otherwise He neither would nor could do, if we would oppose Him with the arrogant pride of our own righteousness.

So then it is not of him that willeth, nor of him that runneth, but of God that sheweth mercy (9:16). This does not mean that God's mercy altogether excludes our willing or running. But the words mean: The fact that a person wills and runs, he owes not to his own strength, but to the mercy of God; for it is He who gives us the power to will and to do. Without this (*power*) man of his own accord is unable both to will and to do. This truth the Apostle expresses in Philippians 2:13 thus: "It is God which worketh in you both to will and to do of his good pleasure." Just that the Apostle says in our text in different words: It is not of him that wills, nor of him that runs, that is, who (*of himself*) accomplishes (*his salvation*), but of God that showeth mercy, that is, who grants to men the gift of His grace.

Here let me add an admonition: Let no one lose himself in speculation (*on this point*) whose mind is not yet sanctified, in order that he may not fall into abyss of terror and despair. Let him rather first purify (*enlighten*) the understanding of his mind by considering the wounds of Jesus Christ (*whose blood flows with salvation for all sinners*). This is theology in the most excellent sense of the term. Of this the Apostle writes in I Corinthians 2:6: "We speak wisdom among them that are perfect." I myself am still a babe that requires milk and not meat (I Cor. 3:2); and so let everyone do who is a babe in Christ, as I am. The wounds of Jesus Christ, the "clefts of the rock" (Ex. 33:22), give us sufficient assurance (*of our salvation*).

The scripture saith unto Pharaoh, Even for this same purpose have I raised thee up, that I might shew my power in thee, and that my name might be declared throughout all the earth (9:17). These words mean: I desired to show you that the power of deliverance lies alone in me and not in the ability, merit and righteousness of any other. For this reason I hardened you and freed Israel. This power he (*the Apostle*), illustrated before in the case of the two brothers, Esau and Jacob, namely, that it is the divine election of grace that saves, and that those surely will be saved who are elected. To this knowledge of divine grace no one would come, if God would not act (*as is here shown*), but would leave every one in his delusion and arrogant opinion that he possesses saving righteousness (*by his own merit*); just as though he must be saved, because he runs, not because God had compassion upon him. Those who called themselves wise, became fools; those who called themselves righteous, became sinners; those who called themselves truthful became liars and vain. So God alone must be called righteous, faithful and good, according to

Psalm 8:9: "O Lord our Lord, how excellent is thy name in all the earth!"

The Elect are Surely Saved Through Faith in Christ

Thou wilt say then unto me, Why doth he yet find fault? For who hath resisted his will? Nay but, O man, who art thou that repliest against God? Shall the thing formed say to him that formed it, Why hast thou made me thus? Hath not the potter power over the clay; of the same lump to make one vessel unto honour and another unto dishonour? What if God, willing to shew his wrath, and to make his power known, endured with much longsuffering the vessels of wrath fitted to destruction: and that he might make known the riches of his glory on the vessels of mercy, which he had afore prepared unto glory, even us, whom he hath called, not of the Jews only, but also of the Gentiles? As he saith also in Osee, I will call them my people, which were not my people; and her beloved, which was not beloved. And it shall come to pass, that in the place where it was said unto them, Ye are not my people; there shall they be called the children of the living God. Esaias also crieth concerning Israel, Though the number of the children of Israel be as the sand of the sea, a remnant shall be saved: for he will finish the work and cut it short in righteousness: because a short work will the Lord make upon the earth. And as Esaias said before, Except the Lord of Sabaoth had left us a seed, we had been as Sodoma, and been made like unto Gomorrah. What shall we say then? That the Gentiles, which followed not after righteousness, have attained to righteousness, even the righteousness which is of faith. But Israel, which followed after the law of righteousness, hath not attained to the law of righteousness. Wherefore? Because they sought it not by faith, but as it were by the works of the law. For they stumbled at that stumblingstone; as it is written, Behold, I lay in Sion a stumblingstone and rock of offence: and whosoever believeth on him shall not be ashamed. (9:19-33).

Thou wilt say then unto me, Why doth he yet find fault? (9:19). The Apostle quotes this question in the sense of those who contend against God in a wicked and arrogant way. Enraged (*at God*), they murmur against Him as if He were a criminal, and indeed, as one who is on the same level as they. (*The Apostle means to say*): Do you dare dispute with your Creator, defy Him, and judge Him? Are you unwilling to yield to Him at least on one little point? Indeed, it is not a sin when in the spirit of reverence, humility and piety one would ask God: "Why hast thou made me thus" (9:20)? Yes, even if under the extreme pressure of trials one would utter an impious word against God, he for that reason would not be damned; for our God is not an impatient and cruel Lord, not even over against the wicked. I say this to comfort those who constantly are troubled by impious thoughts and are greatly alarmed about this fact.

Hath not the potter power over the clay; of the same lump to make one vessel unto honour, and another unto dishonour? (9:21) St. Augustine writes in Chapter 99 of his *Enchiridion*: "The whole race of men is so greatly condemned in its radical apostasy by this righteous divine verdict that not a single person would do right to criticize God's justice, even though not a single one would be free in such a way that some are permitted to remain in their most righteous condemnation, in order that they, (*the elect*), might understand that the whole human race had deserved and to what (*punishment*) the well deserved judgment of God would have to lead them, had not His unmerited mercy rescued them. Every mouth must be stopped (Rom. 3:19), and he that glories, must glory in the Lord (I Cor. 1:31)." These are great and important words, for they humiliate and terrify us greatly. Very aptly St. Augustine shows us why the Apostle wrote these words, namely, to lead us to humility. The words are not written to cause us fear and despair, but to glorify (*divine*) grace and destroy our arrogance.

What if God, willing to shew his wrath, and to make his power known, endured with much longsuffering the vessels of wrath fitted to destruction (9:22). The sense of this verse is: If it is true that God wishes to show His wrath and power, as He before told Pharaoh that he would, why, then, do you contend against His will? For you are the thing that He formed, and if a potter may form the clay (*according to his will*), how much more God, if He were willing to act in this way? So the word "God" here has the emphasis, as it corresponds to the word "potter" in the statement: "Hath not the potter power over the clay?" The conclusion is therefore from the lesser to the greater.

That he might make known the riches of his glory on the vessels of mercy, whom he had afore prepared unto glory (9:23). God endures the reprobates (*vessels of wrath*) in order that He might make His elect fit for glory. He endures them, I say, by allowing them to glory in themselves, to have the rule and to deal with His elect according to their despotic will (*as did Pharaoh*). Man through these words is made to recognize his condemnation and to despair of saving himself by his own powers; for the thought that he has fallen in Adam would otherwise not trouble him. He hopes, yes, he arrogantly presumes to reestablish himself (*with God*) by his own free will. But here he learns that grace alone raises him up before and above his free will.

Esaias also crieth concerning Israel (9:27). Let no one think that the Jews are rejected altogether, because Hosea has said: "I will say to them which were not my people, Thou art my people" (Hos. 2:23). This statement seems to say that God would call only the heathen as a "people" as the Jews were a "people." Against this understanding (*misunderstanding*) Esaias cries concerning Israel that God will call some out of Israel. He speaks of God in the sense as though He were willing to reject the whole people (*of Israel*), but He will leave a few as witnesses of His truth and promise.

Though the number of the children of Israel be as the sand of the sea, a remnant shall be saved (9:27). The term "remnant" is found frequently in (*the writings of*) the prophets. Thus in Isaiah 46:3 we read: "Hearken unto me, O house of Jacob, and all the remnant of the house of Israel." They were called the "remnant" because they were allowed to remain, as is clear from (*the prophecy of*) Isaiah; for while God gave the others up to perdition, He let them remain as the seed for another people.

For he will finish the work, and cut it short in righteousness. (9:28). Almost the entire people (*of Israel*) were carnal and glorified in the flesh—(*their carnal wisdom and work-righteousness*). Therefore God does a work, which is finished and cut short, corresponding to the large number of carnal persons in Israel. It would not have been surprising had all been cut off; for all were children of the flesh and descended from the fathers according to their flesh (*corrupt nature*). Only the Lord allowed a seed to remain unto Himself. He adds, "in righteousness." In Isaiah 10:22 we read: "Though thy people be as the sand of the sea, yet a remnant of them shall return: the consumption decreed shall overflow with righteousness." It is strange that there should be decreed consumption—(*the destruction of the wicked in Israel*)—

that is finished and cut off, and yet also an overflowing with righteousness. But here it is accomplished: the promise of God overflowed with righteousness, yet at the same time it was cut off for almost all. In those in whom the promise was accomplished, it overflowed with righteousness, (*namely, that of Christ unto salvation*).

Israel, which followed after the law of righteousness, hath not attained to the law of righteousness (9.31). The work-righteous will never be justified, because they resist divine grace. But believers are justified because (*by faith*) they accept (*God's*) grace.

As it is written, Behold, I lay in Sion a stumblingstone and rock of offence: and whosoever believeth on him shall not be ashamed (9:33). The righteousness of Christ becomes his who believes on Him; and the sin of him who believes on Him becomes that of Christ. Therefore, sin cannot remain on him who believes, just as man's sin could not remain on Christ. The Hebrew text reads: "He who believes, does not flee." This means that he who believes in Christ need not hurry away or flee, as he will not be terrified. The believer is afraid of nothing, but stands quiet and secure on a firm rock, as the Lord teaches in Matthew 7:24 ff. But he who does not believe will flee and yet cannot escape when he is hard pressed by tribulation and anguish and above all by (*God's*) judgment; for it is the punishment of the damned and their end-less restlessness that they flee God and yet cannot escape.

Romans Ten

Content of the tenth chapter: The Apostle intercedes for the Jews and shows that the righteousness which makes (*man*) worthy of eternal life, comes alone from the Law of Christ (*the Gospel*) and from faith in Christ.

MAN OBTAINS RIGHTEOUSNESS ONLY BY FAITH IN CHRIST

Brethren, my heart's desire and prayer to God for Israel is, that they might be saved. For I bear them record that they have a zeal of God, but not according to knowledge. For they being ignorant of God's righteousness, and going about to establish their own righteousness, have not submitted themselves unto the righteousness of God. For Christ is the end of the law for righteousness to every one that believeth. For Moses describeth the righteousness which is of the law, That the man which doeth those things shall live by them. But the righteousness which is of faith speaketh on this wise, Say not in thy heart, Who shall ascend into heaven? (that is, to bring Christ down from above:) or, Who shall descend into the deep? (that is, to bring Christ again from the dead.) But what saith it? The word is nigh thee, even in thy mouth, and in thy heart: that is, the word of faith, which we preach; that if thou shalt confess with thy mouth the Lord Jesus, and shalt believe in thine heart that God hath raised him from the dead, thou shalt be saved. For with the heart man believeth unto righteousness; and with the mouth confession is made unto salvation. For the scripture saith, Whosoever believeth on him shall not be ashamed. For there is no difference between the Jew and the Greek: for the same Lord over all is rich unto all that call upon him. For whosoever shall call upon the name of the Lord shall be saved (10:1-13).

Brethren, my heart's desire and prayer to God for Israel is, that they might be saved (10:1). Here, according to St. Augustine, the Apostle begins to speak of the hope of the Jews, in order that the heathen might not exalt themselves over the Jews. For as he had

145

to reject the arrogance of the Jews inasmuch as they gloried in their works, he now must oppose the Gentiles, in order that they might not be overbearing as though God preferred them to the Jews.

For I bear them record that they have a zeal of God, but not according to knowledge (10:2). It is commonly said: "The intention is good, and the purpose is true, but the means are misused." The goal which they *(the Jews)* seek is correct; but the way is wrong by which they endeavor to reach the goal. They want to go east and instead they are going west. The arrogant zeal of good intentions does the same today. The Apostle expresses himself very mildly when he says "not according to knowledge." He wishes this to be understood in the sense that they set about with blind zeal, unwise urgency, and foolish purpose. That is the greatest danger *(threatening us)*; and it should serve us as an example that we may speak of the faults of the neighbor with mildness.

This — *(to have zeal not according to knowledge)* — is a terrible thing, which properly and alone resists faith, opposes obedience to God's Word, and makes men stiff-necked and incorrigible, as we perceive this in heretics and schismatics. For they insist upon their "good intentions" with stiff-necked and obstinate opposition, just as though they could not be mistaken; they believe that their salvation is altogether based upon the fact that they have good intentions and zeal of God. Such persons the Bible describes most properly as perverse in heart and corrupt in mind. Therefore we must note that to have a zeal of God according to knowledge means to regard nothing else as greater than always to be ready with fear and trembling to be guided, led and instructed *(by God)* in all that is good, no matter how insignificant it may be.

Moses describeth the righteousness which is of the law, That the man which doeth these things shall live by them (10:5). The word "man" here has strong emphasis, for a man may do the works of the Law and live in them in such a way that he is not slain by the Law. But that does not suffice, for the righteousness of faith *(needed for salvation)* lies beyond man.

The righteousness which is of faith speaketh on this wise (10:6). *(He means to say)*: It teaches nothing else than the faith that Christ died and rose again. By this faith he may live who has not done the works of the Law according to the righteousness (*demanded*) of the Law. For here (*in the righteousness of faith*) no works are necessary, in order that we may live and be saved as this is demanded by the righteousness of the Law. Here faith suffices without works. Thus the Apostle compares the righteousness of the Law and the righteousness of faith and ascribes to the former works, but to the latter faithful trust without works.

Say not in thy heart, Who shall ascend into heaven? (10:6) These words Moses spoke, as we read in Deuteronomy 30:12, but not in this sense (*of Paul*). The Apostle, moved by the Spirit, out of his incomparably clear insight, reveals their real meaning, instructing us, as it were by an important proof, that the whole Bible everywhere speaks alone of Christ when we regard its real meaning, even when the words, outwardly considered as a picture and image, may sound differently. For this reason we also read: "Christ is the end of the law for righteousness" (10:4); that is, everything (*in Scripture*) points to Christ.

Who shall ascend into heaven? (10:6). That is, Christ is ascended into heaven and so you will be saved. Do not doubt that He ascended into heaven; for that is the Word (*Gospel*) which will save you. That in sum is the short way to salvation (*by faith*). The whole righteousness of man which leads him to salvation depends on faith in the Word and not upon knowledge of works. For this reason God, through the mouth of the prophets utters but this one rebuke, namely, that men do not care to hear His voice. To the prophets He entrusted not works, but words or messages to be heard. So he speaks in Isaiah 66:2: "To this man will I look, even to him that is poor and of a contrite spirit, and trembleth at my word." But this is what faith accomplishes, faith in the Word of God. Therefore we must listen to the Word with all zeal and fervor, with simplicity and closed eyes, with all wisdom and sincerity.

If thou. . .shalt believe in thine heart that God hath raised him from the dead, thou shalt be saved (10:9). That is true, for, as we read in 4:25: "Who (*Christ*) was delivered for our offences, and was raised again for our justification." Therefore the Apostle quotes the somewhat obscure statements of Moses — (*those in verses 6 and 7*) — to explain that in truth our righteousness comes not from the law and works, but from the death and resurrection of

Christ. Whoever believes these two facts will be saved as we read in the next verse.

With the heart man believeth unto righteousness (10:10). He means to say: We attain righteousness through no works, no wisdom (*of reason*) no effort, no wealth, no honor. Many want themselves to be regarded as righteous because they know much, read much, teach much, or because they attain to high honors or do great service in the Church. But all this belongs to civil righteousness, which (*for salvation*) is rejected by God. We obtain the true righteousness by believing sincerely the promises of God, as we read in 4:3: "Abraham believed God, and it was counted unto him for righteousness."

With the mouth confession is made unto salvation (10:10). Faith which leads to righteousness does not attain to the goal of righteousness, namely, salvation, unless it culminates in confession. Confession is the chief work of faith; for here man denies himself and confesses God. And he dies (*to himself*) in his confession of God by the denial of himself; for there can be no greater denial of oneself than this, that one dies to confess God. By doing this, he surrenders himself, in order that God may be confirmed and (*his*) confession of Him (*may be confirmed*).

The same Lord over all is rich unto all that call upon him (10:12). This is the new expression. The Apostle might have said, as we read in Joel 2:13: "He is gracious and merciful, slow to anger, and of great kindness, and repenteth him of the evil." But the Apostle means to emphasize the fact that God gives exceedingly abundantly above all that we ask or think, as we read in Ephesians 3:20, so that compared with His gifts, the prayers of those who call upon Him seem poor and modest. Those who call upon Him could never think of such great things (*as He gives*), much less pray for them. So we read in II Corinthians 9:8: "God is able to make all grace abound toward you." He therefore is rich when He gives; we are poor when we pray. He is mighty when He grants us our petitions; we are timid and weak when we ask. We do not pray for as much as He can and will give, for we do not pray according to His ability (*to give*), but far short of His ability, according to our weakness. But he can give only according to His might; therefore He always gives more than we ask for.

SAVING FAITH COMES THROUGH THE PREACHING OF THE DIVINE WORD

How then shall they call on him in whom they have not believed? and how shall they believe in him of whom they have not heard? and how shall they hear without a preacher? and how shall they preach, except they be sent? as it is written, How beautiful are the feet of them that preach the gospel of peace, and bring glad tidings of good things! But they have not all obeyed the gospel. For Esaias saith, Lord who hath believed our report? So then faith cometh by hearing, and hearing by the word of God. But I say, Have they not heard? Yes, verily, their sound went into all the earth, and their words unto the ends of the world. But I say, Did not Israel know? First Moses saith, I will provoke you to jealousy by them that are no people, and by a foolish nation I will anger you. But Esaias is very bold, and saith, I was found of them that sought me not; I was made manifest unto them that asked not after me. But to Israel he saith, All day long I have stretched forth my hands unto a disobedient and gainsaying people (10:14-21).

How shall they call on him in whom they have not believed (10: 14). Here the Apostle meets the arrogance of the proud Jews; indeed, the arrogance of all who teach falsely and are of a haughty mind. Oh, that the false prophets only would heed these words!

How shall they believe in him of whom they have not heard? and how shall they hear without a preacher? (10:14) Even though they say that they hear, they boast in vain, unless they hear true preachers; for to hear false prophets means as much as not to hear. They hear and they do not hear; they have ears, but do not hear, nor do they preach (*the Word of God*). This is a striking statement against all conceited and arrogant hearers and students (*of the Bible*).

How shall they preach, except they be sent? (10:15). This is directed against all conceited teachers and arrogant instructors. These four statements (10:14-15) follow one another in such a way that one leads to the other, but so that the last forms the foundation on which the others rest. Thus, 1. It is impossible that those preach who are not sent. 2. It is impossible that those hear who are without a preacher. 3. It is impossible that they believe who do not hear. 4. It is impossible that they call upon Him who do not believe. To these must be added a last one, namely: 5. It is impossible that they who do not call upon the name of the Lord shall be saved. So, then, the entire source and origin of salvation rests on this, that God sends out someone, (*a true minister of the Word*). If He does not send out any, then they who preach preach falsely, and their preaching is no preaching at all. In fact, it would be better for them not to preach. Then also they who hear, hear error, and it would be better for them not to hear. Then also they who believe, would believe false doctrine, and it would be better for them not to believe. Then also they who call upon Him would call falsely (*upon a false lord*), and it would be better for them not to call. For such preachers do not preach; such hearers do not hear; such believers do not believe; such callers do not call; they will be damned because they would be saved (*by falsehood*). So we read in Proverbs 1:28 ff.: "Then shall they call upon me, but I will not answer; they shall seek me early, but they shall not find me: for that they hated knowledge, and did not choose the fear of the Lord."

In chapter 1:2 the Apostle emphasizes very strongly that the Gospel did not come into the world through any single person. It was promised long before it appeared; it is therefore not a figment of modern times. It came through many prophets of God, and indeed not only through the Word that was preached, but also through that which is in Holy Scripture. Such proof the heretics must show for their doctrine or heresy; they must show where their doctrine was promised before (*in the Old Testament*) and by whom. Then also they must show by whom it was published (*in the New Testament*) and in what Scripture it is written, for they must present as witnesses also the written testimonies. Only they can preach with certainty who proclaim the Gospel without any error.

How beautiful are the feet of them that preach the gospel of peace (10:15). By this quotation the Apostle shows that only those can preach truly who are sent (*by God*). Those cannot preach the divine Word and be messengers of God whom He has not sent and to whom He has not entrusted His Word. With the same words the Apostle also points out the nature of (*spiritual*) peace and its gifts. These blessings are heard only in the divine Word and are apprehended by faith. They cannot be presented in visible form, as the Jews expected.

The word "beautiful" stands for purity, for they (*that preach the gospel of peace and bring glad tidings of good things*) do not proclaim the Gospel for their own advantage or on account of vain glory, as this happens here and there today. They preach solely from obedience to God and for the sake of the salvation of their hearers. But the Hebrew word means also what is lovely and pleasant. Therefore the meaning of the expression is: "For those who are under the Law, the message of the Gospel is lovely and desirable. The Law indeed reveals sin, makes the sinner guilty, and fills his conscience with fear; the Gospel, however proclaims to those who have been terrified the desired healing. The Law pronounces punishment, but the Gospel good things. The Law preaches wrath; the Gospel peace. The Law says, as we read in Galatians 3:10: "Cursed is every one that continueth not in all things which are written in the book of the law to do them." But the Gospel says: "Behold the Lamb of God, which taketh away the sin of the world!" The Law oppresses conscience through the revealed sins: the Gospel frees conscience and gives it peace through faith in Christ.

The expression "good things" refers to the granting of (*divine*) grace and its blessings; "peace," however, to the removal of what is evil. Therefore the Apostle mentions "peace" first and then "good things." For no one will receive this (*spiritual*) peace and these (*spiritual*) good things, unless he has first renounced the peace and good things of the world and by faith is patient under the evil and anxiety of this world and of conscience.

But what is the meaning of "feet"? According to some, the word indicates how ardently the coming of those that bring glad tidings of good things is awaited by all whose troubled consciences are in anguish because of sin. More rightly perhaps this term indicates the words (*of the messengers*) or the announcement of their message, as we read in Psalm 19:4: "Their words (are gone out) to the end of the world"; or in Psalm 147:15: "His word runneth very swiftly."

But they have not all obeyed the gospel (10:16). This verse goes back to what was said before to confirm the four propositions stated above in their proper order. First of all the statement: "Whosoever shall call upon the name of the Lord shall be saved" (v. 13; Joel 2:32). If, then, they did not all obey the Gospel, why do they boast so arrogantly that they call upon the name of the Lord according to the word of the prophet (*Joel*)? How could they call upon Him in whom they did not believe? But the fact that they did not all believe is proved by the words of Isaiah: "Lord who hath believed our report" (Isa. 53:1)?

Verse 16 confirms also the words "How shall they believe in him of whom they have not heard?" (v. 14). He says: "Faith cometh by hearing" (v. 17). This means that unless they hear, they cannot believe. The verse moreover, confirms the statement: "How shall they hear without a preacher" (v.14)? Hearing indeed comes only through the Word of Christ. Lastly, the verse confirms the statement: "How beautiful are the feet of them that preach the gospel of peace" (v.15). The Apostle here emphasizes the fact that he is speaking of a Word which no one can comprehend. It can be apprehended only by hearing it in true faith. At this Word the Jews were offended, for they sought signs and wonders.

I will provoke you to jealousy by them that are no people, and by a foolish nation I will anger you (10:19). That is to say: As you chose for yourselves another god, by which you provoked me, so I will choose (*for myself*) another people by which I will anger you and punish the evil which you have done against me.

These are words of divine grace, for their purpose is to glorify God's grace. He saves only sinners, makes wise only the foolish and the weak, enriches only the poor, and makes alive only the dead. And indeed not those who merely regard themselves as such, but who really are such and acknowledge this. The heathen indeed were not God's people, but a foolish nation, in order that they might acknowledge God's grace when they were saved without their merit and works. The proud, however, who trust in their merit and wisdom, become angry and murmur when there is given to others freely and without their merit that (*salvation*) after which they sought with so much zeal. By this they prove that they did not seek God for His sake, but for their own sakes, because they sinfully loved themselves and hypocritically desired their own advantage. Had they really sought God, they would have been glad that others were saved, and would not have been enraged (*at the conversion of the Gentiles*).

I was found of them that sought me not (10:20). Isaiah writes this against the Jews who boasted of their merits. The Jews certainly do not like to hear that they have been rejected. When

Christ told them that at the time of Elias there were many widows in Israel, but that the prophet was sent only to the pagan widow in Sarepta (*Luke* 4:26), they wanted to hurl Him over a precipice. For they perceived that they were rejected before the heathen and regarded as unworthy (*of salvation*). For them this was an unbearable thought; they were proud of the blood of the Fathers and boasted of the rightcousness of the Law. But here it tells them: I have made myself known to them, (*the Gentiles*), because of my grace and not because of the zeal or merits of any man. Here the word applies: "Whosoever shall exalt himself shall be abased" (Matt. 23:12). All this was written and done in order that the overbearing arrogance of men (*in spiritual matters*) might be suppressed and the grace of God might be magnified, for "he that glorieth, let him glory in the Lord" (I Cor. 1:31).

Romans Eleven

Content of the eleventh chapter: The Apostle rebukes the reviling of the Jews by the heathen, shows the present blinding of the Jews, and the depth of divine wisdom.

THE HEATHEN SHOULD NOT DESPISE THE JEWS, BUT REMEMBER THAT THEY ARE SAVED BY GRACE AS ARE THE ELECT IN ISRAEL

I say then, Hath God cast away his people? God forbid. For I also am an Israelite, of the seed of Abraham, of the tribe of Benjamin. God hath not cast away his people which he foreknew. Wot ye not what the scripture saith of Elias? how he maketh intercession to God against Israel, saying, Lord, they have killed thy prophets, and digged down thine altars; and I am left alone, and they seek my life. But what saith the answer of God unto him? I have reserved to myself seven thousand men, who have not bowed the knee to the image of Baal. Even so then at this present time also there is a remnant according to the election of grace. And if by grace, then it is no more of works: otherwise grace is no more grace. But if it be of works, then it is no more grace: otherwise work is no more work. What then? Israel hath not obtained that which he seeketh for; but the election hath obtained it, and the rest were blinded according as it is written, God hath given them the spirit of slumber, eyes that they should not see, and ears that they should not hear; unto this day. And David saith, Let their table be made a snare, and a trap, and a stumblingblock, and a recompence unto them: let their eyes be darkened, that they may not see, and bow down their back alway. I say then, Have they stumbled that they should fall? God forbid: but rather through their fall salvation is come unto the Gentiles, for to provoke them to jealousy. Now if the fall of them be the riches of the world, and the diminishing of them the riches of the Gentiles; how much more the fulness? For I speak to you Gentiles, inasmuch as I am the apostle of the Gentiles,

I magnify my office: If by any means I may provoke to emulation them which are my flesh, and might save some of them. For if the casting away of them be the reconciling of the world, what shall the receiving of them be, but life from the dead? For if the firstfruit be holy, the lump is also holy: and if the root be holy, so are the branches. And if some of the branches be broken off, and thou, being a wild olive tree, wert graffed in among them, and with them partakest of the root and fatness of the olive tree; boast not against the branches. But if thou boast, thou bearest not the root, but the root thee. Thou wilt say then, The branches were broken off, that I might be graffed in. Well; because of unbelief they were broken off, and thou standest by faith. Be not high-minded, but fear: for if God spared not the natural branches, take heed lest he also spare not thee. Behold therefore the goodness and severity of God: on them which fell, severity; but toward thee, goodness, if thou continue in his goodness: otherwise thou also shalt be cut off. And they also, if they abide not still in unbelief, shall be graffed in: for God is able to graff them in again. For if thou wert cut out of the olive tree which is wild by nature, and wert graffed contrary to nature into a good olive tree: how much more shall these, which be the natural branches, be graffed into their own olive tree? (11:1-24).

I say then, Hath God cast away his people? God forbid (11:1). The Apostle now reaches the end of his discussion and concludes what he began in Chapter 9, where he said: "Not as though the word of God hath taken none effect" (v.6). Or, already in Chapter 3, where he said: "Shall their unbelief make the faith of God without effect" (3:3)? He treats this subject with such great earnestness in order that he may destroy the arrogant boasting of the Jews regarding their merits by emphasizing the firm and immutable faithfulness of God. The Jews might have answered (*the Apostle*): God will not cast away His people, because He has given them His promise. But if what you say is true, then God has truly rejected His people. In this way they wanted to support their arrogance by an appeal to the faithfulness of God; and this they do to this very day.

I also am an Israelite (11:1). Here the Apostle concludes from the smaller to the greater; for had God cast away His people, then above all He would have cast away the Apostle Paul, who had opposed Him with all his might. But now, to prove that he does not reject His people, God accepted even one who was hopelessly lost. In this way the Apostle shows how firm God's (*gracious pur-*

pose of) predestination and election stands, for not even the most desperate circumstances could hinder it (*God's plan of salvation*). So, very rightly, the Apostle adds: "God hath not cast away his people which he foreknew" (v.2). He means to say: This He has proved in my own case, for He has not cast away me; much less has He cast away the others who did not depart from Him (*as did I*).

I am left alone, and they seek my life (11:3). The Apostle argues against them (*the Jews*) with a most effective illustration. He means to say: If you believe that either God is a liar or that none of you is cast away, what are you going to say regarding the case where something similar actually took place? If then it was foolish to think that God will not cast away His people, it is foolish at this time, when experience teaches the same thing. The Jews arrogantly assumed that they were God's people, simply because the heathen were not His people.

I have reserved to myself seven thousand men (11:4). By these words "I have reserved" God's grace and election are wonderfully magnified; for it was He who reserved them unto Himself, so that it was "not of him that willeth, nor of him that runneth, but of God that sheweth mercy" (9:16).

Who have not bowed the knee to the image of Baal (11:4). Baal was an idol. I do not know with what religious ceremonies he was venerated. I know only what the Book of Kings (I Kings 18:26, 27) says about that. They, (*the Israelites*), worshipped the true God under idolatrous ceremonies and names. But just that God had forbidden. They were not to make to themselves any graven image, or any likeness of anything (*Ex.* 20:4). But they were misled by their foolish zeal and argued thus: "It is indeed wrong to make a graven image, if that is the image of an idol. But if we make a graven image (*in honor*) of the true God and worship Him by it, we do well." For this reason in their foolish zeal they killed the true prophets who declared graven images as wrong, for they regarded these prophets as wicked men. All this they did with good intentions and to show their zeal on behalf of God.

Baal is an ominous example of the idolatrous righteousness and piety which in wide areas prevails to this day. Thus the Jews and heretics venerate God according to their own mind, and in their stupid zeal and their eccentric piety they are worse than the ungodly. For God's sake they become enemies of God, and for the fear of God they become scorners of God. Because of piety they become impious; for the sake of peace they disturb the peace; because of their love and holiness they become envious and unholy; in the interest of humility they become proud. Such is the fictitious piety of a stubborn mind and the hypocritical understanding of confirmed obstinacy. So great is (man's) arrogance and his absolutely vain delusion.

Even so then at this present time also there is a remnant according to the election of grace (11:5). These words means to say: As at that time there was a remnant according to God's election of grace, so there is also at this time a remnant according to the election of grace. The Apostle here explains the expression "I have reserved to myself" by the words "according to the election of grace"; for the words "I have reserved" include election and explain and magnify (*divine*) grace.

The election hath obtained it, and the rest were blinded (11:7). The word "election" here must be taken in the sense of "the elect," just as we read in Genesis 12:2: "Thou shalt be a blessing" (*the abstract used for the concrete*).

God Hath given them the spirit of slumber (11:8). The word "spirit" here must not be taken for a created or infused spirit, but for the (*hardened*) mind and will of man, (*as is shown by the word*): "Eyes that they should not see, and ears that they should not hear; unto this day."

Let their table be made a snare, and a trap, and a stumblingblock and a recompence unto them (11:9). The "snare" is scripture itself, namely, inasmuch as it is understood and handed down (*taught*) in a deceitful manner, so that under the show of pious instruction the souls of the deceived and simple are craftily ensnared. Thus St. Augustine in his *Confessions* calls the Manichean Faustus the "great snare of the devil." From one and the same table, or from one and the same Holy Scripture, one draws for himself death and the other life, the one honey and the other poison. Hence nothing else must be treated with so much reverence and so altogether without arrogance as the Word of God. It at once ensnares the proud and traps and offends them, though in a way that they do not perceive: indeed, under a fascinatingly beautiful disguise. This is not the Word's fault, but that of (human) pride, which arrogantly raises its head against it.

The "stumblingblock" consists in this, that they who are ensnared (by false teaching) constantly take offense. For if they are ensnared it is through that which they understand wrongly. To that they cleave and with it they are pleased. So, without realizing it, they permit themselves to be ensnared willingly. But they take offense at what is pointed out to them as the truth from which they turn away. If they cannot avoid it (the truth), they distort it and deny that Scripture must so be understood. At last their eyes are darkened (11:10), so that, while others see, they themselves do not permit themselves to be enlightened; and while all others are raised up they remain perverted in their mind.

Let their eyes be darkened, that they may not see (11:10). When reading such passages as: "Make the heart of this people fat, and make their ears heavy" (Isa. 6:10); or: "Let their table become a snare before them" (Ps. 69:22), we must first think of the opposite, namely: Enlighten the hearts of the believing and humble. God has so ordained it that He does good to those who are humble, namely, His elect. But this cannot take place, unless the proud who do not see this illumination, by this very fact become all the more darkened and all the more offended. So also we say in everyday life, when a person does good to another of which he knows that it displeases a third: "Oh, how I have provoked and offended him!" This our Lord demonstrated and illustrated in Luke 15:25-30 by the example of the proud elder son, (the prodigal's brother). So also the proud are enraged when someone gives to another that which he has promised, as this is illustrated in the Gospel of the laborers in the vineyard, Matthew 20:11-16, by those who murmured against the householder.

And bow down their back alway (11:10). Applied in a metaphorical sense, this means that they who bow down their back, can no longer look up to God. So they no longer observe the righteousness which looks down from heaven, but they regard only their own (*righteousness*), after which they seek and in which they trust.

Have they stumbled that they should fall? God forbid: but rather through their fall salvation is come unto the Gentiles, for to provoke them to jealousy (11:11). (*The next verse adds the thought*): "Now if the fall of them be the riches of the world, and the diminishing of them the riches of the Gentiles; how much more their fulness" (v. 12)? That means: If faith has come to the heathen, because the Jews fell, how much more would it have come to them (*the heathen*), had they stood firm. Hence they, (*the Jews*), did not fall merely "to fall," but rather that they should rise again, encouraged by the example of the Gentiles. He, (*God*), would not win them merely by instructing them. Therefore He sought to win them by inciting them (*to jealousy*) as a loving father commonly does with his son.

If salvation has come to the heathen by their (*the Jews'*) fall, in order that their fall might not be fruitless and their evil not without good, as all things must work together for good to them that love God (Rom. 8:28), how much more must evil work for the good of Christ and God. Indeed, evil must work for good in an abundantly rich measure, if it is God who (*by permission*) works it. In that case it must work for good not only to others, but also to those whose the evil is. In this sense their fall serves the salvation of the heathen: it is not its final object, but that they fell was to induce them to emulate the blessings of those who were raised up (*by faith in Christ*).

Inasmuch as I am the apostle of the Gentiles, I magnify mine office: if by any means I may provoke to emulation them which are of my flesh, and might save some of them (11:13, 14). The Apostle preached to the Jews and was rejected (Acts 13:46). Therefore he magnifies his office among the Gentiles, in order that they, (*the Jews*), might be provoked to emulation. For what we despise when offered to us, we commonly esteem when others take it, as we are influenced by their opinion.

But how does the Apostle magnify his office? By boasting that he, after the fall of the Jews, is preaching the riches (*of Christ*) to the Gentiles. If through his office they, (*the Gentiles*), receive such glorious gifts, which are taken from the Jews, then he truly and solemnly proves the glory of his Gospel ministry. By this the Jews should be moved zealously to seek the riches of this his ministry.

If the casting away of them be the reconciling of the world (11:15). This is not to be understood causally, but it follows as a consequence; for upon the unbelief of these (*the Jews*) followed the reconciliation of the world. But this would have followed no less, had they stood firm, as we clearly learn from Acts 10: 44-48. There we see that the grace of the Holy Spirit was poured out upon the heathen at which the Apostles, who as yet were not sure of the rejection of the Jews, were greatly astonished.

If the firstfruit be holy, the lump is also holy; and if the root be holy, so are the branches (11:16). By means of a twofold analogy the Apostle here supplies proof to magnify God's grace and destroy the arrogant (*Jewish*) boasting of righteousness. In nature this is true: if the firstfruits are good, then also the whole harvest will be good; and if the root is good, then also the tree is good which grows from it. So also here. Were it not for the fact that divine grace is to be glorified, the whole people would share in the same dignity.

Be not highminded, but fear (11:20). The meaning here is the same as in v. 25: "Wise in your own conceits." That is: Be not self-complacent in your thinking, or do not think haughtily about yourselves.

Behold therefore the goodness and severity of God (11:22). From this passage we learn that when we see the fall of the Jews, heretics, and others, we should not so much regard them that fall, as rather the work of God which He does regarding them, so that we may learn from the example of misfortune befalling others to fear God and not boast arrogantly in any way. In contradistinction to this (*lesson*) many exalt themselves in an amazingly stupid manner and call the Jews either dogs or accursed, or they insult them with other abusive words, though they themselves do not know what kind of people they are and what is their standing in God's sight. They want to convert the Jews by force or invective. May God resist them.

If thou wert cut out of the olive tree which is wild by nature, and wert graffed contrary to nature into a good olive tree; how much more shall these, which be the natural branches, be graffed into their own olive tree? (11:24) That the seed of the olive tree does not produce a good olive tree, illustrates that the children born of flesh are not children of God, and that the Jews did not possess the glory — (*the glorious promise and adoption*) of the Fathers simply because they were the seed of the Fathers. The contrary rather is true; (*as flesh born of flesh, they were not heirs of the promise*). As the wild olive tree becomes a good branch, not by nature, but by the art of grafting, so also the heathen become God's people, not by their natural righteousness, or virtue, but by the (*divine*) grace implanted into them.

THE ELECT IN ISRAEL SHALL SURELY BE SAVED

For I would not, brethren, that ye should be ignorant of this mystery, lest ye should be wise in your own conceits; that blindness in part is happened to Israel, until the fulness of the Gentiles be come in. And so all Israel shall be saved: as it is written, There shall come out of Sion the Deliverer, and shall turn away ungodliness from Jacob: for this is my covenant unto them, when I shall take away their sins. As concerning the gospel, they are enemies for your sakes: but as touching the election, they are beloved for the fathers' sakes. For the gifts and calling of God are without repentance. For as ye in times past have not believed God, yet have now obtained mercy through their unbelief: even so have these also now not believed, that through your mercy they also may obtain mercy. For God hath concluded them all in unbelief, that he might have mercy upon all. O the depth of the riches both of the wisdom and knowledge of God! how unsearchable are his judgments, and his ways past finding out! For who hath known the mind of the Lord? or who hath been his counsellor? Or who hath first given to him, and it shall be recompensed unto him again? For of him, and through him, and to him, are all things: to whom be glory for ever. Amen. (11:25-36).

I would not, brethren, that ye should be ignorant of this mystery, lest ye should be wise in your own conceits (11:25). From this passage it is generally concluded that the Jews at the end of the world will be converted to faith (*in Christ*). However, it is true that this passage is so obscure that hardly anyone will be persuaded with absolute clarity, unless he follows the verdict of the Fathers (*Augustine, Chrysostom, Theodoret*) who interpret the Apostle in this sense. The meaning, then, is: The Jews who are now fallen, will be converted and saved, after the heathen according to the fulness of the elect are come in. They will not remain outside forever, but in their own time they will be converted.

So all Israel shall be saved. . .for this is my covenant unto them, when I shall take away their sins (11:26, 27). The Old Testament (*Law*) could not take away sin; it only increased it. The power of man could not take it away. Therefore the New Testament alone, that is, the (*divine*) grace through faith in Christ takes away sin.

The purpose of the whole passage is to incite the people (*the Jews*) to repentance. To understand the Apostle rightly, we must bear in mind that his statement extends to the whole lump of the Jewish people. Even if some among them are cast away, nevertheless, the lump must be honored because of the elect. So we must respect any community because of the good in it, even when they are in the minority over against the wicked. In this sense the Jewish people is a "holy lump," namely, because of the elect, but the Jews are "cut off branches" as regards the castaways. Thus the Jews are both "fulness" and "emptiness." He calls them "lump" to show that he is speaking not of individual persons, but of the whole people, in which there may not be many that are holy. (*Luther at first wavered with regard to the conversion of "all Israel." In Romans he at times speaks as though he believed in the final conversion of all Jews, though he also emphasizes the fact that only the elect will be saved. Later he definitely accepted the opinion of Origen, Theophylact, Jerome, and others, who identified "all Israel" with the number of the elect, to which corresponds the expression "the fulness of the Gentiles." The leading Lutheran exegetes have followed this interpretation and taught that while the elect from among the Gentiles are being brought in through the preaching of the Gospel before Judgment Day, so also are the elect from among the Jews.*)

As concerning the gospel, they are enemies for your sakes (11:28). The word "enemies" must here be taken in a passive sense; that is, they deserve to be hated. God hates them, and so they are hated by the Apostles and all who are of God. This is shown by the opposite term "beloved." They are hated and at the same time beloved. They are hated "concerning the gospel . . . for your sakes." That is to say; As you are loved for receiving the Gospel, so they are hated for rejecting the Gospel. Nevertheless, the lump (*the number of the elect*) is beloved "for the fathers' sakes, as touching the election." This means that some of them because of their election until this very hour are being accepted (*saved*). They are beloved for the Fathers' sakes, because they too are friends (*of Christ, as were their Fathers*).

The gifts and calling of God are without repentance (11:29). This is an excellent statement. God's counsel (*of election and salvation*) is altered by no man's merit or demerit. God never regrets his gift and calling, which He has promised, because the elect are unworthy, and you (*the proud, self-righteous Jews*) are worthy in your own eyes. He does not change His mind. Hence they (*the elect*) will surely be converted and come to the truth of faith — (*salvation without works*).

O the depth of the riches both of the wisdom and knowledge of God! (11:33) This exclamation of the Apostle is to remind us of the fact that in the conclusions stated above there is still something which is hidden and too deep for us to understand. The Apostle had said: "Until the fulness of the Gentiles be come in" (v. 25); or: "That. . .they also may obtain mercy" (v. 31); and: "That he might have mercy upon all" (v. 32). All these sentences say that God permits evil to take place, in order that good may come from it. But it is incomprehensible to us why He does good in this special way, and why He does not at the same time do good and evil to those who are alike. These sentences indeed are strange: "They fell, in order that they might be saved"; or: "They do not believe, in order that they might believe."

How unsearchable are his judgments, and his ways past finding out! (11:33). Those are foolish who, as Aristotle, seek to know the things themselves through the causes, since these are "unsearchable."

According to St. Augustine this is the correct distinction between wisdom and knowledge: To wisdom pertains the contemplation of eternal things; to knowledge, the study of temporal things. Created wisdom thus deals with the things which we can neither see nor understand except through faith alone or through being translated into heaven. But knowledge deals with what is outside God and created. Therefore it is God's wisdom which views all things in themselves before their existence, above their existence, and in their existence. It is His knowledge by which He recognizes the things as they happen. Therefore it is called the intuitive knowledge (*scientia visionis, by which God knows all things outside Himself*).

Romans Twelve

Content of the twelfth chapter: The Apostle instructs the Christians at Rome in what pertains to God and the neighbor (*their duty toward God and the neighbor*).

CHRISTIAN BELIEVERS SHOULD CONSECRATE THEMSELVES TO GOD AS A LIVING SACRIFICE

I beseech you therefore, brethren, by the mercies of God, that ye present your bodies a living sacrifice, holy acceptable unto God, which is your reasonable service. And be not conformed to this world: but be ye transformed by the renewing of your mind, that ye may prove what is that good, and acceptable, and perfect will of God (12: 1, 2).

I beseech you therefore, brethren, by the mercies of God (12:1). After the Apostle, in the preceding chapters, has laid the foundation, namely, the true foundation, which is Christ (I Cor. 3:11), or the firm rock upon which the wise man builds (Matt. 7:24); again, after he has destroyed the false foundation, namely, man's own righteousness and merits, which are the sand upon which the foolish man builds (Matt. 7:26), he now builds upon this foundation (*Christ*) gold, silver, and precious stones (I Cor. 3:12).

Above all, the good works, which are the building, (*the superstructure raised from the foundation of Christ*), must have a sure and dependable foundation, so that the heart (*of the believer*) may resolve immovably to stand and build upon this foundation to eternity, so that the foundation remains laid.

In contradistinction to this (*building good works upon Christ*), the work-righteous come with their good works. They seek to rest their trust on their conscience and believe that they have done enough and are safe, if in their own judgment they have done much — (*many good works*).

For this reason — (*to keep his readers from the false doctrine of work-righteousness*) — the Apostle makes provision that this may not take place. They (*the work-righteous*) strive after good works and regard them as the foundation of their righteousness, the refuge of their conscience, and the solace of their soul, although Christ alone exists (*as the foundation*) before all good works. Has there ever been so foolish a builder who first tried to lay a foundation (*when one already existed*)? Does he not use the foundation which already is laid in the ground? Without our efforts, Christ offers Himself to us as our righteousness, our peace, and our rest for conscience, in order that we may always build upon this (*foundation*) our good works.

So far (*Chs.* 1-11), the Apostle taught how a sinner becomes a new man. He has described the new birth which gives us the new being (*life*), as we are taught in John 3:3. Now he teaches the (*good*) works of the new birth which such a person presumes in vain who has not yet become a new man. For the (*new*) being (*life*) precedes (*good*) works; but before the (*new*) being first comes the "undergoing" (*conversion*). So there follow one upon another: the becoming, the being and the working (*of good deeds*). (*Luther calls the act of conversion an "enduring," or a "suffering" to stress the thought that conversion does not occur, either in whole or in part, through man's free will or cooperation, but alone by faith in Christ which the Holy Ghost works in the heart by means of the Word and the Sacraments. Luther thus uses the Latin word* pati *or the German* erleiden, *that is, suffering. It is understood, of course, that with this "suffering" there is connected no pain; for conversion consists essentially in this, that God, out of pure grace, implants in us faith in Christ.*)

As the Apostle teaches Christian ethics, his greatest concern, to the end of the letter, is to root out (*man's*) own wisdom and self-will. For this reason he begins with this most pernicious pestilence, because it destroys the spiritual birth under the attractive disguise of blessings, annihilating it by its good works. So he says: "I beseech you by the mercies of God," which you have received. Take care that you have not received divine grace in vain, but rather present your bodies a living sacrifice. In the same way he writes in II Corinthians 6:1: "We then, as workers together with him, beseech you also that ye receive not the grace of God in vain." What he means by "present your bodies a living sacrifice," he shows in II Corinthians 6:4 ff., where he says: "In much patience, in afflictions, in necessities, in distresses," etc.

Present your bodies a living sacrifice, holy, acceptable unto God (12:1). The true sacrifice which belongs to God is not outside us nor outside that which belongs to us; neither is it temporal and confined to the hour, but we ourselves are this (*sacrifice*), as we read in Proverbs 23:26: "My son, give me thine heart." It is "living" in contrast to the sacrifices of animals, which were presented dead. But the term may be understood better of the spiritual life which it should bring forth, namely, of that which is good. It is "holy," that is, separated, detached, kept away from what is unclean, as something that is taken from some other use and set apart only for a use worthy of God, and so dedicated, as we read in Joshua 3:5: "Sanctify yourselves: for tomorrow the Lord will do wonders among you." Above all, it signifies the purity which we owe to God. It is "acceptable unto God." This the Apostle writes against man's vain boasting and pride, which commonly turns good into evil. It is greater to be acceptable to God than to be holy; for to displease oneself and not to regard the displeasure of others is exceedingly difficult for those who possess something because of which they are pleased with themselves, as for example, holiness.

Which is your reasonable service (12:1). That is: I say this because you owe (*God*) a reasonable sacrifice and not animal sacrifices, for this is proper according to the new Law (*of love*). The word "service" stands for the sacrifice itself, or the presentation of such a living sacrifice. He says in short: Present your reasonable service, namely, your bodies as a living sacrifice.

Be ye transformed by the renewing of your mind (12:2). In this way the Apostle describes (*Christian*) progress; for he addresses those who already are Christians. The Christian life does not mean to stand still, but to move from that which is good to that which is better. St Bernard (*of Clairvaux*) rightly says: "As soon as you do not desire to become better, then you have ceased to be good." It does not help a tree to have green leaves and flowers if it does not bear fruit besides its flowers. For this reason — (*for not bearing fruit*) — many (*nominal Christians*) perish in their flowering. Man (*the Christian*) is always in the condition of nakedness, always in the state of becoming, always in the state of potentiality, always in the condition of activity. He is always in sin and always in justification. He is always a sinner, but also always repentant and so always righteous. We are in part sinners, and in part righteous, and so nothing else than penitents. No one is so good as that he could not become better; no one is so evil, as that he could not become worse.

This (*fact*) the Apostle expresses very nicely by saying: "Be ye transformed by the renewing of your mind." He adds "By the renewing of your mind" to stress that renewal of the mind, which takes place from day to day and progresses farther and farther, according to the words, II Corinthians 4:16: "The inward man is renewed day by day"; or Colossians 3:10: "Be ye renewed in the spirit of your mind"; or "Put on the new man, which is renewed in knowledge after the image of him that created him."

That ye may prove what is that good, and acceptable, and perfect will of God (12:2). The "good" will of God is that we should do good. The "acceptable" will is that we should be chaste and keep ourselves pure. The "perfect" will of God is that we should desire to please God alone. However, when the Apostle says that the proving of this threefold divine will comes from the transformation or renewing of the mind, he may think of something that goes much deeper than what the words can express, something which we can learn only from experience. Only faith transforms the mind and leads us to where we may prove the will of God. The Apostle speaks of this in Ephesians 3:17: ff.: "That ye. . .may be able to comprehend with all saints what is the breadth, and length, and depth, and height; and to know the love of Christ, which passeth knowledge, that ye might be filled with all the fulness of God."

These words are overflowingly rich in consolation; for just then when afflictions come over us, we should be of good courage, because that is the good will of God. Therefore we should be greatly pleased when things happen to us which displease us. The "good" will of God creates good out of evil. The "acceptable" will of God moves us cheerfully to love such good. It makes this good acceptable to us, and causes us to agree with it, even if it is evil. The "perfect" will of God will eternally perfect and bring to a (blessed) end all who are glad (in Him).

IN CHRIST CHRISTIAN BELIEVERS SHOULD LOVE THEIR NEIGHBOR

For I say, through the grace given unto me, to every man that is among you, not to think of himself more highly than he ought to think; but to think soberly, according as God hath dealt to every man the measure of faith. For as we have many members in one body, and all members have not the same office: so we, being many, are one body in Christ, and every one members one of another. Having then gifts differing according to the grace that is given to us, whether prophecy, let us prophesy according to the proportion of faith; or ministry, let us wait on our ministering; or he that teacheth, on teaching; or he that exhorteth, on exhortation: he that giveth, let him do it with simplicity; he that ruleth, with diligence; he that showeth mercy, with cheerfulness. Let love be without dissimulation. Abhor that which is evil; cleave to that which is good. Be kindly affectioned one to another with brotherly love; in honor preferring one another; not slothful in business; fervent in spirit; serving the Lord; rejoicing in hope; patient in tribulation; continuing instant in prayer; distributing to the necessity of saints; given to hospitality. Bless them which persecute you: bless and curse not. Rejoice with them that do rejoice, and weep with them that weep. Be of the same mind one toward another. Mind not high things, but condescend to men of low estate. Be not wise in your own conceits. Recompense to no man evil for evil. Provide things honest in the sight of all men. If it be possible, as much as lieth in you, live peaceably with all men. Dearly beloved, avenge not yourselves, but rather give place unto wrath: for it is written, Vengeance is mine; I will repay, saith the Lord. Therefore if thine enemy hunger, feed him; if he thirst, give him drink; for in so doing thou shalt heap coals of fire on his head. Be not overcome of evil, but overcome evil with good (12:3-21).

Think soberly, according as God hath dealt to every man the measure of faith (12:3). All this he writes in the interest of unity; for nothing is likely to cause so much division as when people do not stay within the proper bounds of their calling, but neglect their own ministry and break in upon others. God does not give to every person all gifts, as we learn from I Corinthians 12:4-11, where the Apostle unfolds the meaning of our text to its widest extent. Since it is God who distributes all gifts, but does not bestow all of them upon a single person, no one should exalt himself as though he had all and others none; for by this (*arrogance*) the unity of the Church is destroyed. The Greeks have an (*excellent*) saying: "Let every one practice the art which he has learned."

The expression "measure of faith" could be understood in the sense of the extent of faith according to which it is given, exclusive of other gifts. But since the Apostle emphasizes the fact that various gifts are imparted according to the measure of faith, we must take it to mean the measure of the gifts of faith, for with faith many (*spiritual*) gifts are granted. Hence believers who have one and the same faith, nevertheless possess a different measure of gifts. Certainly there is one faith, one baptism, one Church, one Lord, one Spirit, one God, as we are told in Ephesians 4:4-6. Nevertheless, in this one faith, this one Church, this one area of (*Christ's*) dominion there are differing gifts.

Let us prophesy according to the proportion of faith (12:6). The Greek expression means "in agreement with, or according to faith." That is Christians should not go beyond faith and its principles. Faith corresponds to prophecy (*as it trusts in it*). From here on the Apostle unfolds the commandment of love toward the neighbor. It is surprising how little people concern themselves with such important and self-evident instruction, coming from so important an Apostle, indeed, coming from the Holy Spirit Himself. Instead, we choose vanities, such as erection of church edifices, the enlargement of parishes, the accumulation of funds, and so forth. All this we regard as the greatest piety and are not a whit concerned about what the Apostle here commands. Nor will I mention pride, boasting, avarice, luxury, vainglory, and other things connected with these (*vices*).

Or ministry, let us wait on our ministering (12:7). By ministers (*here*) are meant all who serve in ecclesiastical offices such as pastors, deacons, and all who are about holy things; also, besides those dealing with God's Word are such as aid the ministers of the Word, as the Apostle often speaks of his helpers. Against this (*command*) there offend first of all those ambitious persons who, because they despise their own office, desire to teach, though they lack not only the (*necessary*) indoctrination, a thing that might yet be borne, but also the gift of teaching. For it is not sufficient for men to be learned and intelligent, but they must also have God's gracious gift (*of teaching*) to make them truly called by God for teaching. In Matthew 9:38 the Lord says: "Pray ye therefore the Lord of the harvest, that he will send forth labourers into his harvest." Therefore they should be satisfied with their (*lesser*) office who do not know how to preach, or who are not called, even if they (*the latter*) should have the ability (*to teach*).

It is strange how much (*harm*) the good intention does which makes persons believe that by preaching they produce ever so much more fruit, even if they are without the necessary special training, without the (*necessary*) call, and without the gracious gift (*of teaching*). When God calls (*persons to preach*), He calls either those who have this gift, or with the call He grants the gift. Without such (*divine*) grace men either beat the air (I Cor. 9:26), or the fruit of which they boast exists only in their foolish imagination. I will not mention the stupid and altogether incompetent persons who here and there are put into the pulpit by bishops and abbots. We really cannot regard them as called and sent, even if we wanted to, because here incompetent and unworthy (*persons*) are called under God's wrath, which on account of our sins removes from us His Word and permits the increase of babbling, doting talkers.

He that teacheth, on teaching (12:7). Many have the gift of teaching though they do not possess great learning. Others have both, and these are the best teachers as, for example, Augustine, Ambrose, Jerome. Whoever does not use such gifts, but concerns himself with other matters, sins against that which the Apostle, indeed, which God commands. The Apostle here speaks above all of those who are (*divinely*) called. In the same way he, in all his letters, always emphasizes his call, because without the divine call neither the office nor the preaching can prosper. Thus it happens through the working of Satan that as some (*who are not called*) presume to preach, conversely teachers flee from teaching so that the Word of God is hindered in both ways. In I Corinthians

12:28, as here, the Apostle puts the office of a teacher in the third place.

He that exhorteth, on exhortation (12:8). Exhortation and teaching differ from each other in this respect that teaching is meant for the ignorant and exhortation for those who know. The teacher lays the foundation, while the exhorter builds upon the foundation. In I Corinthians 3:6 the Apostle thus writes: "I have planted, Apollos watered"; and in I Corinthians 3:10: "As a wise masterbuilder, I have laid the foundation, and another buildeth thereon." All preachers today must attend to exhortation, for they nurture the faith that already is implanted, unless they work where the Word has not yet been preached. Therefore those who possess this gift (*of exhorting*) and are called into this office should not occupy themselves with other tasks. Today indeed we find it to be true what already Horace, the heathen (*poet*), said: "The lazy ox wants to bear the saddle, while the horse wants to plow." No one is satisfied with his calling, but praises those who walk (*toil*) in other ways. Terrence (*the Roman dramatist*) says: "We are so constituted that we are not satisfied with what is ours (*our work*)." Those who are qualified (*for a certain work*) detest it; those who are unfit, long for it.

He that giveth, let him do it with simplicity (12:8). As they who possess the gifts of teaching and exhorting are tempted by Satan, so that the divine blessing may not be preserved in purity and integrity, so also they that give will not be spared by the Devil. There are two ways in which the commandment of giving is transgressed. First, when we give in order that others (*to whom we give*) may return it with interest. This evil (*custom*) is now spread amazingly in wide areas. We therefore are told in Luke 14:12-14: "When thou makest a dinner or a supper, call not thy friends, nor thy brethren, neither thy kinsmen, nor thy rich neighbours; lest they also bid thee again, and a recompense be made unto thee. But when thou makest a feast, call the poor, the maimed, the lame, the blind: and thou shalt be blessed; for they cannot recompense thee: for thou shalt be recompensed at the resurrection of the just." (*Luther has in mind the unconditional giving that does not expect to be repaid.*)

Secondly, the commandment of giving is transgressed when those who are superior give to those who are under them, or when such give to one another as are equal in rank. This affords still greater pleasure, for then the giver may provide glory in and boast of his giving.

(*Here, however,*) the Apostle speaks rather of such giving as properly refers to those who teach the Word and are (*Christian*) leaders. Of this we read in Galatians 6:6: "Let him that is taught in the word communicate unto him that teacheth in all good things." Such giving should be done in simplicity and not from ulterior motives. God commands this in Deuteronomy 12:19: "Take heed to thyself that thou forsake not the Levite as long as thou livest upon the earth." In Matthew 10:10 the Lord says: "The workman is worthy of his meat." (Cf. also Luke 10:7; I Tim. 5:18.)

He that ruleth, with diligence (12:8). This is what happens to-day: If any one rules, either in state or in church offices, he does this with luxury and laziness, riches and pleasure, glory and honor, force and tyranny. Of such Ezekiel writes: "Woe be to the shepherds of Israel that do feed themselves! should not the shepherds feed the flocks? Ye eat the fat, and ye clothe you with the wool, ye kill them that are fed; but ye feed not the flock. The diseased have ye not strengthened, neither have ye healed that which was sick, neither have ye bound up that which was broken, neither have ye brought again that which was driven away, neither have ye sought that which was lost; but with force and with cruelty have ye ruled them" (Ezek. 34: 2-4). A good norm by which to rule is diligence as the Apostle here writes. Only he can be diligent with respect to others who is unconcerned about himself.

He that showeth mercy, with cheerfulness (12:8). In II Corinthians 9:7 we read: "Let him give: not grudgingly, or of necessity: for God loveth a cheerful giver." Persons do not show mercy with cheerfulness when they feel themselves obliged to help the needy because they are ashamed (*not to give*), or because they fear some other circumstance. Thus today many give alms, yet without any credit (*to themselves*), because they give reluctantly and sullenly. The same is true of such as give, in order that they may not be regarded as misers or rude and merciless persons.

Let love be without dissimulation (12:9). This is a very necessary and significant addition; for as nothing should be so altogether free from hypocrisy as love, so nothing is actually more defiled by it than is love. Everything (*that men may say or do*) is covered with the rouge (*of hypocrisy*) and is veiled under the deceitful appearance of friendship. There is a twofold hypocritical love. One shows itself and glitters outwardly, while there is hatred in the heart. The other does not hide the fact that it is evil (*hypocritical*), nor does it show that really it is hatred. Between these (*two kinds*) there is the hypocrisy of those who speak and do neither what is good nor what is evil.

Abhor that which is evil; cleave to that which is good (12:9). This command seems easy (*to perform*) but it is most difficult because of the emotions of hate, love, fear and hope. There is no one who can (*truly*) say that he abhors what is evil and cleaves to what is good. Still the Apostle gives this command, and certainly with good reason; for man is inclined to what is evil and averse to what is good. His hypocrisy is increased by ignorance of what is good and evil. Everyone calls that good which pleases him, and that evil which displeases him. The Apostle therefore has in mind what is good and evil from the viewpoint of the new man.

Be kindly affectioned one to another with brotherly love (12:10). The Apostle means to say (*when Christians deal with one another*), their love must be of a special degree and more complete than when they deal with strangers and enemies. So the Apostle writes in Galatians 6:10: "Let us do good unto all men, especially unto them who are of the household of faith." The Apostle here uses very strong expressions, for he means to say: Love one another most cordially and with ardent love that becomes brethren.

In honour preferring one another (12:10). In Philippians 2:3 the Apostle writes: "In lowliness of mind let each esteem others better than themselves"; and in Luke 14:10 our Lord says: "When thou art bidden, go and sit down in the lowest room." The Apostle here speaks of the inward preferring in honor which consists in a high esteem and appreciation of the neighbor; for the outward preference in honor often is hypocritical and wants to be repaid with greater honor if it is shown. Oh, it is a great obligation to prefer one another in love! It is much easier to give (*to another*) or to serve (*others*) with the body than to despise oneself and to esteem all others more highly (*than oneself*).

Not slothful in business (12:11). See how love keeps nothing for itself, but seeks alone that which profits the neighbor. In the preceding verses the Apostle taught us to give our possessions and goods to others by giving them our gifts, our mercy and our love. Then he taught us to give to others the honor and esteem that we have for ourselves. Now he teaches us to sacrifice ourselves, for also that belongs to our willing, God-pleasing assistance of others, that we give them our own body — (*our bodily service*) — and so help those in need.

Fervent in spirit (12:11). Against this command all those offend who do their duty indolently, sleep and yawn. In all they do, they only ruin everything. Of such we read in Proverbs 18:9: "He also that is slothful in his work is brother to him that is a great waster." Such persons are hated not only by men, but also by God. For this reason the Apostle directs himself against this capital sin, that is, against "sloth," or against our aversion to do good work. This evil is so widely spread that hardly anyone regards it as proper to exert himself to the utmost. Who does not hate such (*slothful*) persons, and indeed rightly so!

Serving the Lord (12:11). This command is directed not only against those who serve their own avarice, the world, or their belly (*their lusts*), but also, and that much more emphatically, against those who stubbornly adhere to their own good works, instead of doing other (*commanded*) tasks in obedience (*to God*). Therefore they serve themselves rather than God. They refuse to do God's will and persist in such (*works*) as they have chosen for themselves. What fools! They refuse obedience to God in order to obey God (*according to their own sinful way*). They do not know what it means to serve the Lord, for that means to go wherever the Lord calls us, not to resist Him, and not to insist stubbornly upon anything (*against His will*).

Rejoicing in hope (12:12). That is, do not rejoice in that which is present and which you have experienced and learned to know. There is a rejoicing in what we see, but that is a vain and transient joy. So also there is a rejoicing in what we do not see, but possess only by faith. That is a true, eternal and abiding joy. But there is no rejoicing in what is invisible, unless first we have hope. In Matthew 5:4 we read: "Blessed are they that mourn; for they shall be comforted." Such (*mourners*) rejoice in hope. But such rejoicing in hope is ours only when we renounce all (*earthly*) things which we desire, in which we trust, and in which we find delight; indeed, when, in addition, we are so set apart (*from the world*) that we no longer find pleasure in any (*earthly*) boon. If in such cases we willingly endure, then we arrive at hope, and through hope to rejoicing.

Patient in tribulation (12:12). In Romans 5:3-5 the Apostle says: "Tribulation worketh patience; and patience, experience; and experience, hope; and hope maketh not ashamed." That is, hope makes us happy, cheerful and without fear.

Continuing instant in prayer (12:12). This is a loud alarm which all (*Christians*), especially all ministers, should heed and consider. The words describe the complete dedication demanded by (*true*) prayer. Nor is this admonition in vain; for as the ancient Fathers used to say: "There is no work quite so difficult as praying to God." Such prayer demands a broken and contrite mind, yet also an exalted, victorious spirit.

Distributing to the necessity of saints (12:13). The Apostle, as also the whole Bible, means by "saints" all those who believe in Christ. Against this command such sin as are indifferent to the needs of (*afflicted*) Christians. Here the Apostle speaks of such (*believers*) as suffer persecution and are deprived of all their possessions. Today the saints live in obscurity; therefore also their needs are unknown. They are sorely tried by both men and the Devil. We therefore owe them help and comfort, for they suffer injustice.

Given to hospitality (12:13). This duty the Apostle urges in his Epistles to Titus and Timothy (Titus 1:8; I Tim. 3:2) especially upon pastors. But here he addresses all Christians in general. In Hebrews 13:2 we read: "Be not forgetful to entertain strangers: for thereby some have entertained angels unawares." That is, they are not aware that they showed hospitality to angels, as did

Abraham and Lot (Gen. 18:2 ff.; 19: 1 ff.). So today we often give or refuse hospitality to saints, without being aware of it. Here, of course, the Apostle speaks of hospitality that is offered gratis and out of love, without any expectation of pay. The other kind is practiced also by the heathen.

Mind not high things (12:16). The Apostle means to say: Do not regard those who rank highly in the world, and do not be displeased with such as are despised. Take a cordial interest in those that are lowly and have pleasure in them. So St. Augustine says in his "rule": "Do not boast of the high rank of wealthy parents, but of the brotherhood of poor brethren."

Be not wise in your own conceits (12:16). This word is addressed to those who are conceited, stubborn and obstinate. Scripture calls them stiff-necked and unbelieving. It is strange how much all men incline to this vice so that we rarely find such as are entirely free from it. There are persons who accept no advice, even though they have been convinced (*of what is right*) by every argument of reason. They are the cause of dissensions, the most vicious peacebreakers and destroyers of the unity of faith. For this reason the Apostle writes in Ephesians 4:3: "Endeavouring to keep the unity of the Spirit in the bond of peace;" and in Philippians 2:2: "Be likeminded, having the same love, being of one accord, of one mind."

Recompense to no man evil for evil (12:17). In Psalm 37:27 we read: "Depart from evil, and do good." In I Peter 3:9 St. Peter explains this (*verse*) as follows: "Not rendering evil for evil, or railing for railing: but contrariwise, blessing." That is, we should not only do no evil, but we should not repay evil with evil. In Luke 9:55 we are told how Christ rebuked the disciples who wanted to call down fire from heaven (*upon the inhospitable Samaritans*), telling them: "Ye know not what manner of spirit ye are of." So also we are born, "not . . . to destroy men's lives, but to save them" (Luke 9:56).

Provide things honest in the sight of all men (12:17). In I Peter 2:12 we read: "Having your conversation honest among the Gentiles: that, whereas they speak against you as evildoers, they may by your good works, which they shall behold, glorify God in the day of visitation." (Cf. also I Tim. 5:14; Titus 3:1; I Cor. 10:32 f.). From this command stems the excellent rule of St. Augustine: "He is insensible who does not concern himself about a good reputation. For you personally a good conscience is sufficient, but for your neighbor your good reputation is a necessity."

In so doing thou shalt heap coals of fire on his head (12:20). St. Augustine says: "We must understand these words thus: We should incite those who have hurt us to repentance by doing them good. For such 'coals of fire', that is, good deeds, have the power to consume his spirit, or to grieve him." So God converts those whom He does convert by showing them goodness. It is only in this way that we can convert a person, namely, by showing him kindness and love. Whoever is converted by threat or terror is not truly converted, as long as he adheres to the outward form of conversion; for fear causes us to hate those who convert us. But if anyone is converted by love, then the whole person burns against himself and is more angry with himself than anyone else could be angry with him, for he detests himself with the greatest vehemence. It is not necessary to forbid anything to such a person, to watch him, and demand satisfaction from him, for love will teach him all (*right things*). Therefore, benefactions, shown to an enemy are "coals of fire."

Be not overcome of evil, but overcome evil with good (12:21). That is, see to it that he who hurts you does not make you as he himself is, namely, a wicked person. Nor let his wickedness defeat your goodness. But let your kindness overcome his malice and so change him into a good person. St. Gregory writes: "It is more glorious to escape the wrath (*of the enemy*) by silence, than to overcome him by retort." In Proverbs 26:4 we read: "Answer not a fool according to his folly, lest thou also be like unto him." He answers a fool according to his folly and becomes like him who permits himself to be overcome of evil. So he does not improve the fool, but rather falls into the same folly. But he who overcomes evil with good, answers him in such a way that the fool no longer regards himself as wise, but recognizes his folly and detests and regrets it.

Romans Thirteen

Content of the thirteenth chapter: The Apostle teaches subjects to be obedient to their masters and give them love and assistance.

BELIEVERS SHOULD BE SUBJECT TO GOVERNMENTS FOR THE SAKE OF GOD AND CONSCIENCE

Let every soul be subject unto the higher powers. For there is no power but of God: the powers that be are ordained of God. Whosoever therefore resisteth the power, resisteth the ordinance of God: and they that resist shall receive to themselves damnation. For rulers are not a terror to good works, but to the evil. Wilt thou then not be afraid of the power? do that which is good, and thou shalt have the praise of the same: for he is the minister of God to thee for good. But if thou do that which is evil, be afraid; for he beareth not the sword in vain; for he is the minister of God, a revenger to execute wrath upon him that doeth evil. Wherefore ye must needs be subject, not only for wrath, but also for conscience sake. For, for this cause pay ye tribute also: for they are God's ministers, attending continually upon this very thing. Render therefore to all their dues: tribute to whom tribute is due; custom to whom custom; fear to whom fear; honour to whom honour (13:1-7).

Here *in this passage* the Apostle teaches Christians how they should conduct themselves toward those who are without, in particular toward such as have the rule. In contradistinction to the Jewish conception, he teaches that Christians must subject themselves also to the wicked and unbelievers. So also we read in I Peter 2:13-15: "Submit yourselves to every ordinance of man for the Lord's sake. . .for so is the will of God." Even though rulers are wicked and unbelieving, yet is their governmental power good (*in itself*) and of God. So our Lord said to Pilate, to whom

179

He submitted Himself as a pattern for us all: "Thou couldest have no power at all against me, except it were given thee from above" (John 19:11). Christians should not, under the pretense of Christian religion, refuse to obey men (*in authority*) even if they are wicked. So the Jews thought, as we read in John 8:33: "We be Abraham's seed, and were never in bondage to any man." The Apostle therefore commands that Christians should honor the power of governments and not use their liberty of grace as a cloak for their maliciousness. So St. Peter says in I Peter 2:16: "As free, and not using your liberty for a cloke of maliciousness, but as the servants of God."

In the preceding chapter the Apostle taught that Christians must not throw into disorder the institution of the Church. Here he teaches that they must not violate the temporal government; for both these institutions are of God. The former serves the guidance and peace of the inner (*spiritual*) man and his concerns; the latter serves that of the outward (*earthly*) man and his concerns. (*That is, the Church directs people as Christians; the state, as citizens.*) In this life the inward man cannot be without the outward. (*That is to say, the believer serves Christ in His kingdoms of grace and of power.*)

Let every soul be subject unto the higher powers (13:1). Is there (*perhaps*) a hidden meaning in the use of "every soul" for "every person"? Perhaps he means to stress the thought that Christians must show a sincere subjection that comes from the heart. Again, he speaks in this way because the soul is between the body and the spirit. He thus shows that the believer once for all is exalted over all things, and yet at the same time subject to all things. As a dual being, he (*the Christian*) thus bears two forms in himself, just as did Christ. According to the spirit, he (*the believer*) is lord of all things, as the Apostle writes in I Corinthians 3:21,22: "All things are yours; whether Paul, or Apollos. . . or things present, or things to come; all are yours."

By faith the Christian makes all things subject to himself; for he is neither ruled by them, nor does he put his trust in them. He compels them to serve his (*eternal*) glory and salvation. That is what it means (*for us*) to serve God and to rule (*with Him*) as kings. That is the spiritual rule, of which we read in Revelation 5:10: "Thou hast made us unto our God kings and priests: and we shall reign on the earth."

The world is conquered and subdued in no better way than by despising it. The spirit of the believer therefore is subject to no one, nor can it be subject to anyone. It is exalted with Christ, and all things lie subdued at his feet. The "soul" is the same as the "spirit" of man, but inasmuch as it lives and works, and serves the visible world and earthly things, it must be subject "to every ordinance of man for the Lord's sake" (I Peter 2:13). By this subjection it obeys God and desires the same as God. By this subjection it overcomes this temporal world even now.

The powers that be are ordained of God (13:1). Faber Stapulensis explains this thus: "Wherever there are governments of God, there they are ordained." In connection with this he speaks of a twofold (*governmental*) power: one (*divinely*) instituted and the other not (*divinely*) instituted. This exposition, however, I do not favor; for there is no government that is not (*divinely*) instituted. Governments (*at times*) are only usurped and managed in ways not ordained (*by God*). So also other blessings (*of God*) are misused, and yet do not lose their value (*by such misuse*). Money, for example, does not become evil through (*the evil use*) of theft. Hence we must explain the words thus: Wherever there is governmental power, there it is instituted by God. That is, wherever governments exist, they are ordained solely by God. The meaning is the same as (*that of the sentence*): "There is no power, but of God." Therefore, wherever powers exist and flourish, they exist and flourish because God has ordained them.

Rulers are not a terror to good works, but to the evil (13:3). They (*the rulers*) deter us not from good works, as though these should not be done, but from evil. That justifies governments and laudably commends them. Why should we despise rulers, even if (*by this*) we would not displease God? For they do not compel us to do what is evil, but what is good.

He is the minister of God to thee for good (13:4). Even if evil persons (*rulers*) do not desire to serve God, He directs all things in such a way that the good which they possess and which they misuse — (*their ordained governmental power*) — must serve Him. For this reason the King of Babylon, though a wicked idolater, is divinely called "my servant" by the prophets, (*that is, by God through His prophets*) (cf Jer. 25:9; 27:6).

One is amazed at the impenetrable gross darkness that prevails today. There is nothing that angers the clerics, these widely opened mouths avariciously coveting temporal things, more than when the freedom of the churches, with their rights, their possessions and their powers is attacked. Against such "trangressors" they hurl their anathemas. They declare them to be heretics and publicly and with an alarming arrogance condemn them as enemies of God, of the Church, and of Peter and Paul. Meanwhile they are not at all concerned whether they (*themselves*) are friends of God, or at least whether they are no greater enemies of His than those (*who question their rights and powers*). So greatly have they identified faith and obedience with the preservation, enlargement and defense of (*their*) earthly possessions! One may be proud, lascivious, miserly, contentious, irascible, and ungrateful; indeed, one may be guilty of the whole catalog of vices described in II Timothy 3:2 ff.; one's transgressions may even cry to high heaven; nevertheless, he is a most pious Christian, as long as he protects the rights and liberties of the Church. But if anyone should ignore them, then he is no longer a faithful son and friend of the Church.

This practical application (*of this verse*) to present-day circumstances is very profitable for the understanding of the text. I say this at the same time because of my apostolic authority (*Luther's appointment as an official Doctor of Scripture*), since I am invested with the office of teaching. It is my duty to witness wherever I see that wrong is done, even by those who rule.

But here one may ask why the apostle in Galatians 5:13 writes: "Ye have been called into liberty; only use not liberty for an occasion to the flesh, but by love serve one another"; or in I Corinthians 7:23: "Ye are bought with a price; be not ye the servants of men."

To this I reply that the words "liberty" and "servitude" are used in different meanings. He speaks of servitude in a figurative sense, by which a person forfeits his liberty if he engages with others in temporal matters and business transactions.

Again, there is a servitude which is very precious. Of this the Apostle speaks in Galatians 5:13: "By love serve one another." This (*liberty*) the Apostle has in mind also when he says that though he was free, yet he made himself a servant of all, in order that he might gain the more, as we read in I Corinthians 9:19. This servitude is the greatest freedom, which demands nothing, takes nothing, but (*only*) gives and distributes. Therefore the most glorious, indeed the only freedom that is truly found alone among Christians. This the Apostle states also in this chapter, where he writes: "Owe no man any thing, but to love one another" (13:8). This is spiritual servitude in a good sense. All things serve man (*Christians*), for "all things work together for good to them" (8:28). They themselves, however, are servants of none, for they are in need of no one, as already said.

There is yet another servitude of a spiritual nature, and that is the worst. Against this servitude the Apostle fights with all his might on behalf of the Christians. It is this, that people believe that Christians are subject to the whole Law and all its burdens. That is, they are of the opinion that such external works of the Law are necessary for salvation. Those who think and believe this remain servants and will never be saved; for they serve the Law, and the Law rules over them because of their foolish belief and their perverted conscience. To this class belong all those who desire to be saved in any other way than alone by faith in Christ. With anxious care they seek to satisfy the Law by their many works and deeds of righteousness. It is true, also the Apostle and (*other*) spiritual persons have done such works; and they are being done even today, not because they must be done, but because (*such believers*) regard it as their privilege to do them. But those hypocrites bind themselves so tightly to works, as though these were necessary for salvation. They do them from coercion and not of their free will. And yet, they wish it would not be necessary for them to do them, although they believe this. This servitude is widely spread in our time.

On the basis of this (*principle of liberty*) we readily understand, as we read the Book of Acts, why the Apostle desired to purify himself (Acts 21:26) and why he circumcised Timothy (Acts 16:3), though he preached the very opposite of this (*the keeping of the ceremonial Law*). Those who are in the spirit (*the believers*) need not do all these external works.

With reference to temporal government, however, the Apostle does not consider the question of (*Christian*) liberty; for this is not a (*spiritual*) servitude, but rather concerns all men.

BELIEVERS SHOULD LOVE ONE ANOTHER

Owe no man anything, but to love one another: for he that loveth another hath fulfilled the law. For this, Thou shalt not commit adultery, Thou shalt not kill, Thou shalt not steal, Thou shalt not bear false witness, Thou shalt not covet; and if there be any other commandment, it is briefly comprehended in this saying, namely, Thou shalt love thy neighbour as thyself. Love worketh no ill to his neighbour; therefore love is the fulfilling of the law (13:8-10).

Owe no man anything, but to love one another (13:8). That is: Disengage yourselves from all things except from (*brotherly*) love. That (*love*) indeed must remain; and that you must follow ever more and more.

Thou shalt love thy neighbor as thyself (13:9). Man (*by nature*) loves himself in a wrong way; in fact, he loves only himself. This perverse disposition cannot be corrected, unless he puts the neighbor in his place.

Love worketh no ill to his neighbor (13:10). Love does much more, for it does good to him whom it loves. This is the nature of love that it is kindly disposed and does good, even then when it endures evil and is hated.

Therefore love is the fulfilling of the law (13:10). This command can be understood in a twofold sense. First, we are commanded to love both our neighbor and ourself. Again, the command can be understood in the sense that we love only our neighbor, and this alone for love's sake. I like this latter interpretation much better, because man on account of the evil corruption of his nature loves himself above all things. So he seeks himself in all things and loves all things on account of himself even when he loves his neighbor and friends. In all things he looks out for himself only.

This command therefore is immeasurably deep, and every Christian should thoroughly explore himself with respect to it, as he conscientiously examines himself. By the words "as thyself" all hypocritical love is ruled out. Hence, whoever loves his neighbor on account of his money, honor, learning, favor, power and comfort, and would not love him if he would be poor, lowly, ignorant, hateful, submissive and boorish, would manifestly have (only) a hypocritical love. He does not love the neighbor as such, but on account of what he has, and this is his own interest and so not "as thyself." He who loves himself would love himself also if he would be poor, foolish and an absolute "nobody." For who could be so good-for-nothing as to detest himself?

Therefore this command demands of us something that is most difficult, if only we would study it rightly. No one wants to be robbed, harmed, murdered, have his marriage disrupted by adultery, suffer through perjury, be defamed, and have someone else covet what is his own. But if he is not so disposed that he does not want his neighbor to suffer all these wrongs, then already he is guilty of transgressing this command. For this reason this command embraces that of our Lord in Matthew 7:12: "All things whatsoever ye would that men should do to you, do ye even so to them: for this is the law and the prophets."

This command might seem very paltry to those who consider it only superficially and according to its general application. But if it is applied to special cases then we can gather from it an unlimited measure of salutary instruction; indeed, then we may draw from it the most dependable guidance for all circumstances. But that people do not observe it, but transgress it ever so much, even in ignorance; indeed, that even such transgress it as do not desire to heed it, all this stems from the fact that they do not apply this standard to their actual conduct, but are satisfied with their "good intention."

The rich, for example, accumulate treasures in order that the priests may erect churches and monuments. If they would carefully consider the poor, then they would know of themselves what to do, even if the poor would ask nothing for themselves, but desire to have everything given to the Church. Similarly princes and bishops compete with one another to acquire relics; and all wish to be given priority. Yet both (*classes*) continue (*in their search for relics*) and no one yields to the other, though carefully observing the show of piety. Just so the Observantines, (*who most strictly follow the rules of St. Francis*), fight one another for God's sake; yet they do not obey the commandment of love.

But whoever desires seriously to consider this commandment (*of love*) and to apply it (*to his life*) must not depend on "acts awakened within himself," but must measure according to this command, as according to a rule, all works, words and thoughts in his whole life, and must always ask himself, with reference to his neighbor: "What do I want him to do for me?" Keeping that in mind, he would try to act in the same way with regard to his neighbor. Then all wrangling, defamation and discord would soon end, and a whole host of virtues would follow. Every kind of grace, every kind of holiness, and as the Apostle here says, "the fulfilling of the law" would then take place.

He who desires to do this will thoroughly learn to know his faults, humble himself, and fear God; otherwise he will wrongly regard himself as holy. Then also he will very often find himself sluggish in helping his neighbor, although he greatly desires everyone else to be kindly disposed to him, attend to him, and serve him. Then also he will find that he is an enemy and a traitor of his brethren, a slanderer, and full of sins from top to bottom. For this reason the Apostle commands this (*love*) also in Philippians 2:4: "Look not every man on his own things, but every man also on the things—(*the profit*)—of others"; and in I Corinthians 13:5: "Love seeketh not her own." That is, love moves us to deny ourselves and to regard the neighbor, to put off affection for ourselves and put on affection for others, to put ourselves last and the neighbor first. In addition, we would then consider what we would want the neighbor to do for us, and what we or others could do for the neighbor. Then we would know what to do, instructed by this infallible and reliable principle (*of love*).

As many blessings, both temporal and spiritual, as we desire and ask of ourselves, and as much as we do to bring about the fulfilling of our wishes, namely, the utmost, just of so many faults we become guilty by our very desires. For all these things we owe to the neighbor, and yet we find that we are not willing to do them for our neighbor. Or, if we would deny ourselves and desire of others nothing for ourselves that is good, then we would owe no man anything. So deep and far does this commandment reach!

BELIEVERS SHOULD CAST OFF ALL WORKS OF DARKNESS

And that, knowing the time, that now it is high time to awake out of sleep: for now is our salvation nearer than when we believed. The night is far spent, the day is at hand: let us therefore cast off the works of darkness, and let us put on the armour of light. Let us walk honestly, as in the day; not in rioting and drunkenness, not in chambering and wantonness, not in strife and envying. But put ye on the Lord Jesus Christ, and make not provision for the flesh, to fulfill the lusts thereof (13:11-14).

It is high time to awake out of sleep (13:11). After the Apostle has instructed us, he now admonishes us, just as before he distinguished between indoctrination and exhortation. Indoctrination is for those who are ignorant; exhortation for those who know. For this reason the Apostle also uses metaphorical and figurative expressions which are not suited for those who first must be taught.

In I Corinthians 15:34: we read: "Awake to righteousness, and sin not"; and in Ephesians 5:14: "Awake thou that sleepest, and arise from the dead, and Christ will give thee light." There is no doubt that by these words, as also in this verse, the Apostle speaks of that spiritual sleep, in which the spirit, as it were, is asleep by living in sin and being inactive (*in good works*). Against such (*spiritual*) sleep Christ frequently admonishes us in the Gospel where He commands us to be watchful. And indeed He does not speak of those who are (*altogether*) dead in sin and unbelief, nor of (*nominal*) believers who are living in mortal sins, but of Christians who are sluggish in good works and, overcome by the feeling of security, are falling asleep. The Apostle desires that they should advance (*in sanctification*) by serious effort, just as we read in Micah 6:8: "He hath showed thee, O man, what is good; and what doth the Lord require of thee, but to do justly, and to love mercy, and to walk humbly with thy God."

Those who are not concerned (*about their Christian life*), nor watch with fear (*of the Lord*), begin, but do not progress; they put their hand to the plow, yet look back (Luke 9:62). They have "a form of godliness, but (deny) the power thereof" (II Tim. 3:5). With their body they leave Egypt, but in their hearts they return to it. Secure and without the fear of God, they go their way, without feeling, without reverence, but hardened. St. Bernard says of them: "He who does not hurry to repent without ceasing, declares in reality that he does not need repentance." But if he does not need repentance, he also does not need divine mercy; and if he does not need divine mercy, then also he does not need salvation.

For this reason it is a most fitting admonition by which the Apostle here exhorts Christians to awake out of their sleep; though indeed, they would not be Christians, if they were still sleeping (*the sleep of spiritual death*). But to stand still on God's way means to go back; and to go forward means ever to begin anew. So St. Arsenius used to pray: "Help me, O Lord, that I may begin to live to Thee." In I Corinthians 8:2 the Apostle says of wisdom: "If any man think that he knoweth any thing, he knoweth nothing yet as he ought to know." In the same way we may conclude with regard to individual virtues: if any one thinks that he already has apprehended, or that he has already begun, he knows nothing yet as he ought to begin.

Today this class of Christians is represented very numerously and conspicuously. They have changed the repentance which Christ proclaimed into temporal works and external obligations; and if they have done these works, they regard themselves as righteous. Therefore confession (*of being righteous*) often results in damnation, for it is based upon disastrous trust in oneself. Such a confession does not remove the evil (*of sin and guilt*) in spite of the arrogant boasting (*of work-righteous persons who regard themselves as holy*).

"Sleep" in Scripture has various meanings. Thus it denotes bodily sleep, as in John 11:11: "Our friend Lazarus sleepeth." So especially in the Old Testament, as in I Kings 2:10; II Chronicles 9:31, and other passages. In its spiritual meaning it is often used in a good sense, as in Psalm 127:2: "He giveth his beloved sleep." To sleep in this sense means to disregard temporal gifts and to look upon them as a show and shadow rather than as real, in order to gain the blessings that are everlasting. Those who so sleep have by faith become fully awakened and enlightened; so they sleep with regard to earthly matters, that is, they are indifferent to them.

But the word "sleep" is used figuratively also in a bad sense, and this in contrast to the meaning just given. In I Thessalonians 5:6, 7 the Apostle thus writes: "Let us not sleep, as do others; but let us watch and be sober. For they that sleep sleep in the night; and they that be drunken are drunken in the night." Here the word "night" denotes the spiritual night, which is evil. To sleep in this sense means to disregard and despise the blessings that are eternal. Over against these, such sleepers are very indifferent, because they are held captive by the temporal gifts which, wide awake, they see with great greed. What is night for the former (*the believer*) is day for the latter (*the unbeliever*). What the former regards as an awakening, the latter looks upon as sleep, and vice versa. As the gifts differ, so also do the opinions of men.

As Scripture speaks of sleep in a threefold sense, so also it speaks of day and night and of other matters that might be applied in a figurative sense. The spiritual day is faith; the spiritual night is unbelief. So, then, it is clear that the Apostle here does not speak of bodily sleep, nor of the sinister life of sensuality, which is most active at nighttime, (*but of the spiritual sleep of indifference and inactivity in good works*).

The works of darkness, then, are the works of those who sleep spiritually, and that in a bad sense; that is, of those who are asleep in the lusts of the flesh. These works of darkness are not merely such as are commonly regarded as evil — (*fornication, adultery, etc.*) — but also such as are regarded as good. The latter are evil because of the inward (*spiritual*) darkness; that is, because they are not done in faith which is awake.

For now is our salvation nearer than when we believed (13:11). The sense of this verse is the same as that of II Corinthians 6: 1, 2 (Isa. 49:8): "We then, as workers together with him, beseech you also that ye receive not the grace of God in vain. (For he saith, I have heard thee in a time accepted, and in the day of salvation have I succoured thee . . . behold, now is the day of salvation.)" What the Apostle here (*in Rom.* 13:11) touches upon in passing, he there (*in II Cor.* 6:1,2) presents in far greater details. He also describes what he means by "works of darkness" and "armour of light" (v. 12); for in II Corinthians 6:3 ff. he writes: "Giving no offence in any thing, that the ministry be not blamed: but in all things approving ourselves as the ministers of God, in much patience, in afflictions, in necessities, in distresses." Then in II Corinthians 6:7 he says: "By the armour of righteousness on the right hand and on the left." Here (Rom. 13:12) he speaks of the "armour of light"; there (II Cor. 6:7) of the armor of righteousness. So, then, "light" and "righteousness" are the same thing.

Let us therefore cast off the works of darkness, and let us put on the armour of light (13:12). It is a strange antithesis by which the Apostle places in contrast "light" and "darkness," "works" and "armor." And no wonder! For the life of the new Law — (*the new spiritual life in Christ*) — means war and warfare; and for this we need armor (*cf. Eph.* 6:10-20).

Let us walk honestly as in the day (13:13). This is the text by which St. Augustine was converted.

Not in rioting and drunkenness (13:13). The Greek word *kosmos* means banquet, or rather a sumptuous feast, including the extreme waste when such feasts were prepared and managed. What the Apostle here teaches in a negative way, he positively expands and makes clear in II Corinthians 6:5 (*"in watchings, in fastings"*). He desires that Christians should show zeal in fasting and eagerly strive after moderation and temperance.

And indeed, all who study history, at least that of St. Jerome, will find that the six vices (*mentioned in Rom.* 13:13) at that time had gained the ascendancy in Rome and exerted an almost tyrannical sway. For this reason the Apostle wanted to deter the believers, in order that in view of such maniacal patterns of impious Rome they might not be inclined to yield.

So also St. Peter does not pass over the vices of this city, but writes: "For the time past of our life may suffice us to have wrought the will of the Gentiles, when we walked in lasciviousness, lusts, excess of wine, revellings, banquetings, and abominable idolatries: wherein they think it strange that ye run not with them to the same excess of riot, speaking evil of you" (I Pet. 4: 3, 4).

And in II Peter 2:13, 14, he says: "They . . . count it pleasure to riot in the day time. Spots they are and blemishes, sporting themselves with their own deceivings while they feast with you; having eyes full of adultery, and that cannot cease from sin." Indeed, he even calls this city Babylon, because there everything was in chaotic confusion. Alas, modern Rome surpasses ancient Rome by yet greater voluptuousness, so that it seems as though the Apostles were again necessary. Indeed, they are much more necessary now than they were at that time.

In his fight against such vices the Apostle commands that the bishops, the deacons, the men, the elders, the young men and the women should be sober (I Tim. 2:8 ff.; 3:2 ff.; Titus 1:7 ff.; 2:2 ff.). To all he forbids gluttony and drunkenness as though these were a pestilence. So, as we compare our passage (in Rom. 13) with those (in Tim. and Titus) we gain a correct understanding (of the words) of the Apostle. Here (in Rom. 13) he points out what he does not want; there (in Tim. and Titus) what he demands.

Not in chambering and wantonness (13:13). That is, they (*the believers*) should be watchful and chaste, as in the passages above he commands chastity and watchfulness, above all, to the bishops, but then also to the elders and all others. This is an excellent sequence; for gluttony and drunkenness are the fertile soil in which unchastity or debauchery thrive. For this reason the pious Fathers declared that whoever desires to serve God, must root out, above all, the vice of gluttony. That is a prevailing vice which causes much trouble. If this vice is not altogether extirpated, it makes the soul dull for divine things, even if it should not lead to unchastity and debauchery as among aged men. Hence fasting is a most excellent weapon for the Christian, while gluttony is an outstanding pit of Satan.

Not in strife and envying (13:13). After having instructed the Christian for his own benefit to be temperate, watchful and chaste, the Apostle now instructs him with reference to the neighbor. Christians should live in concord and love with one another. This commandment the Apostle inculcates in all his Epistles, as in I Timothy 2:8; 3:2 ff.; Titus 1:7.

"Strife" is a fight by means of words in which everyone presumes to be true, honest and right, while all others are regarded (*as wrong*). So no one is willing to yield to the other.

The word "envying" allows many applications. "Envying" means loving jealousy or jealous love, both being mingled in it: love and jealousy. It is a bitter love and bitterness permeated by love. However, the word is not always used in the same sense in Scripture.

Put ye on the Lord Jesus Christ (13:14). (*We do this*) by following Him and by being renewed in His image, in suffering, fasting and (*other*) good works.

Make not provision for the flesh, to fulfil the lusts thereof (13:14). The Apostle desires that Christians should take care of their bodies in such a way that no evil desires are nurtured thereby. St. Victor says: "He who nurtures the flesh, nurtures an enemy"; and again: "He who destroys the body, destroys a friend." We should not destroy the body, but crucify its vices or evil passions.

Romans Fourteen

Content of the fourteenth chapter: The Apostle admonishes those that are strong in the faith not to despise the weak, nor to give them offense, but to build them up in the spirit of peace.

BELIEVERS STRONG IN THE FAITH
SHOULD NOT DESPISE THE WEAK

Him that is weak in the faith receive ye, but not to doubtful disputations. For one believeth that he may eat all things: another, who is weak, eateth herbs. Let not him that eateth despise him that eateth not; and let not him which eateth not judge him that eateth: for God hath received him. Who art thou that judgest another man's servant? to his own master he standeth or falleth. Yea, he shall be holden up: for God is able to make him stand. One man esteemeth one day above another: another esteemeth every day alike. Let every man be fully persuaded in his own mind. He that regardeth the day, regardeth it unto the Lord; and he that regardeth not the day, to the Lord he doth not regard it. He that eateth, eateth to the Lord, for he giveth God thanks; and he that eateth not, to the Lord he eateth not, and giveth God thanks. For none of us liveth to himself, and no man dieth to himself. For whether we live, we live unto the Lord; and whether we die, we die unto the Lord: whether we live therefore, or die, we are the Lord's. For to this end Christ both died, and rose, and revived, that he might be Lord both of the dead and living. But why dost thou judge thy brother? or why dost thou set at naught thy brother? for we shall all stand before the judgment seat of Christ. For it is written, As I live, saith the Lord, every knee shall bow to me, and every tongue shall confess to God. So then every one of us shall give account of himself to God (14:1-12).

Him that is weak in the faith receive ye (14:1). In this chapter the Apostle commands two things, namely, first, that the strong should not despise the weak, and that both should not judge one another; and secondly, that the strong should not give offence to the weak. For so he writes in 14:13: "Judge this rather, that no man put a stumbling-block or an occasion to fall in his brother's way." The occasion for this teaching was that in the Old Testament Law various kinds of food were forbidden and this as a shadow of what was to come. Some of the weak and simple in the faith could not understand that the symbols were no longer in force, and that all things had become clean, (that is, allowed to believers). They believed that certain kinds of food should not be eaten because of their common use (by heathen). Such (persons) should not be despised, but tolerated. Again, those who had a clear understanding (about such foods) were not to be judged, as though they did evil when partaking of various foods. About this question there was a most disturbing controversy. The first church convention (Acts 15:6 ff.) concerned itself with this question; indeed, even St. Peter was rebuked by St. Paul in the same matter (Gal. 2:14).

In all his letters the Apostle treats this subject and condemns the false apostles who, being of Jewish extraction, taught that the (ceremonial) laws must be observed to obtain salvation. A similar occasion (for controversy) was the meat offered to idols for believers of Gentile origin, as we learn in I Corinthians, chapters 8-10. (There the Apostle writes): "Whatsoever is sold in the shambles (market), that eat."

When the Apostle here speaks of the "weak," he has in mind those who were of the opinion that they were obligated to certain laws, to which in reality they were not obligated. His words, however, are directed above all against the Jewish error, which some false prophets taught, distinguishing between certain kinds of food. Against them he writes in I Timothy 1:3-6: "I besought thee . . . that thou mightest charge some that they teach no other doctrine, neither give heed to fables and endless genealogies, which minister questions, rather than godly edifying which is in faith . . . now the end of the commandment is charity out of a pure heart, and of a good conscience, and of faith unfeigned: from which some having swerved have turned aside unto vain jangling." Similar admonitions we find also in Galatians 4:9 ff.; Colossians 2:16; Hebrew 13:9.

He treats the matter more in detail in I Corinthians, Chapters 8-10, where he sets forth the same doctrine as here (*in Rom.* 14).

What the Apostle teaches is that in the new Law (*the Gospel covenant*) everything is free and nothing necessary (*for salvation*) for those who believe in Christ, except "charity out of a pure heart, and of a good conscience, and of faith unfeigned" (I Tim. 1:5). In Galatians 6:15 he writes: "In Christ Jesus neither circumcision availeth any thing, nor uncircumcision, but a new creature."

It does not belong to the new Law (*the Gospel covenant*) to regard some days as feast days and others not, as this had been commanded in the Law of Moses. Nor does it belong to the new Law to select certain kinds of food and distinguish them from others, as the Law of Moses does in Leviticus 11:4 ff.; Deuteronomy 14:7 ff. Nor does it belong to the new Law to regard some days as holy and others as not. Nor does it belong to the new Law to build such or such churches, to adorn them so or so, or to sing in this way or another. Nor are organs, altar decorations, chalices and pictures necessary, and whatever else we now find in the houses of worship. Nor is it necessary for priests and monks to be shaved or appear in special garments as in the Old Testament. All this is "shadow" and "token" of the new reality (*worship*) and puerility.

On the contrary, every day is a feast day, and a holy day; and every kind of food is permitted. So also every kind of garment is allowed. All is free, and only humility, love, and what else the Apostle inculcates must be observed. Against this (*Christian*) liberty, for which the Apostle contends, many false apostles raised their voice to mislead the people to do certain things as though these were necessary. Against such errorists the Apostle took the offensive with an amazing zeal.

So what? Should we then confirm the heresy of the Picardists (*an extreme sect of the Hussite Brethren*) who have adopted this rule (*that all ceremonies are forbidden in the New Testament*)? Should we abolish all churches, all ornaments, liturgical acts of service, all sacred places, all fast days and holy days? Should we discard all differences between priests, bishops and monks regarding their ranks, garments and ecclesiastical acts, observed for many centuries to this very day? Should we declare all the convents and religious establishments, all benefices and benefactions as things that must be abrogated?

By no means! In contrast to this (*error*) stands that which the Apostle himself taught and did; for he circumcised Timothy, offered sacrifices and purified himself in the temple (Acts 13:3; 21:26). So, then, all things are free (*in the New Testament*), but so that a Christian out of love may willingly (*vow to*) offer this or that sacrifice (*to God*). But as soon as this is done, then he must do it, not indeed from the nature of the thing, but because of the vow, made freely and in love. Then also he (*who has vowed*) must be careful to keep it with the same love with which he has vowed it. If the vow is observed without love and against his will, then it would have been better not to vow. He may keep it with his body (*outwardly*), but in his heart he does not fulfill it; and so is a transgressor for not keeping the vow freely.

But return to the text. The Apostle desires above all that those who are weak in the faith should be tolerated and instructed by the strong. Nor should they condemn the weak. In this way he admonishes them (*his readers*) to peace and unity, for we must take care of the weak, in order that they may become strong. We must not forsake them in their weakness as those do who turn away from them in disgust and consider only their own salvation. So, then, the strong should instruct the weak, and the weak should be ready to be instructed. The peace and love will govern both (*the strong and the weak*).

But not to doubtful disputations (14:1). That is, no one should judge the opinion or conviction of the other. The strong has his own opinion which is determined by his (*special*) reasons. Just so the weak has his opinion. Therefore the Apostle says in v. 5: "Let every man be fully persuaded in his own mind." That means that every one should remain sure and certain in the opinion which his conscience suggests.

This, however, does not mean that we should bear the superstitious piety, or rather the show of piety of our own time, simply because it flows from weakness of faith. Those who do these works of piety do them because of their gross ignorance. They are not aware that they themselves first must become different, and then their works. In Galatians 5:13 the Apostle admonishes the Galatians that they should not use their liberty for an occasion to the flesh, as this now is done in Rome where no one any longer troubles himself about the (*divine*) Word. There everything is swallowed up by disputations. This liberty they have in a perfect measure, but the other things which the Apostle commands, they ignore entirely, and so they use their liberty as an occasion to the flesh, indeed, for a cloke of maliciousness (I Pet. 2:16).

Let every one therefore examine himself carefully when he prays or brings an offering, or enters the choir, or what else he may do, to discover whether he does all this of his own free will (*and not by coercion*). Then he will find out what he is before God, (*namely, a sinner, not serving Him willingly*); for if he would not do it in case it were left to his choice, he would not do anything at all (*that is good*) since he is a menial and a hireling.

We fail to take into consideration that we should do all things (*good works*) not under the pressure of coercion, or driven by the goad of anxious fear, but moved by a cheerful and fully free will, if they are to please God. In all we do, we must consider not what we have done, or what there is to be done; not what we failed to do or what we should fail to do; also not what good we have done or what good we have omitted, or what evil we have done or omitted. But we should rather consider of what nature and how strong our (*good*) will has been, and the readiness and cheerfulness of our heart with which we have done all or intend to do all. Therefore the Apostle writes in I Corinthians 16:12, though he might have commanded Apollos: "As touching our brother Apollos, I greatly desired him to come unto you with the brethren: but his will was not at all to come at this time." So also he beseeches Philemon on behalf of his slave: "Without thy mind would I do nothing; that thy benefit should not be as it were of necessity, but willingly" (Philem. v. 14).

Essentially, there lies at the bottom of this error — (*doing good works from necessity*) — the Pelagian view. For although now there are none that (*openly*) confess Pelagianism and call themselves Pelagians, yet there are many who in reality and in their views are Pelagians though perhaps they are not aware of it. They believe very definitely and boldly that if they could only produce a "good intention," then "infallibly" they would obtain infused grace. So they go about their way most securely, expecting of course very definitely that the good works which they do are pleasing to God. Therefore they have no more fear or anxiety so as to ask God for grace. They are not afraid of acting wrongly, but are sure that they are doing rightly. Why? Because they do not understand that God permits the wicked to sin even in their good works (*such as they themselves regard as good*). Hence they do not fear that their good might be evil, but they are full of self-confidence and regard themselves as sure (*to please God*).

St. Peter admonishes (*his readers*) in I Peter 2:17: "Fear God." So also St. Paul writes in II Corinthians 5:11: "Knowing therefore the terror of the Lord, we persuade men;" and in Philippians 2:12: "Work out your salvation with fear and trembling." In Psalm 2:11 we read: "Serve the Lord with fear, and rejoice with trembling." The saints (*believers*) seek the grace of God with fear and anxiety, praying for it without ceasing. They do not trust in their "good intention," or in their zeal in general, but always fear that their works may be evil. Humiliated by such fear, they seek after divine grace and pray for it. And by their humble prayers they obtain God's favor. The greatest pestilence today are those preachers who proclaim the signs of present (*infused*) grace, in order to render their hearers secure. It is by humility that we obtain God's grace, and through (*divine*) grace we become willing to do good works. Without it we are unwilling to do them.

God hath received him (14:3). With these important words the Apostle closes the mouths (*of those who despise and those who judge*). He who despises or judges another (*believer*) despises and judges not merely man, but God. Therefore very forcefully the Apostle urges them to consider each other in humility and to bear with one another.

Who art thou that judgest another man's servant? (14:4) It is contrary to the Natural Law and to all human custom to judge the servant of another man. So the conduct of these men (*who despise and judge others*) is opposed not only to God, but also to human judgment and convention. The Apostle (*in particular*) meets the motivations of their arguments, as when the weak thinks that the strong is falling, or when the strong believes that the weak has already fallen; for he says: He who stands, stands to his master; and he who falls, falls to his master. Therefore you cannot excuse your judging or despising; for even if what you think is true, it is not lawful for you to judge and despise.

Again, the Apostle meets the argument of those who ask: "Who knows whether he (*who eats or eats not*) will stand?" He replies: "God is able to make him stand."

Let every man be fully persuaded in his own mind (14:5). The meaning of these words is that every man should be sure of his opinion or thoughts (*concerning the controverted question*). Neither should he judge another who thinks otherwise, nor should he punish him with contempt, in order that he who is weak in the faith and so has his own opinion, conviction, or conscience, may not become confused and misled by what the other person thinks. By this he may be induced to act contrary to his own convictions and since he thinks differently in the matter, be moved to sin against his conscience. For though in his weakness he cannot judge otherwise than that this or that is not allowed, nevertheless he does what the others (*the strong*) do, so as not to be despised by them, although his conviction forbids him to do so.

In I Corinthians 8:4-7 we read: "We know that an idol is nothing in the world, and that there is none other God but one . . . Howbeit there is not in every man that knowledge: for some with conscience of the idol unto this hour eat it as a thing offered unto an idol; and their conscience being weak is defiled." That is, they cannot judge any other way than that this is forbidden and so they eat against their own judgment (*and violate their conscience*). This defilement is caused by the pride of the strong who eat such meats offered to idols in their sight, and while doing so, look upon them (*the weak*) with contempt. They rather should take care of them (*the weak*) and instruct them. Or, if these, because of their weakness, could not receive instruction, then because of (*Christian*) love they should also become weak and refrain from idol meats, despite their inner conviction and conscience. For though all things are allowed, yet for the sake of the brother's salvation, we dare not maliciously make a show of our liberty. It is better that one surrender his liberty outwardly than that a weak brother should perish.

So in one and the same work, which is allowed, one sins and the other does well because of the difference of their conscience. Therefore the Apostle says: "Let every man be fully persuaded in his own mind." That is, let every one be sure and firm and at peace. On account of the scruples of the weak, the strong should not change his conviction, nor should the weak for the sake of the strong act against his conviction. Let the weak permit him (the strong) to act (as he thinks), but let the weak be true to his own conscience. (Luther's concern in this exposition is that the strong Christian should not by his unwise use of adiaphora offend his weak brother and cause him to sin against his conscience.)

None of us liveth to himself, and no man dieth to himself (14:7). Here he faces them (who judge and despise) with the judgment seat of Christ. There we all must be judged. See, with what great threats he deters us from despising one another and especially the weak. He uses every argument against this, namely, God, man (human laws), Christ's suffering, reign, and last judgment. He deters us from judging by emphasizing the divine judgment. He means to say: It is foolish to judge those who will be judged by Christ. But also be careful in order that you who judge may not be judged yourself (by God).

As I live, saith the Lord (14:11). When God swears, He swears by Himself. In Isaiah 45:23 we read: "I have sworn by myself, the word is gone out of my mouth in righteousness, and shall not return, That unto me every knee shall bow, every tongue shall swear." That this is said of Christ, the incarnate God, is clear from the verses that precede and that follow.

Every knee shall bow to me, and every tongue shall confess to God. (14:11). It is certain that this does not take place now in time. Therefore in these words, which are unshakably firm, the resurrection of both the good and evil is indicated. "Every knee" and "every tongue" means all members of the (risen) body. The prophet prefers "every knee" and "every tongue" to "all men" to emphasize all the more and express the completely preserved condition (*of man*) in the resurrection.

Believers Should Not Give Offence to One Another

Let us not therefore judge one another any more: but judge this rather, that no man put a stumblingblock or an occasion to fall in his brother's way. I know, and am persuaded by the Lord Jesus, that there is nothing unclean of itself: but to him that esteemeth any thing to be unclean to him it is unclean. But if thy brother be grieved with thy meat, now walkest thou not charitably. Destroy not him with thy meat, for whom Christ died. Let not then your good be evil spoken of: for the kingdom of God is not meat and drink; but righteousness, and peace, and joy in the Holy Ghost. For he that in these things serveth Christ is acceptable to God, and approved of men. Let us therefore follow after the things which make for peace, and things wherewith one may edify another. For meat destroy not the work of God. All things indeed are pure; but it is evil for that man who eateth with offence. It is good neither to eat flesh, nor to drink wine, nor any thing whereby thy brother stumbleth, or is offended, or is made weak. Hast thou faith? have it to thyself before God. Happy is he that condemneth not himself in that thing which he alloweth. And he that doubteth is damned if he eat, because he eateth not of faith; for whatsoever is not of faith is sin (14:13-23).

I know, and am persuaded by the Lord Jesus (14:14). This, then, is the sum of the chapter: first, that the strong should not despise the weak; secondly, that they (*the strong*) should not give offence to the weak. Both acts are contrary to (*Christian*) love, which cares for the weak, does not seek its own, but seeks the edification of the weak. The Apostle shows himself a pattern (*in this respect*) when in II Corinthians 11:28, 29 he writes: "Besides those things that are without, that which cometh upon me daily, the care of all the churches. Who is weak, and I am not weak? who is offended, and I burn not?" In I Corinthians 9:22 he says: "To the weak became I as weak, that I might gain the weak: I am made all things to all men, that I might by all means save some." That the Apostle could so burn, (*though he was not offended with those who were offended*), is clear from this passage, in which, with burning words, he turns against such as despised (*others*) and gave offense.

The words "I know, and am persuaded" here must not be understood in the sense "I hope," but in that of absolute certainty: "I am sure and certain." In fact, we may almost translate with "I am bold," or "I dare," as the Apostle before said of Isaiah: "Esaias is very bold, and saith" (Rom. 10:20). In II Timothy 1:12 the Apostle writes: "I know whom I have believed, and am persuaded." That is to say: I do not deceive myself. He therefore means to say: I know and say it with boldness. And just because I am in the Lord Jesus, I teach this (*truth that nothing is unclean*) so boldly. He uses this forcible expression because of the fear of others, who were timid and skeptical with regard to this sentence, but especially also in view of the lying prophets who taught the opposite (*namely, that certain things are unclean of themselves*).

There is nothing unclean of itself (14:14). Nothing (*no adiaphoron*) is unclean of itself, that is, because of its nature or its inner constitution, but only according as it is judged by men from without or because of their conscience. That is clear from the words: "But to him that esteemeth any thing to be unclean, to him it is unclean." In Acts 10:15 we read: "What God hath cleansed, that call not thou common" (*unclean*).

But if thy brother be grieved with thy meat, now walkest thou not charitably (14:15). Note here the climax and emphasis. The Apostle says: "With thy meat" (*thou grievest thy brother*); that is, for so trivial a matter you disregard the eternal salvation of your brother. One might understand this: If you would do it on account of money, or honor, or your life, or the welfare of your body, or any other matter that is more durable than is food; for food merely serves your momentary benefit and enjoyment. Hence the Apostle in these words sharply rebukes and reproaches the utter lovelessness of those who look with contempt upon a brother on account of food.

Again, with the same emphasis the Apostle says: "Thy brother," and not: "The enemy." Not even a friend or acquaintance, but a brother, to whom a Christian owes much more than to anyone else, since he is a brother (*in Christ*)! "Brother" here means about as much as "neighbor." Why, then, should anyone want to serve his stomach and palate, which are bound to perish, rather than the brother who will live forever (*with him in glory*)?

In the third place, the Apostle says: "If thy brother be grieved";

that is, he becomes confused and his conscience is violated. That means much more than that he suffers loss of money or other possessions. And all this only for the sake of food. Again, the Apostle does not say: "If you grieve him," but: "If thy brother be grieved." With these words the Apostle aptly cuts off the subterfuge of those that might answer him: "We do not grieve him, but we are only doing what we are allowed to do." Or, "Can we not use our rights and do in our affairs as we please?" It is not sufficient for you to live according to your rights and do in your affairs as you please, but you must also care for your brother and so be guided by God (*His Word and will*). Indeed, let me say that you have neither right nor privilege to act (*as you please*), if you cause your brother grief, for in that case these things are no longer your private affairs; but, regarded from the spiritual viewpoint, they do concern your brother, who, because of his doubts and scruples of conscience, is troubled by them. So, then, you act contrary to what is right, if you so act that your brother is grieved. Today everyone regards only what is his and what he may do according to his "right"; but he does not consider what he owes to others and what edifies both himself and his neighbor. In I Corinthians 6:12 the Apostle writes: "All things are lawful unto me, but all things are not expedient."

In the fourth place, the Apostle says: "Now walkest thou not charitably." So you walk a wrong way, even if (*in your opinion*) you walk grandly and admirably. In I Corinthians 13:2 the Apostle writes: "Though I have all faith, so that I could remove mountains, and have not charity, I am nothing." This is indeed terribly terrifying! Because of (*the unwise use of*) food a person can render all his good works totally worthless. Nevertheless, such fools everywhere place love at the end and trouble themselves with many good works, so that in them is fulfilled the word of Ecclesiastes 10:15: "The labour of the foolish wearieth every one of them, because he knoweth not how to get to the city."

Destroy not him with thy meat, for whom Christ died (14:15). That is, it is serious enough that you grieve and offend him and violate (*brotherly*) love; but in addition to all this you are a cruel murderer, for you destroy your brother. And it is indeed a most cruel crime to murder a brother. Again (and this also far surpasses all cruelty and ingratitude) you disregard the death of Christ for your brother: for certainly He died also for him. See, then, what a great evil he does who despises his brother and so fails to walk charitably! So also we read in I Corinthians 8:12: "When ye sin so against the brethren, and wound their weak conscience, ye sin against Christ." And in the preceding verse (v. 11): "Through thy knowledge shall the weak brother perish, for whom Christ died?" The Apostle (*thus*) compares food and the death of Christ with each other. He means to say: Take care that food may not please you so greatly that you prefer it to the death which Christ suffered for the brother. This is a most severe admonition.

Let not your good be evil spoken of (14:16). That is, you sin against both the Church and yourselves; for your "good," that is, that which you are in God and have from God, will be so regarded by the heathen that they will flee from it rather than desire to obtain it. So you will be the cause why many will perish that otherwise might be saved. It is indeed both serious and dreadful that not only your wrong, but also your good is spoken evil of, and that merely because of your food.

The Apostle calls that "good" which we are because of Christ. He means to say: Be careful that the heathen may not blaspheme your faith, your religion, and your whole Christianity. They rather should be attracted by its sweet savor, and by its goodness they should be built up by you. In II Corinthians 6:3 the Apostle says: "Giving no offence in anything, that the ministry be not blamed"; and in Romans 12:17: "Provide things honest in the sight of all men."

For the kingdom of God is not meat and drink (14:17). That is you claim the kingdom of God for yourselves in vain, if you disturb the peace (*of the Church*) for the sake of food, pretending to champion meat and drink, as though that were essential to God's kingdom. This, alas, is now being done everywhere. The external food (*problem*) causes more disturbances (*in the Church*) than inward (*true*) religion.

But righteousness, and peace, and joy in the Holy Ghost (14:17). Righteousness is here used with reference to God; for this we have (*from God*) through faith, or trust (*in Christ*). Peace here relates to the neighbor; for it is achieved by mutual love, by which one cares for the other and is of help to him. Joy in the Holy Ghost is said with relation to the believer himself. Joy in the Holy Ghost is not joy in the flesh, but rather joy in the crucifixion of the flesh — (*the corrupt nature of the believer*).

We have joy in the Holy Ghost by hope, and by putting our trust in God and not in the works which we do either for the neighbor or for God. Be cheerful for yourself, but toward the neighbor be a lover of peace, and in your relation to God be righteous. Nothing disturbs peace more than the offense or resentment which is given to a brother especially in matters violating the conscience. We have peace with the neighbor when in mutual love we serve and edify one another. This peace is broken when we contemptuously judge the weak and violate their conscience. The Apostle therefore desires not only that we should live in peace with one another, but also that we should establish peace by (*the spirit of*) peacefulness and modesty.

He that in these things serveth Christ is acceptable to God, and approved of men (14:18). The believer who serves Christ in these things is acceptable to God for doing what is right; he is approved of men because he works for peace. In the preceding verse the Apostle places "joy in the Holy Ghost" last; for first the Christian must be acceptable to God and then he must seek not his own but the profit of his neighbor. Of those who create disturbances and confuse others, we commonly say that they do not have peace, because they themselves do not permit others to live in peace. In I Thessalonians 5:13, 14 the Apostle writes: "Be at peace among yourselves"; and: "Warn them that are unruly. . .be patient toward all men."

Let us therefore follow after the things which make for peace (14:19). That is, follow after those things which do not disturb others, but edify them and give them peace. But which are these things? This cannot be specified in detail, but love will teach them, as opportunity (*for them*) is offered us from time to time.

And things wherewith one may edify another (14:19). The word "edify" is a favorite term of the Apostle. He might have said: "Wherewith one may *profit* another," that is, by word and deed toward salvation. So also he writes in I Corinthians 10:23: "All things are lawful for me, but all things edify not."

For meat destroy not the work of God (14:20). The Apostle calls the Christian brother "the work of God," just as he says in I Corinthians 9:1: "Are not ye my work in the Lord?" In I Corinthians 3:17 he writes: "If any man defile (*destroy*) the temple of God, him shall God destroy." To destroy the work of God for food means not only to insult God, but also to fight against God and to tear down that which He builds up. It thus means to war against God without ceasing.

Whatsoever is not of faith is sin (14:23). Here the Apostle has in mind those who indeed believed that they were saved by Christ, yet also feared that in such matters (*as eating or drinking*) they might sin, even against Christ. Everything that is not of faith is sin, because it goes counter to faith and conscience; for we must beware with all possible zeal that we may not violate our conscience. Therefore we must not incite the (*weak brother*) to act according to the weakness of his faith, but we must rather strengthen him and build him up, in order that he may grow in the knowledge of our Lord Jesus Christ. So we read in II Peter 3:18: "Grow in grace, and in the knowledge of our Lord and Saviour Jesus Christ."

There are some who explain "faith" here in the sense of "conviction" or "conscience." But "faith" here can be taken as meaning trust in Christ. So I understand this passage despite my high regard for other interpreters. He who is weak in faith, believes; and again, he also does not believe. He is right inasmuch as he believes. He is wrong inasmuch as he does not believe. If in addition, he is misled to misbelief, then he sins in act (*in his conduct.*)

Romans Fifteen

Content of the fifteenth chapter: The Apostle admonishes the strong (*Christians*) to bear with the weak and to help them do what is right. Then he excuses himself for not having visited the Christians at Rome in person. This chapter is an appendix to the preceding; for he concludes (*his instruction*) by pointing to the pattern of Christ. Hence the repetition of the exhortation that they (*the Christians at Rome*) should receive one another (*in love*) and that one should not despise the other.

BELIEVERS SHOULD NOT PLEASE THEMSELVES, EVEN AS CHRIST DID NOT PLEASE HIMSELF

We then that are strong ought to bear the infirmities of the weak, and not to please ourselves. Let every one of us please his neighbour for his good to edification. For even Christ pleased not himself; but, as it is written, the reproaches of them that reproached thee fell on me. For whatsoever things were written aforetime were written for our learning, that we through patience and comfort of the scriptures might have hope. Now the God of patience and consolation grant you to be likeminded one toward another according to Jesus Christ: that ye may with one mind and one mouth glorify God, even the Father of our Lord Jesus Christ. Wherefore receive ye one another, as Christ also received us, to the glory of God (15: 1-7).

We then that are strong ought to bear the infirmities of the weak (15:1). From the special case (*of food*) the Apostle now gathers a general lesson; for what he taught of weakness of faith in matters of food, he applies (*in general*). As here, so also in all other weakness and failings we must bear the weak and not despise them, just as Christ has borne us. Thus (*Christian*) love bears all people and all things. So Moses and the prophets bore Israel. In Galatians 6:2 the Apostle writes: "Bear ye one another's burdens, and so fulfil the law of Christ." In the preceding verse (v. 1) he writes: "If a man be overtaken in a fault, ye which are spiritual, restore such an one in the spirit of meekness; considering thyself, lest thou also be tempted." In Philippians 2:5 he writes: "Let this mind be in you, which was also in Christ Jesus."

And not to please ourselves (15:1). Such as please themselves desire to bear (*receive*) the advantages of the neighbor, but not his burdens. Indeed, they want to be borne by all, but they themselves do not want to bear any one. All they do is to revile, judge, defame, accuse and despise others. They do not bear with them, but are enraged (*at them*) and regard no one as good except themselves. So the Pharisee acted, of whom we read in Luke 18:10 ff. He criticized, reproved, accused and condemned the publican and all other men and vainly rejoiced in his own righteousness. Therefore St. Augustine remarks about this Pharisee in his exposition of Psalm 71: "Ah, it gives you (*Pharisee*) great joy that you are good and that the other one is evil! But what does he add? 'Extortioners, unjust, adulterers, or even as this publican!' That no longer is joy, but scorn!" This scorn is a peculiar trait of such as please themselves. They do not rejoice, because they are righteous, but rather, because others are unrighteous. If the others would be as righteous as they are, they would not rejoice at all. In fact, that would greatly displease them.

Let every one of us please his neighbour for his good to edification (15:2). Here where the Apostle teaches that we should not please ourselves, he also teaches that we should please the neighbor. And to please the neighbor means not to please ourselves. True love for ourselves is hatred toward ourselves, as our Lord says: "He that hateth his life in this world shall keep it unto life eternal" (John 12:25). In I Corinthians 13:5 the Apostle writes: "(Love) seeketh not her own." Hence he who hates himself and loves the neighbor, loves himself truly; for then he loves himself, away from himself, and so he loves himself in an unselfish way, as he loves the neighbor.

For this reason I say, without desiring to contradict the opinion of others and despite my high regard for the Fathers; that the understanding concerning the love for the neighbor, namely, that in the commandment (*"Love thy neighbor as thyself"*) one's love for himself is the measure of one's love for the neighbor, is unfounded. I do not believe that with the provision "as thyself" a person is commanded to love himself, but these words show us our wrong love, with which we love ourselves. The words teach us that we love ourselves (*in a wrong, unselfish way*) and that we cannot be freed from this love, until we cease to love ourselves and begin to love our neighbor in utter forgetfulness of ourselves. The sinful nature (*of this love*) shows itself in our desire to be loved of all men and in all things to seek what is our own. In I Corinthians 10:33 the Apostle writes (*showing true Christian love*): "I please all men in all things, not seeking mine own profit, but the profit of many, that they might be saved."

The Apostle adds: "For his good to edification." That is, we should please the neighbor so that he is moved to do what is good, in particular that he may be edified. The Apostle usually contrasts edification with offense and vice versa. In 14:19 he thus says: "Let us . . . follow after the things which make for peace (by which others do not take offense), and things wherewith one may edify another." That is, by which we do not give offense to others. Peace stands in contrast to "occasion to stumble"; edification in contrast to offense; and brotherly reception of the weak in contrast to despising him. Therefore the Apostle has emphasized these three things (*causing the brother to stumble, giving him offense, and despising him*) above in 14:21 where he writes: ". . .whereby thy brother stumbleth, or is offended, or is made weak."

The reproaches of them that reproached thee fell on me (15:3). This is said not only of the reproaches inflicted upon Christ by the Jews, for then it would not fit into the scope (*of the chapter*). The Apostle rather refers to Christ as an example as He has borne all infirmities (*of all men*). So we read in Isaiah 53:4: "He hath borne our griefs, and carried our sorrows." As we glorify God by good works, so we dishonor Him by evil works, and with these we cover Him with reproaches, for by doing evil we cause Him to be reviled. Of these the Apostle wrote in 2:24: "The name of God is blasphemed among the Gentiles through you." Therefore we pray: "Hallowed be thy name" (Matt. 6:9). That is, God's name should be reverenced and revered as holy. It is really the guilt of our sin which fell upon Christ; for that he suffered punishment and for that He made atonement. Had he desired to please Himself, or had he loved Himself, He certainly would not have done this (*for us*). But He loved us, and hated Himself and emptied Himself (*of his divine majesty and glory according to His human nature*) and so He gave Himself up for us totally. Hence it is love which causes us to please our neighbor and to show patience toward him. Love does not permit us to please ourselves, for love is patient. Without such (*Christian*) love we are impatient and please only ourselves, for then we are righteous in a proud (*sinful*) way.

Whatsoever things were written aforetime were written for our learning (15:4). The Apostle says that all these things written afore were written indeed of Christ, but for our learning, in order that we might show patience toward the neighbor and have hope through the comfort which the Scriptures give. Here the Apostle meets the possible objection: But what has all this to do with us? For literally considered, it pertains only to Christ. The Apostle replies: What is written of Christ is written for us, in order that we may learn to imitate Him. Hence we must understand this as something which is presented to us of Christ, not merely in a speculative way, but by way of example for us to follow. From this passage we therefore learn the important truth that all that Christ did is recorded for our instruction, for he says: "Whatsoever things were written aforetime were written for our learning."

That we through patience and comfort of the scriptures might have hope (15:4). This is a very fine grouping together (*of patience and hope*). We have hope through both the patience and the comfort which the Scriptures offer. Hope, of course, is not a tangible thing, for if we were able to see a thing, why should we hope for it? But hope excludes all things that we can see. Therefore patience here is necessary. And that we may not weaken as we are patient (*in hope*), the Apostle puts the word "comfort." By this we are upheld, in place of the things (*which men can see*). It is therefore something grand to surrender the whole tangible reality for the (*divine*) Word and Scripture. That can be done only by those who have died to all (*temporal*) things, at least, so far as the ardent desire (*for these*) is concerned. Though they actually use these things, they do so, not willingly, but impelled by their need. Such are the Christians who heed the Word of their (*divine*) Master: "Whosoever he be of you that forsaketh not all that he hath, he cannot be my disciple" (Luke 14:33); or that of the Apostle: "They that use this world, as not abusing it" (I Corinthians 7:31). Their whole life is dedicated to God. They serve Him in all their works, for in none of them they seek after their own (*interests*).

The God of patience and consolation grant you to be like-minded one toward another according to Christ Jesus (15:5). (*He means to say*): You do not have these two (*blessings, namely, patience and consolation*) of yourselves, but God grants them to you. The Apostle (*here*) prays for those whom he instructs, for that is the obligation of a pious teacher. He must not only water, but also ask God to give the increase. First, he must labor; then he must teach; lastly also he must pray for them (*his students*). So St. Bernard, in his writing *Regarding the Consideration of Eugene III*, explains the threefold: "Feed my sheep" (John 21:15-17), which our Lord inculcated upon St. Peter.

Wherefore receive ye one another, as Christ also received us to the glory of God (15:7). "To the glory of God" means that God might be glorified by his good work. And this indeed is a wonderful glorification of God, that He is glorified when we receive the sinners and the weak. For it is to His glory that He deals with us as a Benefactor. Therefore this serves His glory, that is to say, it becomes an occasion to Him to manifest His friendliness, when we bring people to Him who are to receive a blessing (*from Him*). Therefore we should not bring (*to Him*) those who are strong, holy and wise (*proud and work-righteous unbelievers*). In them He cannot glorify Himself, because He can impart to them no (*spiritual*) blessing, since they (*as they think*) are not in need of them.

AS A MINISTER OF THE HEATHEN THE APOSTLE DESIRED TO VISIT ROME AND SPAIN

Now I say that Jesus Christ was a minister of the circumcision for the truth of God, to confirm the promises made unto the fathers: and that the Gentiles might glorify God for his mercy; as it is written, For this cause I will confess to thee among the Gentiles, and sing unto thy name. And again he saith, Rejoice, ye Gentiles, with his people. And again, Praise the Lord, all ye Gentiles; and laud him, all ye people. And again, Esaias saith, There shall be a root of Jesse, and he that shall rise to reign over the Gentiles; in him shall the Gentiles trust. Now the God of hope fill you with all joy and peace in believing, that ye may abound in hope, through the power of the Holy Ghost. And I myself also am persuaded of you, my brethren, that ye also are full of goodness, filled with all knowledge, able also to admonish one another. Nevertheless, brethren, I have written the more boldly unto you in some sort, as putting you in mind, because of the grace that is given to me of God, that I should be the minister of Jesus Christ to the Gentiles, ministering the gospel of God, that the offering up of the Gentiles might be acceptable, being sanctified by the Holy Ghost. I have therefore whereof I may glory through Jesus Christ in those things which pertain to God. For I will not dare to speak of any of those things which Christ hath not wrought by me, to make the Gentiles obedient, by word and deed, though mighty signs and wonders, by the power of the Spirit of God; so that from Jerusalem, and round about unto Illyricum, I have fully preached the gospel of Christ. Yea, so have I strived to preach the gospel, not where Christ was named, lest I should build upon another man's foundation; but as it is written, To whom he was not spoken of, they shall see; and they that have not heard shall understand. For which cause also I have been much hindered from coming to you. But now having no more place in these parts, and having a great desire these many years to come unto you; whensoever I take my journey into Spain, I will come to you; for I trust to see you in my journey, and to be brought on my way thitherward by you, if first I be somewhat filled with your company. But now I go unto Jerusalem to minister unto the saints. For it hath pleased them of Macedonia and Achaia to make a certain contribution for the poor saints which are at Jerusalem. It hath pleased them verily; and their debtors they are. For if the Gentiles have been made partakers of their spiritual things, their duty is also to minister to them in carnal things. When therefore I have performed this, and have sealed to them this fruit, I will come by you into Spain. And I am sure that, when I come unto you, I shall come in the fulness of the blessing of the Gospel of Christ. Now I beseech you, brethren, for the Lord Jesus Christ's sake, and for the love of the Spirit, that ye strive together with me in your prayers to God for me; that I may be delivered from them that do not *believe in Judea; and that my service which I have for Jerusalem may be accepted of the saints; that I may come unto you with joy by the will of God, and may with you be refreshed. Now the God of peace be with you all. Amen* (15:8-33).

Now I say that Jesus Christ was a minister of the circumcision for the truth of God (15:8). The Apostle here explains why he admonished them, (*namely*), in order that they might glorify God, because in Christ He had accepted them out of pure grace. They (*the Gentile Christians*) were not such as were the Jews to whom Christ had been promised, and who therefore received Him (*as their Messiah*) assured to them by a (*divine*) promise. Therefore, as he had said: "As Christ also received us," stressing the mercy (*of God*) which is given freely and gratis, so immediately he shows also in what respect it is mercy that is given so freely. (*That is, the heathen received the same divine mercy promised and given to the Jews.*)

As it is written, For this cause I will confess to thee among the Gentiles, and sing unto thy name (15:9). The Apostle here says that the heathen do that, which, according to the word of the Psalmist, Christ does among them. That is not an improper use (*of Scripture*), nor is it a contradiction. But it is really true that Christ among the heathen, and the heathen in Christ, glorify God, and indeed by the (*Holy*) Spirit. For Christ was not among the heathen bodily, nor did He (*in His body*) sing unto His (*God's*) name.

And again he saith, Rejoice, ye Gentiles, with his people (15:10). This call goes forth from Jerusalem, that is, from the Lord's people to others, namely, to the heathen who are not (*members of*) Jerusalem. Therefore the Apostle adds "Gentiles," and he explains the term "Jerusalem" with "his people." The passage represents different passages in the Psalms, as Psalm 67:5: "Let the people praise thee, O God; let all the people praise thee"; or Psalm 97:1: "The Lord reigneth: let the earth rejoice; let the multitude of isles be glad thereof," (*which passages predict the Lord's rule among all nations*).

There shall be a root of Jesse (15:12). Here "root" is the stump itself, which, so to speak, remains after the tree has died. This stump, nevertheless, grows in a marvelous way to be a great tree. This "root" is Christ who has spread Himself out into a large Church. In a similar way Christ describes Himself as a "corn of wheat" (John 12:24), or as a "grain of mustard seed" (Matt. 13:31), which becomes a tree (v. 32). The term "root" suggests the suffering and death of Christ, who has been humiliated so that He became as nothing, and then again was exalted. In Isaiah 53:2 we read: "He shall grow up before him as a tender plant, and as a root out of a dry ground." Christ's suffering and death are thus described by means of a figure.

By all this the Apostle removes the dissension between the Jewish and the heathen (*Christians*), so that they should not be at variance with each other, but receive each other, as Christ also received them. For out of pure mercy He has received not only the Jews (who therefore should not exalt themselves), but also the Gentiles. Therefore both have reason enough to glorify God and not to contend with each other.

According to His human nature, Christ has David and the patriarchs for his "root" for from them He stemmed; but spiritually He Himself is the "root" out of which the whole Church has grown. In that respect He is the flower, but from this latter point of view they (*David and the patriarchs*) are His flowers.

The God of hope (15:13). God is both the Source and Goal of the (*Christian*) hope. The expression "the God of hope" is indeed strange. Nevertheless, by this expression the Apostle distinguishes between the true God and false gods. The idols are gods over things that are tangible. They rule over those who have no hope, but rely on material things. But whoever trusts in the true God forsakes all these (*earthly*) things and lives alone by hope. Therefore the expression "the God of hope" means the same as "the God of those who have hope"; for He is not the God of those who fear and despair. He is rather their Enemy and Judge. In short, God is "the God of Hope" because He is the Giver of hope, or rather, because He is honored by hope. For wherever there is hope, there God is worshiped.

Fill you with all joy and peace in believing (15:13). That is to say, with an appeased conscience and mutual concord. The Apostle places joy first and then peace, because it is joy that gives peace to men, engendering it in their hearts. If a person has obtained peace (*through faith in Christ*), then it will be easy for him to live in peace with others. But whoever is morose and troubled (*in his conscience*) will be morose and irritable also over against others. But this — (*to have joy and peace*) — is possible only to him who believes, because joy and peace do not rest upon tangible things, but upon that which lies outside these, and so upon hope. Otherwise God would not be the God of hope, who gives these hidden blessings, namely, joy in personal sorrow and grief, and peace despite opposition and persecution. He who does not believe will fall when sorrow and persecution become his lot, because then everything disappears in whose tangible possession he trusts. Through persecution (*of believers*), however, hope becomes inexpressibly rich, as the Apostle writes in 5:4: "Experience (worketh) hope." This indeed takes place through the power of the Holy Spirit. For experience does not work hope by our own powers. (*Without the Holy Ghost*) we would be too weak and helpless in times of persecution. But "the Spirit helpeth our infirmities" (Rom. 8:26). Through Him we obtain the victory and also become perfected and triumphant.

I myself am persuaded of you . . . that ye are full of goodness (15:14). We should always think the best of our neighbor. The Apostle (*with these words*) modestly excuses himself for teaching them so much, as though they were ignorant, although he could praise them in so many great things. Observe here the logical sequence. The Apostle first puts "full of goodness" and then "filled with all knowledge." Without love which edifies, knowledge puffs up. Those cannot admonish one another who are not full of love, for they who have only knowledge (*and not love*) retain it for themselves, are puffed up, and regard it beneath their dignity to instruct others. They only desire to be seen and look with contempt upon others. But they who love freely share their knowledge and edify. They who love, teach by word, yet refrain also from all works that give offense.

I should be the minister of Jesus Christ to the Gentiles (15:16). With this word "minister" (*Greek: leitourgos*) the Apostle glorifies most wonderfully his ministry and teaches that we should preach the Gospel as something holy, and so with all sacredness and solemnity. The expression "offering up" alludes to the office of the (*Old Testament*) priests. He means to say: My sacrifice consists in this that I preach the Gospel and so offer up and sacrifice the Gentiles to God through the Gospel. With the phrase "to the Gentiles" he begins to praise his office, meaning to say: Since you are Gentiles, you belong to my office, which I have received for the benefit of the heathen. Above, in 1:5, he said: "We have received grace and apostleship, for obedience to the faith among all nations, for his name." The words "ministering the gospel" mean: I am the priest who offers up the Gospel as a sacrifice. Through this sacrifice the heathen, who are offered up and who receive this offering, become acceptable to God.

I have therefore whereof I may glory through Jesus Christ (15:17). The Apostle means to say: It is not I who speak and act in all that I speak and act, to make the Gentiles obedient by word and deed (v. 18), but it is Christ (*who does all things*). So he writes in II Corinthians 13:3: "Ye seek a proof of Christ speaking in me."

I will not dare to speak of any of those things which Christ hath not wrought by me (15:18). (*With these words*) the Apostle removes from himself all presumption and rebukes the lying apostles who preached more from vainglory than because of a call. He means to say: I do not dare to speak or do anything, unless Christ speaks and works through me. Hence I glory, not because it is I who have done this — (*making the Gentiles obedient*) — but because it is Christ who works through me. Through Him my glorying is valid before God.

Through mighty signs and wonders, by the power of the Spirit of God (15:19). The might of the signs and wonders makes (*the Gentiles*) attentive; (*but*) it is the power of the Holy Ghost that renders the signs and wonders effective. Also sorcerers and false Christs show forth signs and wonders, but not by the power of the Holy Ghost.

So have I strived to preach the gospel, not where Christ was named, lest I should build upon another man's foundation (15:20).

By doing this — (*building upon another man's foundation*) — the Apostle would have denied his apostolic office, for they (*the apostles*) were sent out to found the Church, they themselves being foundation stones of the Church (*by virtue of their teaching* — Eph. 2:20; Rev. 21:14). He speaks of "another man's foundation," not as though the other apostles had preached another Gospel, but the same Gospel was preached through the service of some other apostle. In 2:16 he said: "According to my gospel," that is, the Gospel which was proclaimed through my ministry.

What shall we say to all this? Was the Apostle vainglorious? Does he set vainglorious persons a (*bad*) example, giving them the right to refer to him for their vainglorious boasting? By no means! For above he glories through Jesus Christ (v. 17). Had he sought honor for himself, his glorying would have been null and void. He therefore sought glory for other (*and valid*) reasons.

In the first place (*he writes this*) in order that the dignity of his apostolic office might not be diminished, for in this there would have been a hindrance for him to bring the heathen to faith (*in Christ*), he being their apostle.

In the second place, the Apostle says this — (*"Lest I should build upon another man's foundation"*) — out of his overflowing love. Because he desired to save many souls, he did not wish to preach where Christ was already known; for then he would have been kept from preaching Christ to those who as yet did not know Him. This is proved by his quoting (*in v. 21*) the words of Isaiah 52:15: "For that which had not been told them shall they see." That is, he must preach Christ where He is not yet known, in order that he, by preaching Him where He already was known, might not waste valuable time in which he might have preached to strangers. Also this is significant that the Apostle does not say: "Where the other apostles already have preached:" for that would have been arrogant and vainglorious, as though he did not care to preach where other Apostles had preached. But he says: "Not where Christ was named," to indicate that he declined to preach where it was not necessary. He wanted to preach only where there was need of it.

In the third place, the ministry of the Gospel is an office which is greatly despised. So it was then and so it is now. It does not offer the preacher honor or glory, but commonly only disgrace and persecution. For this reason Christ says (*by way of warning His ministers*) in Luke 9:26: "Whosoever shall be ashamed of me and my words, of him shall the Son of man be ashamed, when he shall come in his own glory, and in his Father's, and of the holy angels." So also the Apostle writes in I Corinthians 4:9: "I think that God hath set forth us the apostles last, as it were appointed to death;" and in 4:13: "We are made as the filth of the world, and are the offscouring of all things unto this day." Nevertheless, although the ministry of the Gospel does not offer the preacher honor and glory, the Apostle, with a wonderful and fully apostolic love, regards that as glory for himself which is disgrace, in order to help others in this way (*to regard the Gospel ministry highly*).

To preach where Christ was already known would not have been disgraceful, since there the initial disgrace had been endured and overcome. But where Christ was not yet known, there the dishonor would have been new (*for the Apostle*) and so all the harder to bear. This the Apostle had in mind when in Romans 1:14 he said: "I am debtor both to the Greeks, and to the Barbarians; both to the wise, and to the unwise;" and again 1:16: "I am not ashamed of the gospel of Christ." This is to say, I regard this as my ministry of glory (*to preach the Gospel*); indeed, I seek my glory in that of which others, because of the disgrace (*involved*), are terrified. So also in 15:17 he says: "I have therefore whereof I may glory through Jesus Christ in those things which pertain to God." He means to say: (*I glory in Jesus Christ before God*), though in the world I am dishonored by (*wicked*) men. In the same way we read in Psalm 119:46: "I will speak of thy testimonies also before kings, and will not be ashamed." That is, I am not ashamed, but regard it as my glory to speak of Thee, (*O God*).

In the fourth place, the Apostle here means the glory of a (*good*) conscience before God. In other words, he glories not with an evil, but with a good conscience, as he writes in II Corinthians 1:12: "For our rejoicing is this, the testimony of our conscience." He hastens to preach the Gospel only where Christ was yet unknown, to have the testimony of his commanding conscience before

God that he administered his (*apostolic*) office most faithfully. For it is our conscience which before God either covers us with shame or robes us with glory. It is therefore pure praise of the Gospel when the Apostle extols his office. And what is more necessary than such praise before men who detest the Gospel or even fight against it!

Whensoever I take my journey into Spain, I will come to you: for I trust to see you in my journey, and to be brought on my way thitherward by you, if first I be somewhat filled with your company (15:24). All these words seem to be superfluous, and yet they are full of love; for the Apostle here offers himself most readily, whereas people should have desired with great zeal to possess so precious a treasure. The proverb says: "It is not the manger that longs for the cattle, but the cattle long for the manger." Here we find the reverse. And he says all this to exemplify to his readers what he had taught concerning love: "(Love) seeketh not her own" (I Cor. 13:5).

It hath pleased them of Macedonia and Achaia to make a certain contribution for the poor saints which are at Jerusalem (15:26). With admirable propriety the Apostle moves the Christians at Rome to make a contribution (*toward the collection for the poor at Jerusalem*). For what other reason should he have mentioned this matter to them? But he wants to incite them that they, induced by the example of the others rather than by a demand, do of their own free will, and without any coercion, what there is to do. (*The Apostle means to say*): I demand nothing of you, but I will gratefully accept what you willingly contribute. This obligation and ministry of love was enjoined upon St. Paul before the other Apostles. We read of this in Galatians 2:9, 10: "They gave to me and Barnabas the right hands of fellowship. . . . Only they would that we should remember the poor."

It hath pleased them verily (15:27). "It hath pleased them verily" means that (*they gave*) willingly and with joy.

I will come by you into Spain (15:28). (*He means to say*): See, with what zeal I am ready to serve others. What (*then*) ought *you* to do!

When I come unto you, I shall come in the fulness of the

blessing of the gospel of Christ (15:29). It is the blessing of the Gospel to make (*Christians*) abound in progress and (*cause them*) to grow in the knowledge of the Lord. So we read in II Peter 3:18: "Grow in grace, and in the knowledge of our Lord and Saviour Jesus Christ." The Apostle does not promise to bring the blessings of temporal gifts, but only the Gospel.

That I may be delivered from them that do not believe in Judea (15:31). The Apostle knew of the persecution that awaited him. It is described to us in Acts, 21-28. From this it is clear that this letter was written thirty years after the death of our Lord, namely, during the time of Nero.

The God of peace be with you all. Amen (15:33). "The God of peace" means the God who is worshiped in peace, just as the "God of hope" means the God who is glorified through our hope. The idols, however, are gods of contention. It is questionable whether the Apostle got to Spain. Faber Stapulensis, on the basis of an apocryphal passage, affirms this. But I believe that he did not get there.

Romans Sixteen

Content of the sixteenth chapter: The Apostle presents to us for imitation a number of pious people and directs us to remain faithful.

The Apostle Commends Phoebe, Greets Various Christians, and Admonishes All to be Faithful

I commend unto you Phebe our sister, which is a servant of the church which is at Cenchrea: that ye receive her in the Lord, as becometh saints, and that ye assist her in whatsoever business she hath need of you: for she hath been a succourer of many, and of myself also. Greet Priscilla and Aquila, my helpers in Christ Jesus: who have for my life laid down their own necks: unto whom not only I give thanks, but also all the churches of the Gentiles. Likewise greet the church that is in their house. Salute my wellbeloved Epenetus, who is the firstfruits of Achaia unto Christ. Greet Mary, who bestowed much labour on us. Salute Andronicus and Junia, my kinsmen, and my fellowprisoners, who are of note among the apostles, who also were in Christ before me. Greet Amplias my beloved in the Lord. Salute Urbane, our helper in Christ, and Stachys my beloved. Salute Apelles approved in Christ. Salute them which are of Aristobulus' household. Salute Herodion my kinsman. Greet them that be of the household of Narcissus, which are in the Lord. Salute Tryphena and Tryphosa, who labour in the Lord. Salute the beloved Persis, which laboured much in the Lord. Salute Rufus chosen in the Lord, and his mother and mine. Salute Asyncritus, Phlegon, Hermas, Patrobas, Hermes, and the brethren which are with them. Salute Philologus, and Julia, Nereus, and his sister, and Olympas, and all the saints which are with them. Salute one another with a holy kiss. The churches of Christ salute you. Now I beseech you, brethren, mark them which cause divisions and offences contrary to the doctrine which ye have learned; and avoid them. For they

221

that are such serve not our Lord Jesus Christ, but their own belly; and by good words and fair speeches deceive the hearts of the simple. For your obedience is come abroad unto all men. I am glad therefore on your behalf: but yet I would have you wise unto that which is good, and simple concerning evil. And the God of peace shall bruise Satan under your feet shortly. The grace of our Lord Jesus Christ be with you. Amen (16:1-20).

I commend unto you Phebe our sister (16:1). This letter was sent through Phebe, was written by the hand of Tertius, and was dictated by the Apostle in Corinth. Cenchrea was a port or harbor of the Corinthians.

As becometh saints (16:2). By "saints" we are to understand, not those who are to be received, but those who are to receive. For not only should the saints receive the saints, but (*all men should receive them*) whoever they may be. But this especially becomes and behooves the saints. So Christ says in Matthew 5:46: "If ye love them which love you, what reward have ye? do not even the publicans the same?"

Here we might ask how the Apostle could enumerate their names, though as yet he had not been in Rome nor had seen them, but longed to see them, as he tells us in 1:11; 15:23. In reply I suggest that he had heard of them by way of report. So he writes in 1:8: "Your faith is spoken of throughout the whole world." Of course, it seems strange how well he describes their (*Christian*) works, which rather he first should have learned (*while in Rome*). However, I judge, they all were people from Achaia and Corinth whom here the Apostle recommends, so that they (*the Christians at Rome*) might become acquainted with them and salute them (*receive them as brethren*). He here apparently follows the Hebrew custom according to which all names (*of the members*) were recorded in the synagogues according to their tribes.

THE APOSTLE SENDS GREETINGS FROM FRIENDS, A FAREWELL BENEDICTION AND A CORDIAL DOXOLOGY

Timotheus my workfellow, and Lucius, and Jason, and Sosipater, my kinsmen, salute you. I Tertius, who wrote this epistle, salute you in the Lord. Gaius mine host, and of the whole church, saluteth you. Erastus the chamberlain of the city saluteth you, and Quartus a brother. The grace of our Lord Jesus Christ be with you all. Amen. Now to him that is of power to stablish you according to my gospel, and the preaching of

Jesus Christ, according to the revelation of the mystery, which was kept secret since the world began, but now is made manifest, and by the scriptures of the prophets, according to the commandment of the everlasting God, made known to all nations for the obedience of faith; to God only wise, be glory through Jesus Christ for ever. Amen (16:21-27).

Now to him that is of power to stablish you according to my gospel, and the preaching of Jesus Christ, according to the revelation of the mystery (16:25). By "mystery" the Apostle here understands the mystery of Christ's incarnation (*and redemption*). The Gospel is nothing else than the proclamation of Christ. So he himself writes in 1:1-4: "Separated unto the gospel of God . . . concerning his Son Jesus Christ our Lord, which was made of the seed of David according to the flesh; and declared to be the Son of God with power, according to the spirit of holiness, by the resurrection from the dead."

Which was kept secret since the world began (16:25). The words "Which was kept secret since the world began" may be understood in the sense that it was "kept secret from all eternity."

By the scriptures of the prophets (is) *made known to all nations for the obedience of faith* (16:26). The question here might be asked how the Gospel was kept secret and yet was known to the prophets. (*We answer that both are true*). it is not merely made manifest now, but it was known already to the prophets.